BLACK POLITICS/
WHITE POWER

BLACK POLITICS/ WHITE POWER

CIVIL RIGHTS, BLACK POWER, AND THE BLACK PANTHERS IN NEW HAVEN

By Yohuru Williams
Delaware State University

Blackwell
Publishing

© 2008 by Blackwell Publishing Ltd

BLACKWELL PUBLISHING
350 Main Street, Malden, MA 02148-5020, USA
9600 Garsington Road, Oxford OX4 2DQ, UK
550 Swanston Street, Carlton, Victoria 3053, Australia

First published 2000 by Brandywine Press
First reprinted 2008 by Blackwell Publishing Ltd

2   2008

ISBN 978-1-881-089-60-5

A catalogue record for this title is available from the British Library.

The publisher's policy is to use permanent paper from mills that operate a sustainable forestry policy, and which has been manufactured from pulp processed using acid-free and elementary chlorine-free practices. Furthermore, the publisher ensures that the text paper and cover board used have met acceptable environmental accreditation standards.

For further information on
Blackwell Publishing, please visit our website at
www.blackwellpublishing.com

Table of Contents

TABLES

FIGURES

ABBREVIATIONS

AIM   American Independent Movement
BPP   Black Panther Party
CCC   Coalition of Concerned Citizens
CORE   Congress of Racial Equality
CPI   Community Progress Incorporated
FBI   Federal Bureau of Investigation
HNU   Hill Neighborhood Union
HPA   Hill Parents Association
NAACP   National Association for the Advancement of Colored People
RG   Record Group
SAC   Special Agent in Charge

PREFACE
War Without Bloodshed?

It's funny about the Mississippi white man. He admires any man who stands up for what he believes. They admired Medgar. They didn't particularly love him, but they admired him. That's why, when I go all over the country, people criticize me when I say that in Mississippi we are freer than Negroes in Chicago and New York. Because we know where this man stands. In Chicago and New York you wonder. They rub you down and they grin in your face and they stab you in the back.

> —Charles Evers, brother of slain civil
> rights leader Medgar Evers, 1963

In 1958, political scientist Harold D. Laswell offered what has become a widely accepted definition of politics as the system that decides who gets what, when, and how. But how then do we define black politics, politics for a people who for the majority of the nation's history have not been invited to share in the decision making? Whatever sway African Americans have wielded over political decisions has generally come of white fear or paternalism rather than a genuine acceptance of the political presence of black Americans.

The historian Rayford Logan spoke to this phenomenon when he described Radical Reconstruction after the Civil War as the "betrayal of the Negro." Despite momentous legislation aimed at establishing the franchise and giving blacks a fair chance in the South, subversion of the law, intimidation, and terror ruled the black political experience, and African Americans found little solace in the Federal government or the Supreme Court. In the end, many liberal whites blamed blacks for the failures of Reconstruction, pointing to the large number of blacks who had been elevated to public office. They concluded that incompetence alone would explain the collapse of black political power later depicted in Thomas Dixon's cantankerous novel *The Klansman*. Few recognized then that the black politician had been little more than a pawn in a game between two powerful white interests that shared at least one basic assumption: the Negro was no more than a problem or a tool. One of these interests, the Republican Party, ultimately sacrificed black civil rights to ensure its continued dominion over the political process.[1]

The same can be said for the alliance between white female suffragists and black abolitionists. The defection of prominent women such as Susan B. Anthony and Elizabeth Cady Stanton from the camp of black civil rights indicates the extent to which blacks were usually a part of the agenda of others. When "Negro" rights were no longer compatible with the primary interests of their benefactors, they were discarded. In denouncing the extension of universal manhood suffrage promoted by the Fifteenth Amendment, for instance, Stanton and her supporters pled directly to the superiority the Anglo-Saxon race assumed of itself. In their writings against the Amendment, they capitalized on white women's dread and contempt of black people by, according to historian Ellen Carol Dubois, "implying that poor black men were more responsible for women's disenfranchisement than rich white ones."[2] Appealing to "American women of wealth, education, virtue and refinement," Stanton exposed the elitism of her feminism and the depth of her own racism. In her controversial diatribe against universal manhood suffrage, she challenged white females,

> . . . if you do not wish the lower orders of Chinese, Africans, Germans and Irish, with their low ideas of womanhood to make laws for you and your daughters, . . . to dictate not only the civil, but moral codes by which you shall be governed, awake to the danger of your present position and demand that woman, too, shall be represented in this government![3]

Black participation in the farmer's alliance movements of the 1880s and 1890s tells the same story. The Populists courted the black vote but, in the aftermath of defeat, turned on blacks as the source of their political ill fortune. The liberal optimism of a unified political movement among white farmers and black farmers soon degenerated into what historian C. Vann Woodward has termed a "capitulation to racism." As he observed, "The blind spot in the Southern Progressive record, as for that matter, in the national movement—was the Negro, for the whole movement in the South coincided paradoxically with the crest of the wave of racism."[4]

Blacks in the twentieth century have been even more disposable in accordance with white political dealings. White politicians have had the power to designate with whom they will deal and what issues they will address. The visibility of black power brokers has derived from their association with white politicians. In exchange for the ear of the "master race," black leaders are expected to marshal support for the white politician even when a position he takes is unpopular or against the interest of the community as a whole. This serves to perpetuate the myth of black Americans as politically unsophisticated.

The political process has alternatively been described as "war without bloodshed." If so, black politics should be a study in black casualties. White power brokers have sought to gain the black vote through minimalist means. Political gestures worth more symbolically than substantially have been the rule. Black leaders who subscribe to the idea that politics are the key to improvement are perpetually at risk. Any politics involves compromise, but black politicians have not been invited to ask for compromises in return. In an interview with journalist Robert Penn Warren in 1963 Adam Clayton Powell Jr., arguably one of the most well known black politicans of the twentieth century, best illustrates the dilemma which besets the black politcian. Commenting on his interaction with his southern counterparts, Powell explained,

> I have very good relations with men from the South. People on both sides of the fence would be amazed if they knew how well we get along. Because I know their situation. Right now I have two or three outstanding Southern Congressmen from the deep, hard-core South who are begging me to attack them in public, because they're afraid they might lose the primary.[5]

It seems inconceivable that Powell, despite his own tumultuous legal troubles and struggles within Congress, could be oblivious to the fact that these same men would be unable to return the favor in any capacity lest they offend the same constiutents who would rally around a candidate in a public fued with him. Powell may have imagined this as playing politics, but in reality it was merely the extension of black politics as defined by the white power structure.[6]

Oddly enough when asked about the role of white liberals in the civil rights movement, Powell remarked, "Not to be abrupt . . . Follow Black Leadership." Powell's comments appear all the more curious since in many northern communities, white liberal politicians, at least on the surface, welcomed black political participation. Black politics, for them, meant a means of guaranteeing a consistent voting bloc. The "Negro" vote, from the perspective of most white politicians, did not have to be approached intelligently. It did not have to be courted or cultivated through programs geared toward improving conditions for blacks. It could be bought, bartered, and sold with empty promises and minor political appointments. The chief agent of the white political machine was the black politician, who more often than not was heavily associated with some denomination of the African-American church, either as a minister or prominent member. The very nature of the church as a conservative body had a profound impact on the demands of its leaders. Many were willing to accept the symbolism of minor political appointments or conversations with the city's chief executive as signs of progress. The desire to have a black appointed to some board or commission often took precedence over more serious concerns facing the masses of African Americans.[7]

After World War II, increasing numbers of blacks shifted their allegiance to the Democratic Party. As the Republican Party once cultivated its image as "the party of Lincoln," by 1960, white Democrats were held up as the friends of the black race. Yet again blacks found themselves restricted to dealing with politicians who were quick to become too comfortable with the arrangement and ignored demands by blacks for better jobs and housing. Even when they did respond, it was always in exchange for black conformity on some issue. This exchange was decidedly one sided since blacks were expected to vote the ticket, support the party and keep a lid on political dissent.

The North was held up by white politicians and many blacks as a Mecca for black advancement. National civil rights agencies, such as the National Association for the Advancement of Colored People (NAACP), seemed to fixate almost exclusively on the South as the region in need of massive protest initiatives. Many northern white politicians were called upon to put pressure on their southern counterparts and took great pleasure in donating money to the organization to fight southern apartheid. However in their 1973 study of urban rioting, *Ghetto Revolts*, Joe Feagin and Harlan Hahn observe that the "apparent tardiness in the partcipation of northern blacks in civil disobedience actions is more than a matter of historical negelct."[8] The authors maintain that the relative inactivtiy of northern blacks reflected the character and demands of migration. "In the peak periods of migration in the forties and fifties," they argue, "northern ghetto residents were probably preoccupied with the fundamental problem of migrant survival in and integration into, the urban sphere." But by the the early 1960s, "increasingly large numbers of ghetto dwellers were native born or long time residents." Among them "thousands had been in the cities long enough to experience on many fronts and in many situations the lack of control over the important decisons that affected their lives. The essentially political goal of seizing control of the decision-making machinery was apparently becoming widespread."[9]

As Blacks began to put pressure on northern politics, they discovered that white politicians were as paternalistic as southern planation owners. Troublesome blacks had to be dealt with lest they influence the sheeplike majority. It was important to silence opposition to the designated "Negro" leadership. Many black leaders and spokespersons for civil rights called for calm among northern blacks, or urged the primacy of the southern struggle. Black political enlightenment was not to be celebrated, but controlled. Attempts by blacks to seize control of the decision-making apparatus would be met with force. Agitators were accused of being outsiders. If they could not be assimilated or turned they would be destroyed. The agents of their destruction were those sworn to serve and protect, the police.

Police harassment was generally attributed to the poverty or ignorance of the class of blacks who did the challenging. Three years before black frustration devastated Watts, author and poet James Baldwin wrote, "The only way to police a ghetto is to be oppressive. None of the Police Commissioner's men, even with the best will in the world, have any way of understanding the lives led by the people; they swagger about in twos and threes patrolling. Their very presence is an insult, and it would be, even if they spent their entire day feeding gumdrops to children."[10] "They represent the force of the white world," Baldwin continued, "And that world's real intentions are, simply, for that world's criminal profit and ease, to keep the black man corralled up here, in his place. The badge, the gun in the holster, and the swinging club, make vivid what will happen should his rebellion become overt . . ."[11]

"Political involvement of the police," explains Jerome Skolnick in his study of anti-establishment protest, "is not per se a new phenomenon. Indeed, it is well known that in the days of the big city political machines the police were in politics in a small way. They often owed their jobs and promotions to the local alderman and were expected to cooperate with political ward bosses and other sachems of the machines."[12] In the later half of the twentieth century, the police were all the more political agents of the white power structure since the policemen themselves shared the politicians' and white community's fear of black people. A report in March of 1969 by the Group for Research on Social Policy at John Hopkins University concludes that "The police have wound up face to face with the social consequences of the problems in the ghetto created by the failure of other white institutions—though, as has been observed, they themselves have contributed to those problems in no small degree." "The distant and gentlemanly white racism of employers," the report continues,

> the discrimination of white parents who object to having their children go to school with Negroes, the disgruntlement of white tax payers who deride the present welfare system as a sinkhole of public funds but are unwilling to see it replaced by anything more effective—the consequences of these and other forms of white racism have confronted the police with a massive control problem of the kind most evident in the riots.

With regards to black social unrest, the Hopkin's report is in line with the sentiments of sociologist Morris Janowitz in his essay on the dynamics of race riots in Hugh Davis Graham and Ted Gurr's edited *Violence in America*. Janowitz observed that northern police officers lack of expereince in dealing with blacks made their reaction uniform in favor of the whites. The Hopkins Group likewise concluded, ". . . we found the police were inclined to see the riots as the long range result of faults in the Negro community—disrespect for law, crime, broken families etc.— rather than as responses to the stance of the white community."[13]

The advent of the civil rights movement and the increased migration of southern blacks to northern cities encouraged northern white politicians to define black politics more equitably. The active challenging and maneuvering of black people influenced this greatly. However, many black organizations fed the desire among northern white political leaders to believe that they were inherently different from their southern counterparts, because they provided jobs or gave money. The white political establishment was willing to experiment with offering more patronage jobs or creating a few programs but the push for self-sufficiency and self-determination within the black community was met with raw power.

Out of frustration northern African Americans turned to more radical organizations based in black power politics. Black power politics corresponds more closely with the definition of black politics offered by Marcus Pohlmann in his 1998 study *Black Politics in Conservative America*. According to Pohlmann, "Black politics is the sum total of actions, ideas, and efforts aimed at creating better conditions for African-descended people in the United States." Pohlmann's definition allows for a consideration of black politics outside of the political mainstream. The radical black activists are involved in politics only to the extent that they remain the sharpest critics of politicians and their programs. Generally seen as the radical fringe, in many ways they represent the true interests of all the poor and oppressed. It is their presence that keeps the black politician from becoming completely irrelevant to white power brokers. They stir up enough trouble to remind people of the potential dangers associated with ignoring the plight of the oppressed. Knowing black politics to be an extension of the white power structure, they speak outside the political system, and in so doing put pressure on it, whether it be conservative or liberal. In the late 1960s, the Black Panther Party claimed to adopt the Maoist notion that power flowed through the "barrel of a gun." The Chicago Panther leader Fred Hampton was fond of repeating the often quoted axiom that politics is nothing but "war without bloodshed." The rhetoric of the Panthers came along at a time when many black northerners were beginning to revolt against northern apartheid. Although Malcolm X had spoken to the same issues, it was not until the rash of long, hot, riotous summers, that many northern white politicians began to appreciate that "two societies separate and unequal" existed in their cities as well. And they had not the means that southern white politicians had once had at their disposal: literacy tests, poll taxes, and the threat of mob violence. So black radicals, though apparently speaking from outside mainline politics, were able to make a mark on it.[14]

By cultivating an image of progressive thinking while pursuing an agenda of oppression, then, white politicians created a Frankenstein monster. An accounting of the best known liberal Democrats of the late 1960s including Chicago Mayor Richard Daley and Philadelphia Police Chief Frank Rizzo reads like a who's who of some of the most notorious agents of repression in recent United States history. But what of the unknown or forgotten leaders? In the 1960s, the small city of New Haven, Connecticut, was heralded as a model community. Its mayor, Richard C. Lee, enjoyed a record sixteen years as mayor and presided over what was lauded as the most efficient bureaucracy in the nation. Lee combined enlightened administration with a good degree of paternalism. Although he attracted some of the most capable political scientists and civil engineers to New Haven, in the face of social problems, Lee nonetheless opted for an antiquated approach toward his black constituents. He was more than willing to patronize the national civil rights movement, but attempted to micromanage civil rights in his city by making the black church and civic leaders responsible to him and him alone. Lee even served as head of the National Council of Mayors, where he and his police chief, James Ahearn, distinguished themselves as enlightened public officials. In the process, he helped to undermine legitimate indigenous protest. He fostered a human renewal program, the Community Progress Incorporated (CPI), that attempted to do the job of a civil rights organization but also stifled legitimate dissent and protest within its ranks. Less than a year after it came into existence, the organization lost some of its workers, who complained that the CPI was little more than a front for the mayor's office and was not truly committed to improving the lot of the city's less fortunate. There had always been rumblings of black discontent in New Haven, which Lee chose to address by playing politics rather than creating meaningful programs. This initially left meaningful community organizing to a local group of activists known as the Hill Parents Association and later to the infamous Black Panther Party. In 1970, New Haven became the site of the so-called "trial of the century" when three Black Panthers were prosecuted for the murder of a suspected police informant.

While the popular image of the Black Panther Party continues to be one of a violent revolutionary group, at the community level it served as an agent for concrete community organization and social change. In

New Haven, the Black Panther Party was a significant force in local civil rights activities. It established a freedom school, a free health clinic, a community-run breakfast for children program, and an anti-drug campaign, as well as involving itself in the principal problems facing the city's African-American population, including an increasingly hostile white community and city government.

While the Black Panthers claimed to speak for the disfranchised and ignored black masses, in many cases its leaders were drawn from the same stock as the middle-class black students who led the Student Non-Violent Coordinating Committee. Huey Newton and Bobby Seale were both students in college, training grounds for the bourgeoisie, when they first formed the BPP. Despite enunciating a more humanist than racial program in its middle period, 1968–1971, state and local officials used the presence of the BPP as a means of discrediting local indigenous black protest movements. Blaming discontent among their black residents on the influence of outside agitators made white politicians more comfortable than acknowledging and arousing local resistance; especially resistance with the potential to cut across race and class lines. In New Haven it is evident that civil rights organizations had failed until the HPA and BPP emerged. The BPP provided a cover for the local organizing that really produced and sustained the Panther programs in New Haven. The BPP became the draw for support, but local people kept the programs going long after the shadow of the Panther had faded. While the national BPP suffered, the local BPP continued for a time to contribute to community leadership.

Notes

1. As John Hope Franklin has observed, "So little is known of the history of the Republican Party in the South because the presumption has generally been that Lincoln's party was, on its face, hostile to Southern mores generally and anxious to have Negroes embarrass white Southerners." Franklin has concluded however that "had historians been inclined to examine with greater care the history of the Republican Party in the South, they would have discovered even more grist for the Democratic Party mill." John Hope Franklin, "Black History Since 1865 Representative or Racist?" Gerald N. Grob and George Athan Billias, *Interpretations of American History* Volume II Since 1877. Sixth edition. (New York: The Free Press, 1992), 154.

2. Ellen Carol Dubois, *Feminism and Suffrage* (Ithaca, New York: Cornell University Press, 1980), 177–178.

3. Ibid.

4. C. Vann Woodward, *The Strange Career of Jim Crow* (Oxford: Oxford University Press, 1974), 89–94. See also *Tom Watson: Agrarian Rebel*.

5. Robert Penn Warren, *Who Speaks for the Negro?* (New York: Random House, 1965), 144.

6. In a follow-up paragraph Warren editorializes, "It is easy to understand how Congressman Powell has good relations with even his collegues from the

South. He is a man of enormous magnetism. And he does understand their situation. He is a political animal." Ibid, 144. It is curious given Powell's moderate tone, that he has been credited with coining the term Black Power as Stokeley Carmichael, aka Kwame Ture, would later use and define it in the mid-1960s. In actuality, Powell's behavior may be viewed more judicously as an extension of black politics. The more militant sentiments he masked for Penn Warren were very visible in his dealings with his black constiutents. His rhetoric however did not protect him from mounting political scandals within the House where he was the subject of numerous investigations beginning in 1958 when he was acquitted on a charge of tax evasion and ending with his censure by that body in 1965 after charges of misconduct. Harold Cruse, *The Crisis of the Negro Intellectual* (New York: Quill, 1984), 427.

7. There are numerous obvious exceptions to the scenario described here. For example in Chicago, in the 1920s, Edward H. Wright and Oscar De Priest were able to fashion a strong black political machine and were able to win major concessions for blacks and create many opportunities for the black masses on their own. In his study of black education in Chicago, Michael Homel notes, however, that in the decade after Wright and De Priest's tenure, Democratic Mayor Edward Kelly (1933–1947) "gave blacks the same mix of symbolic recognition and jobs" that had served earlier Republican political machines within the city. The patronage of Kelly combined with Franklin D. Roosevelt's national New Deal, awakened the "friend of the Negro" mentality among Chicago's black leaders. Switching in large numbers to the Democratic Party, blacks soon discovered that they had in Homel's words, "less bargaining power," within the powerful Democratic party machine to which they were new converts. As more pressing concerns began to manifest themselves such as the quality of Chicago's public schools, Homel notes that black politicians were forced to operate in "closely defined limits if they wished to retain the favor of the Kelly Organization." Michael Homel, *Down From Equality, Black Chicagoans and the Public Schools 1920–1941* (Chicago: University of Illinois Press, 1984), 147–151.

8. Joe R. Feagin and Harlan Hahn, *Ghetto Revolts* (New York: Macmillan Publishing Co., 1973), 93–94.

9. Ibid.

10. James Baldwin, *Nobody Knows My Name* (New York: Dell, 1962), 65–67.

11. Ibid.

12. Jerome Skolnick, *The Politics of Protest* (New York: Ballantine, 1970), 268.

13. David Bosel, Richard Berk, et al, "White Institutions and Black Rage," (March 1969) reprinted in Ibid, 260.

14. Marcus D. Pohlmann, *Black Politics in Conservative America* (New York: Longman, 1999), 10.

CHAPTER ONE

Introduction:
When the Colored Began Moving In,
We Knew Our Neighborhood Was
In Trouble

We've been told by the Supreme Court to integrate. That is hurt-
ful because I think it is driving parents out of the city and we'll
eventually have the same situation in Westville as Dixwell. No
place to go except out to the suburbs. . . . Hamden hasn't one
housing project. No Negroes in Woodridge.

> —Harold M. Mulvey, while serving as
> Connecticut Attorney General, 1966

I've never been able to figure out why people could stand and
applaud, tears in their eyes, when a black just scored the winning
basket—and then have chills go down their spine if they sat next
to him at dinner.

> —Bob Dole, United States Senator,
> Kansas, January 1971

Nestled on the banks of the southern Connecticut coast, New Haven is
one of the oldest cities in the United States. It was founded in 1638 by
the Puritans and holds the distinction of being one of the first "planned"
cities in the world. It was divided into seven principal areas that corre-
spond with its present divisions: Wooster, Fairhaven, Dixwell, West
Rock, Hill, Newhallville, and Dwight. These areas served as the basis for
representation in the local assembly. They also strengthened community
ties and made colonial affairs easier to manage (see Figure 1.1).

Included among the first settlers to New Haven were several blacks.
They were slaves and had no political rights within the colony. Connecticut lawmakers partly abolished slavery after the American Revolu-

1

Figure 1.1
NEGRO NEW HAVEN

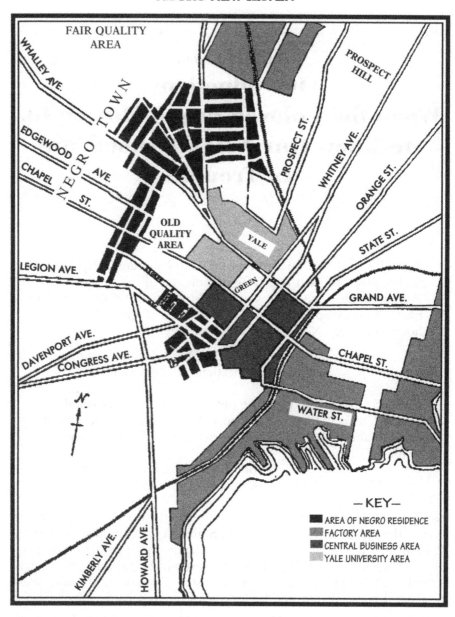

A map identifying primary areas of Negro residence in New Haven. Adapted from Robert Austin Warner, *New Haven Negroes, a Social History.* New York: Arno Press, 1969, 196.

tion. The Gradual Emancipation Act of 1784 provided that children of slaves would be emancipated upon reaching the age of twenty-five, later amended to twenty-one. Full emancipation would not be granted until 1848. The act also recognized free people of color as citizens of the state. While the act redefined the legal status of blacks, it offered little opportunity for social or economic advancement. Blacks were excluded from the lucrative skills. They were prohibited from serving as apprentices and worked largely as servants performing all types of menial labor. In addition, rigid segregation practices kept the races completely separate. In 1811 the Artisan school was established to provide instruction to New Haven's "colored students." A second segregated school was requisitioned in 1825. The physical condition of these schools was poor and little money was provided for necessary resources. Black students were provided with a primary school education alone. There were no provisions made for secondary schooling.[1] Blacks generally occupied dwellings in the poorest areas of the city. They were forced to settle in segregated sections or among poor whites.

A group of white abolitionists known as the African Improvement Society of New Haven conducted a study in 1829 that identified two distinct clusters of blacks in New Haven; one law-abiding and respectful, the other unlawful and incorrigible. The society complained that the troublesome minority generally garnered more attention. One black section of the city known as New Liberia was singled out as a haven for lawlessness. Its reputation for vice, the society concluded, harmed both the respectable and the bad blacks. Among the more scandalous activities reported by the society was open cohabitation between blacks and whites.[2]

For most of its history blacks were prescribed to the area of New Haven known as Dixwell, where the first officially sanctioned African-American church, the United African Society, was founded around 1824. An escaped slave named James Pennington served as its first minister. He was succeeded by Amos Beman, a noted black abolitionist. In this period, Connecticut's black population remained relatively stable. In 1820 there were 267,000 whites, 7,800 free blacks, and 97 black slaves in the state of Connecticut. Between 1790 and 1820 the total number of blacks living in New Haven increased from around two hundred to just over six hundred.

Connecticut had the worst record among all northern states for its treatment of blacks in the decades before the Civil War. Historian Howard Jones has observed that racial attitudes in the state greatly resembled those of the South. As he explains, "Although people in the State opposed slavery and did not favor its spread into western territories, this did not mean that they welcomed blacks." At no time was antagonism more evident than in the 1830s. In his well-established study of anti-abolitionist mobs, Leonard Richards writes, "Connecticut remained the most inhospitable of the New England states." From 1833 through 1837, antislavery journals reported sixteen anti-abolition and anti-Negro mobs there. Within the state, New Haven was the scene of much of the violence.

Problems began in 1831 when a white congregationalist minister and pastor of a black church, Simeon Jocelyn, proposed the creation of a college for blacks in New Haven. Describing the citizens as "friendly, pious, generous and humane," Jocelyn and his supporters assumed that cosmopolitan New Haven, home to Yale college, would embrace the humanitarian gesture. Instead his proposition was greeted with public outrage. His proposal roughly coincided with the bloody uprising in South Hampton County, Virginia, known as Nat Turner's rebellion. Many feared that a "Negro" college would expose the city to an outbreak of violence similar to what had occurred in Virginia. Others worried that an increase in the city's black population might hurt the city's economy and its relationship with Yale.[3] Opponents of the proposed college pointed to the proliferation of vice in black areas and raised the specter of racial amalgamation.

The controversy led to numerous assaults on white abolitionists, black people, and their property. Blacks were openly insulted and beaten in the streets. Tensions came to a head in September of 1831 after "the best citizens in New Haven, led by the mayor and a number of Yale professors and students staged a riot before the homes of supporters of the college." A few weeks later a vigilante mob stormed into New Liberia and apprehended eighteen whites, four women and fourteen men, for abiding and socializing with blacks.[4]

The college remained a volatile issue in 1833 when hostilities again flared. The situation had begun innocently enough when a black girl, Miss Sarah Harris, was granted admission to the formerly all white female academy in nearby Canterbury. Parents complained and then began removing their daughters from the school. Prudence Crandall, a white school teacher, resolved to convert the academy into a school for black females. With the support of William Lloyd Garrison she was able to recruit a number of black students from outside the state. She reopened her school "for young ladies and little misses of color" in April of 1833. The state government reacted swiftly. On May 24, 1833, the Connecticut General Assembly passed the "Black Law." It declared that no "colored" person from outside the state should be allowed instruction in any but the free public schools unless a town granted explicit consent. Students at the academy were victimized daily by irate citizens who hurled eggs and stones. Miss Crandall was jailed briefly and suffered through two criminal trials while angry citizens sought other means of destroying her school. In January of 1834 there was a failed attempt at arson. Several months later, on the evening of September 9, 1834, a well-organized mob smashed all of the windows and doors. The school was forced to close its doors permanently the next day.[5]

The final incident on the surface appears to be in stark contrast with the first two. It took place in August of 1839 when a Spanish slave ship, the *Amistad*, drifted into Long Island Sound. The cargo had mutinied, killing all but two of the crew, whom they compelled to take them back to Africa. The ship was captured by federal authorities on August 26, and the mutineers were sent to the New Haven County jail to await a hearing on their status. Sentiment in the city was largely in support of the Africans. Citizens brought food and clothing for the slaves and raised money for their legal defense. The Africans were ultimately ordered to be released to the President and returned to Africa. The case had been decided by Judge Andrew T. Judson, who a few years earlier had been one of Prudence Crandall's most outspoken critics. The apparent paradox demonstrates the limits of liberal-minded New Haven. The *Amistad* Africans' temporary respite was essentially different and far more acceptable than the prospects of an invasion of black students into the Elm city. Black people were fine in small numbers as long as they knew and understood their place or were not staying in New Haven.[6]

Abolitionist sentiment increased widely in Connecticut as a whole during the 1840s and 1850s. Rodger Sherman Baldwin, who had defended the *Amistad* slaves, was elected governor in 1844. He served for two years pushing for the franchise of blacks and the complete abolition of slavery. He also attempted to enact a provision to limit the operations of slave catchers in the state. Baldwin was defeated on all three fronts. During his last year in office the State Assembly created a great deal of optimism among blacks when it proposed an amendment removing the qualifying word "white" from the State Constitution. Amos Beman and Reverend Pennington helped to draft an appeal to the voters that called on them to support equality. "We do not want to be pointed at as the degraded class in the community," they wrote. "We appeal to you in the sacred name of justice. We appeal to you as Christians and ask you in the name of Christians: Is it Christ-like to treat the heir of common salvation thus invidiously?" Despite their eloquence, the amendment was soundly defeated in a statewide referendum the following year by a vote of more than three to one.[7]

By 1850, the number of blacks living in New Haven fluctuated at around one thousand of the city's twenty thousand total population. The emphasis among politicians remained on keeping large numbers of blacks out of the city and the state. In 1853 the State General Assembly even entertained a bill to sponsor black emigration to Africa. Citing the lack of progress made by blacks in Connecticut, the bill reported,

It has been decided that here they can never rise to a social or political equality. Call this prejudice, or patriotism, or philosophy, the fact is certain. Recent efforts to break down this sentiment have resulted in their greater depression, and their political enfranchisement has been refused by a vote of about four to one.[8]

Time brought some improvement. As Robert Austin Warner has written, "the prewar enthusiasm for Negro betterment secured equal protection for colored people in the improved education which until then they had been denied." The New Haven school board in 1860 adopted a new agenda with regard to black education. Stating its belief that black children were capable of making the same strides in education if provided with the same quality of instruction, the board announced plans to repair the physical condition of the black schools and also hired white teachers to replace their black instructors. Many concerned parents responded by signing a petition to request the hiring of qualified black instructors, but the board demurred citing the scarcity of well-trained black educators.

The Civil War renewed optimism within the city's black population. In 1865 the board presided over the opening of a new "Negro" school which was vastly superior in quality to the existing white schools in New Haven. Black parents, however, had become dissatisfied with the continuation of separate schools no matter how well constructed or how well staffed. The Thirteenth, Fourteenth, and Fifteenth Amendments encouraged black New Haveners to demand full equality. They began agitating for admission to all the public schools in New Haven. In July of 1869 the board of education took its first steps toward incorporating black students into the majority schools. Separate elementary schools were completely abolished in 1871. At the closing of the last segregated school in 1874 the school board concluded,

> The result of the war changed—and who will say unfairly or unjustly—the entire relation of people of color to the State and to its inhabitants. It made them citizens; it opened to them all offices of honor and emolument; it destroyed color. All were to be Americans alike. Whatever their descent, each was eligible to any state offices, from the lowest to the highest. By law, no discrimination could be made in the schools of Connecticut on account of race or color.[9]

The school board's forecast for the future would prove overly hopeful. Despite gains made during the Civil War and Reconstruction, from 1850 to the nation's entrance into the First World War blacks continued to face segregation and economic hardship in Connecticut. During the bustling years of the late nineteenth century social practice restricted clerical, business, and commercial positions to New Haven's white population.

In the large-scale foreign immigration to New Haven brought on by industrialization the Irish and the Germans came first. By 1870, twenty-eight percent of the population was foreign-born. Italians and Eastern Europeans followed in the 1880s. Despite initial discrimination in jobs and housing, the new immigrants were allowed to mix with the old stock Anglos. Between 1900 and 1910 the total population increased by twenty-five thousand, rising from 108,000 to 133,000. The immigrants were largely responsible. A study conducted in 1910 revealed that one third of New Haven's population was foreign-born and another third had at least one immigrant parent.[10]

Around the turn of the century a small but steady stream of immigrants from the West Indies also began to trickle into New Haven. They came largely from Nevis and Jamaica. Although West Indians faced the same limitations as other blacks their shared experience produced little unity. Cultural differences accounted for the greatest gulf between the two groups. Native-born blacks generally resented their foreign-born competition and mocked their accents and social customs. The West Indians on the other hand regarded themselves as superior to black Americans. Constance Baker Motley, a former New Haven resident, remembers, "My father never discussed race relations as such, but he always expressed his views on black Americans who he thought were generally lazy, no good, undisciplined and lacking middle class values. He had the same myopic view of American blacks as most whites."[11]

With the new immigration came an increase in business activity. Essential city services, however, were unable to keep up with the population growth. New Haven's harbor, once a thriving port, was virtually neglected. The New Haven railroad, in the words of Jeanne R. Lowe, "tottered on the brink of receivership." By 1920, New Haven was already experiencing the exodus of middle and high income families from the city. Between 1920 and 1930, New Haven suburbs grew more than sixty percent in population. While all of the city's remaining residents suffered, blacks were in a particularly precarious position. Racism and discrimination limited employment opportunities for blacks. Census reports prior to 1920 revealed that no black female clerks and only a few black bookkeepers and typists were employed by the city. Blacks typically engaged in the same type of menial labor they had performed in the years before the Civil War.[12]

During World War I, however, blacks had been able to acquire semi-skilled work in certain defense factories. These opportunities continued to grow after hostilities in Europe came to an end, and between the First and the Second World War, New Haven hosted a great influx of black migrants. Large contractors such as Winchester Arms, suffering from the city's decline in population, suspended discriminatory hiring practices and encouraged southern blacks to move to New Haven for jobs. The city's second largest employer, Yale University also welcomed blacks to work in its janitorial and dining services. This fit the pattern of black migration nationwide, impelled by the prospect of better jobs and the desire to escape from the southern caste system.

By 1930 blacks constituted two percent of New Haven's total population. The number of West Indians alone living in New Haven had risen to four hundred. One of these was Constance Baker Motley. Her family had moved from Nevis to New Haven in 1902. Like many longtime black residents she experienced little overt racism in New Haven. She lived in an integrated neighborhood and attended integrated schools. "There were very few black children in my elementary schools," she says, "so racial hostility was not a problem." The war industries paid well and Yale University provided many blacks with an abundance of employment opportunities. "When I was growing up, all of my male relatives seemed to work at one Yale eating club or another," Mrs. Motley recalls. "We seemed to have no more and no less than everyone else. Fear and racial conflict were simply not a part of the landscape."13

Although some families like Constance Motley's lived in integrated areas, from the late 1940s up until the mid-1960s, Dixwell remained the nucleus of black activity in New Haven. Black churches and the city's few black businesses lined its streets. In this period the Dixwell Congregational Church, which emerged from the original church founded by the United African Society, would serve an important function in civil rights activities in New Haven. The church and the local branch of the National Association for the Advancement of Colored People, chartered in 1917, were closely connected. The leading members of the church doubled as the officers and membership of the local NAACP. In their ranks were a few doctors and lawyers, and of course ministers, but most of the church congregation and members of the NAACP were working-class, employed as domestics, janitors, and support staff at prestigious Yale University. These groups, along with the professionals, constituted the black elite in New Haven. Their numbers were small and they were for the most part completely assimilated.

Between 1930 and 1950 New Haven's black population grew from five thousand to more than 9,500. The city experienced its greatest wave of black migration in the 1950s when the city's African-American community more than doubled from 9,825 in 1950 to 22,665 in 1960. Most of the city's new residents were southern-born. A study conducted in the mid-1960s revealed that three fourths of black heads of household in New Haven had been born in the South. The arrival of blacks, primarily from Virginia and North and South Carolina, as well as continuing migration from Puerto Rico led to a substantial increase in the nonwhite population of the inner city (see Tables 1.1–1.2). As the number of blacks residing in New Haven increased the tolerable conditions described by Mrs. Motley began to change.

Table 1.1

**Black Migration from the South to
New Haven, Connecticut, 1945–1970**

Era	Net Black Migration	Annual Average Rate
1945–1950	550	110
1950–1955	1280	256
1955–1960	2500	500
1960–1965	2708	541
1965–1970	2334	460

Source: Cleo Abraham, *Protests and Expedients in Response to Failures in Urban Education: A Study of New Haven, 1950–1970*, diss., University of Massachusetts, 1971, 31.

Table 1.2

New Haven Population by Race, 1950, 1960, 1967, and 1970

	1950	1960	1967	1970
Total Population	164,443	152,048	141,752	137,707
White	154,618	129,383	108,116	99,986
Black	9,825	22,665	33,636	37,721
Percent Black	6.0	14.9	23.7	27.4

Source: U.S. Department of Commerce, Bureau of Census, U.S. Census of Population and Housing; 1950, 1960, 1967, and 1970.

The growth in the black population brought little unity among blacks in New Haven. Many longtime residents describe a "plantation mentality" among blacks regarding labor, leisure, and skin color. Black professionals along with those employed in the Yale service industries considered themselves as distinct from those who worked in factories. Blacks who could "pass" for white enjoyed a special status since their color might allow them to escape from second-class citizenship. This affected all aspects of their social dealings such as who they associated with, what organizations they joined, and what behavior they deemed appropriate. Constance Baker Motley remembers, "Just as my father kept his distance from working-class blacks, established middle-class blacks shunned the newly arrived West Indians. As a result, my parents' friends were largely other West Indians."[14] When large numbers of southern blacks began moving into the city the hierarchy became more complex. Many whites expressed concern for the future of the city. In response to a question about de facto education, for example, Connecticut State's Attorney and New Haven resident Harold Mulvey remarked, "I suppose all parents are concerned with the education of their children and Negro parents are no different. By the same token, Negroes from the Carolinas are not interested in anything except finding a job and existing." According to Fred Harris, who was born in New Haven in 1938 and would head up its most notable local civil rights organization, the Hill Parents Association, many blacks had accepted the long perpetuated notion that there were essential differences that made northern blacks superior. "They would say 'you're not like those people,'" Harris recalls, and many blacks responded by treating the new migrants contemptuously. Some blacks recognized what they considered to be divide and conquer tactics by whites and upper-class blacks to keep down the new arrivals.[15]

For the most part, black migrants to New Haven arrived poorly equipped for urban living and lacked marketable skills. They inhabited the worse housing available. Jeanne Lowe's *Cities in a Race with Time*, reports that by 1950, one third of black New Haven housing was substandard. In addition, the schools were in poor physical condition. A 1963 study by the NAACP revealed that de facto segregation existed in New Haven schools. Nine buildings that were designated as "Negro" schools in use in 1963 had been described in 1909 as outdated.[16]

The story of the Louis family was typical. Charles Louis was born in 1938 and his brother Joe in 1943. Their five-year age difference is reflected in their experience in New Haven.

Like Mrs. Motley, Charles Louis recalls attending integrated schools made up of poor and lower middle-class blacks, Jews, and Italians. Nicholas Pastore, who served as New Haven's chief of police, and United States Senator Joseph Liberman were both classmates of Charles. In 1940 the Louis family moved into one of the first public housing complexes ever built in New Haven. Charles notes that the public housing projects did not carry the same stigma they have today. Residents were required to maintain the property. As Charles remembers, the city even distributed lawn mowers in the summer and shovels in the winter to ensure compliance.[17]

By the time Joe started school New Haven had already experienced several waves of black migration from the South, while large numbers of whites began to move into other areas of the city. The demand for public housing increased and the quality of available housing spiraled. Many of the newly arrived blacks moved into the dilapidated houses and flats vacated by earlier waves of European immigrants. They also placed a new burden on the school system and forced the city to confront its latent racism. Since black migration coincided with white exodus out of New Haven the number of total students had not grown and yet the schools were allowed to deteriorate.[18]

Many of these problems would come to a head during the administration of Mayor Richard C. Lee, who was first elected in 1953 and served sixteen years as mayor. Between 1954 and 1969 Lee embarked on a massive urban renewal project designed to rehabilitate both the physical structure and the public image of the city. Attendant on it was a program aimed at social rebuilding that the mayor labeled as "human renewal" and "people programs." The mayor's program attracted significant national interest and a substantial amount of federal money flowed into New Haven to support it. The city became a great experiment in urban redevelopment, earning federal recognition as a "Model City." The city would maintain this honor until the summer of 1967 when civil unrest shattered this facade.

New Haven's urban renewal program sparked a great deal of scholarly interest in the city for its innovative approach to government. In 1961 New Haven received an honorable mention in Jane Jacobs's classic study, *The Death and Life of Great American Cities*. Jacobs observed that New Haven, with a population in 1961 of 165,000 people, was small enough that administrators and staff members could easily communicate with one another. She also maintained that the relative size of the municipal government allowed city officials the opportunity to stay abreast of the most current thinking about urban redevelopment and apply it to New Haven, creating an informed and able cadre of civil administrators.[19] Jacobs's study underscores the optimism New Haven generated about urban renewal at the start of the 1960s. The mayor and city officials were featured in numerous newspaper and magazine articles praising their work for initiating a program that took into account the "human" factor. Mayor Lee, in particular, was hailed as a new type of political leader at the vanguard of a new civil service consisting of politicians, business leaders, and experts working together to improve the nation's urban centers.

The acclaim that New Haven administrators received caused some to question who was really in charge in New Haven. In 1962, Robert Dahl, a professor of political science at Yale University, sought to identify the power behind decision making in New Haven. In *Who Governs? Democracy and Power in an American City*, Dahl probed the evolution of changing patterns of political leadership there. Employing sociological methods of investigation, he sought to identify the "ruling elite" in New Haven.

According to Dahl, between 1900 and the end of the First World War New Haven's old social notables had begun a gradual withdrawal from the city, moving into the suburbs and enrolling their children in private schools. In their place came a new class of civil administrators, ethnic in character, liberal in economic development, and socially conservative. Though the old economic and social notables no longer controlled politics in New Haven, they still exerted great influence, especially in social policy. The rise of a new class of ethnic civil administrators, so recently themselves the victims of prejudice and poverty, would not spell the end of divisions based on race. According to Dahl, an aspect of the new order was the growth in New Haven of an underclass predominately African-American and Puerto Rican.[20]

Dahl's study demonstrates the conservative nature of New Haven between 1956 and 1971. The new men in government that Dahl speaks of were men like Mayor Lee, who had grown up as part of the ethnic European underclass but benefitted from the departure of the old economic and social notables. In the 1960s when African Americans in New Haven began to clamor for more political power and equal educational opportunities they necessarily threatened the new position that individuals like Lee had so recently inherited. Despite a liberal progressive program of urban renewal, the mayor had not intended to unleash the social forces that gave rise to cries for social equality in New Haven. As the new middle class began to move out to the suburbs, the increasingly black and Puerto Rican population of New Haven suffered from an urban renewal program principally directed against black ghettos.

William Lee Miller's *The Fifteenth Ward and the Great Society: An Encounter in a Modern City*, published in 1966, was one of the first to examine this dynamic. Miller was part of the civil government in New Haven. He served as an alderman for the fifteenth ward, which Dahl referred to as the wealthy fifteenth, the very last of the old "social and economic notables." Miller, however, was part of the new class of politicians. Like the mayor, he stood firmly behind an urban renewal program that continued to receive national praise: in 1965 Robert Kennedy told a New Haven audience, "What my brother hoped to do with the New Frontier, Dick Lee is doing in New Haven." Miller reveled in the optimism of the period. As a civil administrator, Miller witnessed what he describes as the ethnic immigrants' sourness toward any social program devoted to the plight of African Americans. Many of the Irish, Italians, Jews, and Poles resented what they perceived to be special help extended to African Americans that had not been available to their fathers and grandfathers. Calling this the comparative grandfather response, Miller remarks, "this argument is so pervasive and spontaneous as to represent an unmistakable reality of popular feeling."[21]

The attitude of the older immigrants to the newly arrived underclass described by Dahl and Miller helps to explain the strong reaction against urban renewal in certain areas. In the predominately Italian neighborhood of Wooster Square, for instance, residents unfairly blamed the new arrivals for the generation-old problem of the slums and poor city planning in New Haven. Wooster was the first of the seven city neighborhoods slated for improvement. During the later years of the nineteenth century it had been transformed from a middle- and upper-class community into an Italian ghetto. In the decade from 1890 to 1900 the number of Italian residents in Wooster Square rose from five percent to almost a quarter of the neighborhood's residents. Wooster became known as "Little Naples," a classic ethnic ghetto. Poverty was rampant, tenements lined the streets, and there was an explosion in petty crime. Miller observes that twentieth-century problems of neglected city services, traffic, and physical obsolescence were most responsible for Wooster Square's further decline. "Negro migration to the city," writes Allan Talbot, "accompanied the decline rather than caused it as some New Haveners believed." The fact was lost on the Wooster Square resident who remarked, "When the Colored began moving in, we knew our neighborhood was in trouble."[22]

Part of the problem as Miller analyzes it was the apathy of blacks in New Haven toward civil rights. He notes that New Haven's African-American community showed little initiative and when the lines were drawn reacted only reluctantly to racism and discrimination. Miller credits the articulate "middle-class Negro leadership" for attempting action but complains that the mass of African Americans were not involved. To emphasize his point, Miller cites someone he describes as a "middle-class Negro politician" as commenting on the mostly black residents of a low income housing project, "You can't get those people . . . out for anything—you'd have to blast them out." For the most part Miller's observations were collaborated by most researchers looking at New Haven in the late 1960s. Their unfavorable appraisal of African-American organizations resulted from what they perceived as the lack of leadership and the level of political infighting within organizations like the NAACP, which was split on whether to adopt a more radical agenda or to maintain its working relationship with the mayor.

Miller's account raises serious questions that this study will address. Who were the leaders of the local NAACP? What issues excited the mass of African Americans who Miller claims were uninterested in civil rights? What was the reaction of the local government?

Miller's book was followed in 1967 by Allan R. Talbot's *The Mayor's*

Game: Richard Lee of New Haven and the Politics of Change. Like Miller, Talbot had worked in the Lee Administration. He served from 1960 until 1965. He began preparation for the book in 1961 by keeping a personal record that he supplemented with taped interviews. As a city administrator, Talbot enjoyed full access to the mayor's office and contact with city officials. His account is primarily an insider's view of the mayor's urban renewal program.[23]

Talbot argues that the Lee Administration developed a formula for success in New Haven that relied on the personal charisma of the mayor. "Lee has always enjoyed his visits in the Negro areas of the city," Talbot explains. "He has always seemed more indignant and emotional in his trips through Negro slums, and as a result, he has given his best fire-and-brimstone speeches before Negro audiences." Lee's fiery rhetoric, however, masked his true feelings. Lee's attitude toward the black leadership was paternalistic. Talbot recorded that Lee regarded most black politicians as frauds and believed that he could garner more votes without them. But the mayor, who had once resided in one of the city's largest black neighborhoods, was happy to keep good relations with the leaders of a black community increasing in demographic importance: as the city's total population fell during his sixteen-year tenure by fifteen thousand, the number of black residents would grow by thirteen thousand.[24] Lee enjoyed a special relationship with the NAACP. He was responsible for hiring more black city workers than any mayor before him. He also worked to get blacks hired in the business and trade industries. His efforts on behalf of African Americans endeared him to the more stable black residents of the city who were in a position to benefit from his program. "Blacks with a college education, high school diplomas, or high potentials were able to move relatively quickly into middle class jobs in New Haven," writes Cleo Abraham. "They had marketable skills to offer the community, requiring little additional training by employers. Some found employment in business and industry (banks, retail stores, etc.). The majority, however, were placed in jobs by Community Progress, Inc. (CPI)."[25] Allan Talbot recalls:

> While this city hall patronage obviously had little effect on the majority of New Haven Negroes, it did help to establish a bond between Lee and the Negroes. Though no one could say precisely what was thought of Mayor Lee, the election returns and the personal contacts strongly indicated a widespread feeling that this was one white official who really wanted to help.[26]

For the new arrivals, however, the Lee Administration seemed cold and unfeeling. Without the skills to find better work, they were forced into the lowest rung of menial labor within New Haven. The physical renewal program typically targeted black ghettos and blacks were disproportionately displaced. As Cleo Abraham comments: "Some Black residents have benefitted from urban renewal. Some live in attractive, new integrated town houses along Dixwell, while less fortunate neighbors live in dilapidated housing on the Hill." Propertied and professional black residents concentrated on access to previously restricted openings to social and economic advancement; lower income blacks were concerned over substandard housing, and the need for imaginative social welfare programs. In the midst of Lee's ambitious urban renewal program they were restricted along with indigent whites and Puerto Ricans into the worst neighborhoods in the city. The Hill became the last refuge for those displaced by urban renewal. By 1966, thirty-eight percent of all families residing there had incomes of less than $4,000, and fifteen percent had incomes below $1,500.[27] In that year, the Hill had the highest concentration of Puerto Ricans and the second highest concentration of blacks in the city. Urban renewal accentuated the difference between the rich and the poor and the differences between them in interest helped to define the struggle for civil rights in New Haven between 1953 and 1963 (see Table 1.3).

Table 1.3

***Racial Composition of New Haven, Connecticut,
by Neighborhood (1966)***

Neighborhood	Population	White	Black	Puerto Rican
The Hill	23,000	49.9%	42.5%	7.6%
Dwight	8,000	48.0	50.1	1.9
Dixwell	6,000	10.5	85.1	4.4
Newhallville	10,000	24.2	74.5	1.3
Fairhaven	14,000	59.1	35.5	5.4

Source: Alan Mallach et al., "CPI Manpower Division Inner City Survey, Final Report," Community Progress, Incorporated, 1966, in Fred Powledge, *Model City* (New York: Simon and Shuster, 1970), 81.

Between 1956 and 1963 a bitter struggle developed within the NAACP over Lee's relationship with the branch. This contest between more militant factions and the Lee supporters ultimately resulted in the decline of that organization as a viable vehicle for social change in New Haven. The trouble in the NAACP eased the way for more radical organizations like CORE, which emerged on the scene in 1961. Between 1961 and 1963 CORE claimed to represent New Haven's less affluent African-American community. The leadership of CORE deliberately remained independent of Lee and by focusing on the disruptive nature of urban renewal on the city's poor offered for a brief moment, in 1962 and 1963, a significant challenge to the Lee Administration.

Talbot candidly explains:

> During the nineteen-fifties . . . no one perceived—or at least identified—any special Negro problems in the slums. Not many racial agencies kept racial records, no one was writing popular books which described Negro "self-hate" or the "invisible poor," or making a case for the peculiarity of the Negro condition in urban society.[28]

And unlike Miller, Talbot was willing to concede that the city was partially at fault for the condition of African Americans in New Haven. But Talbot was not critical enough in his assessment of the mayor. Despite considerable effort to depict Mayor Lee in the role as "friend to the Negro," Talbot only succeeded in underscoring the paternalism of the Lee Administration toward the city's black population. Like Miller's book, Talbot's account was published before the civil disturbance in the summer of 1967. And although Talbot discusses the racial situation in New Haven with a somewhat more critical eye toward the mayor's program, he never mentions the Hill Parents Association or black militant organizations by name, referring to protest organizations collectively as "an established group of ministers, ward heelers, and outright con artists who portrayed themselves as spokesmen for New Haven Negroes." Talbot attributes this situation to what he describes as the lack of "mature" grassroots leadership within the community itself.

A year before the civil disturbance that exposed New Haven's "other America," Miller boastfully observed, "there has been no invasion of the city or major violence in the streets since July 5, 1779." In the summer of 1967, however, a riot broke out over the shooting of a Hispanic man by a white store owner. The riot resulted in property damage and deaths. The actions of the police during the civil disturbance came under scrutiny and began to undermine the liberal progressive image of New Haven. It also fixed attention for the first time on the New Haven police force.

An article on the riot in the January 1968 issue of *Progressive Architecture* was the first to broach the issue of the city's unfair treatment of African Americans. The authors placed squarely on the mayor and urban renewal the blame for the plight of New Haven's African-American population. The article was the first to take seriously the efforts of militant organizations like the Hill Parents Association. The article was also the first to discuss what Robert Bowles, the executive director of the New Haven Urban League, described as "a break HPA" movement directed against the organization by the New Haven police. Dahl had observed that power concentrated in the hands of the few would be unequally distributed in all strata of society. *Progressive Architecture* underscored the possible abuses that could occur from that maldistribution, especially with regard to the police. It set the tone for a reassessing of New Haven's urban redevelopment program by outsiders looking to evaluate the scope, successes, and failures of urban renewal. After 1967 the liberal progressive image of New Haven was beginning to come under attack.

William Lee Miller, Allan Talbot, and Cleo Abraham all speak of the masses of African Americans who were not involved in local civil rights activity under the NAACP, CORE, and the Urban League. Who were these people? Where did they come from? What were their social and economic backgrounds, their political affiliation? What was the role of the African-American church, labor unions, and other civil rights organizations? Why did the New Haven black community react so favorably to the Black Panther Party, especially in light of its national reputation? What was it about the BPP program that spoke to the needs of the city's black residents, or was it that the BPP was willing to make their agenda its own? Discovering those masses will tell much about the future of racial problems and racial struggles in New Haven.

The historiography on New Haven demonstrates the lack of attention given to the presence and activities of African Americans in the city between 1950 and 1970. In the literature, black organizations appear to be passive rather than active agencies for change. Mayor Lee and his ambitious program are the most likely reason for this portrayal. Most of the studies of New Haven centered on the impact of Lee's programs on African Americans, rather than on the African-American community itself. This study seeks to redress that imbalance in attention by exploring the nature of black organizations in New Haven between 1950 and 1970. It places African Americans at the center, while examining the effect of local, state, and national issues on these organizations. The aim of this work is to contribute to our understanding of northern, urban black organizations during the civil rights era. It also seeks to answer why New Haven, despite the liberal progressive leanings of Mayor Lee was "No Haven" for African Americans.

This introduction covers an analysis of urban renewal and the state of race relations in New Haven before the start of widespread direct action protest in that city in 1961. Chapter Two details the efforts of the New Haven branch of the NAACP to win concessions on civil rights in New Haven between 1953 and 1961. It concentrates on internal problems within the chapter, most notably, the chapter's relationship with Mayor Lee. Chapter Three examines more closely the efforts of Mayor Lee in subverting the efforts of civil rights organizations in New Haven. Most of the chapter deals with the emergence of a local chapter of CORE.

It also discusses the creation of Community Progress, Incorporated (CPI), the mayor's own civil rights organization, along with the battle for school integration in New Haven in 1963. The emergence of a local militant group in 1966, the Hill Parents Association, is the subject of Chapter Four, which explores the activities of the HPA in more detail, specifically its campaigns against substandard schools and its involvement in a statewide movement for welfare reform. The chapter concludes with a discussion of the efforts of HPA to create a parallel community program in the summer of 1967. Chapter Five, which tells of the 1967 riot, describes the scope of local surveillance of the HPA and other militant organizations in New Haven and the clamor for law and order that developed in the city after 1968.

Profiling the Black Panther Party, Chapter Six outlines its birth and development, its national activities, its problems with law enforcement, and the circumstances under which the Party sanctioned a chapter in New Haven, Connecticut. Chapter Seven recounts the activities of the BPP in New Haven, including a discussion of its programs and its support base within the New Haven community. It also discusses the escalation of local and federal surveillance of the BPP in New Haven and the circumstances leading up to the murder of Alex Rackley in 1969. The trial of the New Haven Black Panthers sets the context for Chapter Eight. The chapter examines the nature of local and federal surveillance of the Party, looks at national and local support for the New Haven Black Panthers, and examines the activities of the New Haven chapter in the aftermath of the trial, its community programs, and the continuance of federal surveillance. It discusses community programs that have remained in place and the impact of the wiretap settlement, while evaluating the New Haven chapter in light of the efforts of other civil rights organizations in New Haven.

Notes

1. Robert Austin Warner, *New Haven Negroes* (New York: Arno Press and the New York Times, 1969), 72–73.

2. Ibid., 28.

3. Warner, 53–61; Howard Jones, *Mutiny on the Amistad* (New York: Oxford University Press, 1987), 96–99; Leon Litwack, *North of Slavery: The Negro in the Free States, 1790–1860* (Chicago: University of Chicago Press, 1961), 155–162; Jarvis M. Morse, *A Neglected Period of Connecticut's History, 1818–1850* (New Haven, Conn.: Yale University Press, 1933), 193–196; Leonard L. Richards, *Gentlemen of Property and Standing: Anti-Abolition Mobs in Jacksonian America* (New York: Oxford University Press, 1970), 38–40; C. Peter Ripley, ed., *The Black Abolitionist Papers Volume II* (Chapel Hill: The University of North Carolina Press, 1986), 82.

4. Ibid. See also Philip Foner and George Walker, eds., *Proceedings of the*

Black State Conventions, 1840–1865, 2 vols. (Philadelphia: Temple University Press, 1979–1980), 2: 86; William M. Banks, *Race and Responsibility in American Life* (New York: W.W. Norton, 1996), 11–12.

5. Warner, 59; Litwack, 126–131; Jones, 96–99; Dwight L. Dumond, *Antislavery: The Crusade for Freedom in America* (Ann Arbor: University of Michigan Press, 1961), 211–217; Albert E. Van Dusen, *Connecticut* (New York: Random House, 1961), 211–212; Edmund Fuller, *Prudence Crandall: An Incident of Racism in Nineteenth Century Connecticut* (Middletown, Conn.: Weslyan University Press, 1971); Phillip S. Foner and Josephine Pacheco, *Three Who Dared: Prudence Crandall, Margaret Douglass, Myrtilla Miner—Champions of Antebellum Black Education* (Westport, Conn.: Greenwood, 1984), 5–46; Alice Felt Tyler, *Freedom's Ferment: Phases of American Social History from the Colonial Period to the Outbreak of the Civil War* (Minneapolis: University of Minnesota Press, 1944), 506–508.

6. Warner, 66–67; Jones, 96–99; Clifton Johnson, "The *Amistad* Case and Its Consequences in US History," *Journal of the New Haven Colony Historical Society* 36, no.2 (1990); Constance Baker Motley, "The Legal Aspects of the *Amistad* Case," *Journal of the New Haven Colony Historical Society* 36, no.2 (1990) 23; Van Dusen, 213; Richard Hegel, *Nineteenth-Century Historians of New Haven* (Hamden, Conn.: Archon Books, 1972), 14–15.

7. Warner, 94–96.

8. Warner, 107.

9. New Haven Board of Education (1874) reported in Robert Austin Warner, 119.

10. Robert Dahl, *Who Governs* (New Haven: Yale University Press, 1961), 32.

11. Constance Baker Motley, *Equal Justice Under Law* (New York: Farrar, Straus and Giroux, 1998), 14–15; see also Robert Warner, 192–195.

12. Claudia Scott, *Forecasting Local Government Spending* (Washington, D.C.: The Urban Institute, 1972), 13.

13. Motley, 23 and 14–15.

14. Ibid., 15.

15. Fred Harris, interview by author, telephone tape recording, 9 April 1999; Harold Mulvey would ultimately be named judge in the trial of the New Haven Panthers in 1970 and 1971. His comments would come back to haunt him. Mulvey's comments recorded in "Koskoff Discusses Trial," *Connecticut Daily Campus*, 12 November 1970, 1–2. See also "Interview with Harold Mulvey," *People's News Service*, newspaper of the Connecticut State Chapter of the BPP, 21 June 1970, 9–11.

16. Jeanne R. Lowe, *Cities in a Race with Time* (New York: Random House, 1967), 514.

17. Mr. Charles Louis and Mr. Joe Louis, interview by author, tape recording, Washington, D.C., 22 May 1999.

18. Ibid.

19. Jane Jacobs, *The Death and Life of Great American Cities* (New York: Vintage, 1961), 411–412.

20. Dahl, 229.

21. William Miller, *The Fifteenth Ward and the Great Society: An Encounter in a Modern City* (Boston: Riverside Press, 1966), 99.

22. Allan Talbot, *The Mayor's Game: Richard Lee of New Haven and the Politics of Change* (New York: Harper & Row, 1967), 137.

23. Ibid., x.

24. Talbot, 169–170.

25. Cleo Abraham, *Protests and Expedients in Response to Failures in Urban Education: A Study of New Haven, 1950–1970* (Ph.D. diss., University of Massachusetts, 1971), 5.

26. Talbot, 168.

27. Scott, 13.

28. Talbot, 166.

CHAPTER TWO

The Babylon of
Black Togetherness

At its apex, the Black Panther Party in New Haven was successfully based in the community. Other black organizations such as the National Association for the Advancement of Colored People, the Congress of Racial Equality, and the Urban League, although active at various times in New Haven, seemed far less effective in addressing the needs of blacks within the city. The relative success of the BPP, and the lackluster performance of other local groups, find their explanation in New Haven politics before the rise of the BPP. The groundwork was done during the mayorship of Richard C. Lee. He was a central figure in New Haven politics, intimately involved with black groups in pursuit of his model city. The mayor's interaction with such groups as the NAACP goes a long way toward explaining the appeal of the BPP over a decade later.

"Babylon of Black Togetherness," comes from a letter written by John Barber, president of the local NAACP, to Mayor Lee in 1963 lamenting the political infighting and disorganization that hampered black organizations in New Haven in the late 1950s and early 1960s. Barber's letter, ironically, was to one of the people most responsible for those problems.

The NAACP was one of the first national civil rights organizations to form a chapter in New Haven. Chartered in 1917, the local chapter enjoyed great success in its early years. According to Robert Austin Warner, who published a study of New Haven blacks in 1940, its membership was a blend of white religious liberals and "the mass of solid civic minded Negroes." The leadership of the organization was clearly dominated by the liberals. Warner found that between 1917 and 1940 chapter presidents included, "a Jewish Rabbi, a Unitarian and a Congregationalist Minister—all white," but only one "Negro Pastor."[1]

Concerning itself with issues of more national import than local, the organization peaked between four and five hundred members. The local

21

Youthful John Barber at
Moorehouse College. *(Courtesy,
of Earl Williams and John
Barber Jr.)*

chapter followed the agenda of the national office and W. E. B. Du Bois
and other leaders regularly visited New Haven. But by the late 1930s the
organization entered a sharp period of decline. The nation's entry into
the Second World War and the increase in wartime employment in New
Haven might be two explanations. Warner offered his own conclusion:

> While the organization resisted local discrimination in the
> Y.M.C.A. and in public-school teaching appointments . . . no
> outstanding fight has occurred in New Haven. Perhaps for that
> reason interest and membership have now declined, and the
> younger thinkers term the agency either as moribund or defunct.
> Only a local race conflict would test the hidden loyalties to this
> organization and to its ideals and methods.[2]

By the late 1940s and early 1950s that conflict was on the horizon in
New Haven.

The local chapter was revitalized in the mid-1940s, when it became
closely associated with the Dixwell Congregational Church. At that time,
the Dixwell area was well known as the black neighborhood in New
Haven. Eighty-five percent of its inhabitants were black.

Under Mayor "Honest John" Murphy in the late 1940s the members worked to have blacks appointed to positions within the city government, including the police and fire departments, the board of education, and the police board of commissioners. Although their efforts were largely unsuccessful, a steadily increasing African-American migration from the South promised greater influence in politics. In 1940, four thousand blacks had lived in New Haven. By 1950 that number had doubled to 9,500, six percent of the city's total population. While Mayor Murphy, a Democrat, and his successor William Cellantano, a Republican, could justify ignoring the small but growing black population in the late 1940s, the NAACP reasoned that the next mayor of New Haven could not. The chapter eventually attempted to use the increase in black population to leverage concessions from the mayor.[3]

In the election of 1953, the NAACP backed the Democratic candidate Richard Lee, primarily because he actively courted the African-American vote. Lee had twice tried to unseat the Republican incumbent William Cellantano and had twice been defeated in close elections, losing by seven hundred votes in 1949 and by only two votes in 1951. In 1953, however, he won by a comfortable 3,582 votes. Lacking a solid African-American vote, he would have lost.[4]

Once Lee was in office, the NAACP attempted to hold him accountable for the promises he had made during the campaign. In particular, the branch chapter wanted him to do something about police brutality

Mayor Richard C. Lee pictured here in a publicity photograph for Allan Talbot's 1962 book *The Mayor's Game.* Lee's record sixteen years as mayor of New Haven coincided with the rise of militant black protest in the city. *(Copyright* Washington Post; *Reprinted by permission of the D.C. Public Library)*

in New Haven. In the late 1940s and early 1950s the New Haven chapter of the NAACP was particularly concerned with ending police brutality and placing blacks on the police force. As early as 1954 the new mayor made major strides with the branch after he took more proactive measures in dealing with these concerns.

On February 17, 1954, Branch Secretary Charles A. Hubbard sent a resolution to the mayor expressing the group's doubts about the "proper training of police officers on human relations." Mayor Lee responded by inviting Hubbard and the NAACP to meet with him about their concerns.[5]

This first meeting was cordial. The branch wanted to know what Lee's position was on the investigation into the police shooting of Donald Williams, a black motorist, on December 26, 1952. Representatives presented Lee with a copy of a petition it had sent to his predecessor, Mayor Cellantano, back in January of 1953, demanding an investigation and observing that "a police officer is not justified in having recourse to his gun in an arrest involving a minor motor vehicle violation, even though it might mean losing the operator temporarily through flight." Although the first meeting resolved little in the way of the NAACP's original petition, Mayor Lee had demonstrated a level of openness that endeared him to many within the branch.[6]

Lee remained relatively aggressive in his dealings with the organization, reacting swiftly when it brought problems to his attention; for example, in his response to the demand by the NAACP for an investigation into the arrest of a thirteen-year-old black girl named Margaret Harris. After being accused of a minor infraction Harris had been handcuffed and paraded two blocks to the police station at 5:00 in the afternoon. The mayor promptly arranged to meet with the branch. In a resolution delivered in advance of its meeting with the mayor, the NAACP called for some form of "public disciplinary action" against the officers involved and asked Lee for "Some assurance . . . that measures of education in human relations are being taken in the police force against recurrence of such unfortunate displays of poor judgement."[7] At the meeting on March 11, 1954, neither of the NAACP's issues was resolved. But the branch president Harold Fleming informed the mayor that the NAACP appreciated the "genuine attention" Lee was giving the matter and said that he was appointing a special mayor's committee to serve as "an official liaison group between your office and the New Haven Branch of the NAACP."[8] In a speech a few weeks later, the mayor mentioned the need for better training for the New Haven police. In response, Branch Secretary Charles Hubbard wrote to Lee expressing his "appreciation for the forthright stand you have taken, regarding the training and conduct of the New Haven Police."[9]

The creation of a mayor's committee within the NAACP came at the time Lee was in the process of creating his own citizens' group, called the Citizens Action Commission. Lee boasted that the CAC represented *the finest* in community participation. Many disagreed, however, arguing that the commission was not an expression of community support for the mayor but had been created and sustained by Lee and the Redevelopment Agency to give the appearance of popular backing. And not everyone in the New Haven branch of the NAACP was satisfied with the mayor's relationship with the organization. William Nathan Hamilton, the chairman of the Legal Redress Committee in New Haven, was particularly cautious about Lee and worried that the close connection between the mayor and the NAACP might hurt the branch in the long run.

When Hamilton apprised the mayor of an incident of police misconduct involving a black motorist, Lee wrote his newly appointed police chief, Francis V. McManus, "If this happened the way it was described the officer in question deserves to be hauled up before the Board and suspended." Noting the sensitive nature of the complaint, Lee advised McManus to "sit down with the Police Brass and go over this thing." Lee concluded, "Please get going on this immediately. One of the many reasons I named you Chief was for your ability, I thought, to handle things like this, and here's a test of your metal." In the meanwhile, Lee wrote Hamilton, "There is no need to tell you, I am just as concerned about the incident involving Mr. Norwood [the motorist] as you are."[10] Yet Hamilton and the NAACP were again frustrated in persuading the mayor publicly to censure the police force. McManus called a meeting and invited the branch to attend. At that meeting, however, McManus denied that an assault had occurred and refused to honor the NAACP petition requesting that the matter be brought before the police review board. Lee meanwhile refrained from any further intervention, stating that the incident was a police matter, and in effect accepting the version of the story given by McManus and the officers.

Despite the frustrations of Hamilton and others, the mayor's relationship with the NAACP continued to blossom. While Lee's interest in maintaining peace with the black community was genuine, he also continued taking steps to turn the NAACP into a tool of his political machine. In 1955, for instance, Lee prompted Edward Logue, one of his advisors in the mayor's office and head of the Redevelopment Agency, to join the NAACP. President Fleming quickly appointed Logue to the mayor's committee but Logue's response betrayed the direction in which the mayor hoped to see the NAACP head. As Logue wrote Fleming, "I am very pleased to accept the appointment. Dick is very hopeful that this Committee working with the Human Relations Committee of the Citizens Action Committee will develop real importance in our common life here."[11]

But the political connection hurt the NAACP in two ways: by preventing the chapter from expressing any substantive criticism of the mayor and by splitting loyalties among members into pro-Lee and anti-Lee factions. Lee was particularly close to some of the older members of the branch who appreciated his willingness to engage in dialogue. As the older group of leaders within the organization became less active or in some cases passed on, Lee's hold on the chapter began to fade. After the death of Branch Secretary Charles Hubbard in 1957, the debate within the NAACP intensified over the chapter's relationship with Lee.

After 1957 the character of the New Haven branch of the NAACP changed. A younger and more vocal group of leaders emerged with a broader program than maintaining cordial relations with the mayor. National events made the chapter much more militant in identifying the social, political, and economic forces that limited black people in the United States. Between 1954 and 1957 the civil rights struggle began to shift from the NAACP's legal attack on segregation to direct action protest. The national attention afforded to direct action protests, including the Montgomery bus boycott of 1955 and 1956 and the Little Rock school desegregation battle of 1957, had a strong effect on elements within the New Haven chapter. Finally, throughout the late 1950s and early 1960s a parade of leaders in the southern civil rights movement such as Daisy Bates, the NAACP president from Little Rock Arkansas, came through New Haven on speakers' tours and fund-raising endeavors.

At about the same time the Dixwell Ministerial Alliance, a group of local ministers and church leaders committed to improving the quality of life for African Americans in New Haven, became more radical as well. John Daniels, a lifelong NAACP member and member of the Dixwell Congregational Church, notes that the Dixwell church had always been closely associated with the NAACP. According to Daniels a number of leaders of the NAACP had come out of the Dixwell church and the two organizations had worked closely together in the past. On one occasion however, the Alliance was more militant than the NAACP.[12]

In the winter of 1957 the branch chapter had become embroiled with the police over the demotion of Clarence Jacobs, New Haven's only black detective. Jacobs was removed after he was arrested during an incident of domestic violence. The situation struck an uneasy chord with Reverend Theodore Ledbetter, who was head of the Dixwell Ministerial Alliance and served on Lee's Human Relations Council. It was the Dixwell Ministerial Alliance, therefore, that intervened on behalf of Jacobs.

During a meeting held with New Haven's four police commissioners and Chief of Police McManus on Tuesday, February 26, 1957, Ledbetter took a very militant stance. Angered by the commissioners' stubborn refusal to reconsider Jacobs's punishment, Ledbetter warned, "New Haven is building up for an explosion." Asked what he meant Ledbetter replied, "I mean a race riot. Unless you come up with the right solution there will be trouble and it will be on your conscience."[13]

Soon after the meeting, Ledbetter resigned or was forced to leave his position on the Human Relations Council. Lee took the situation very seriously, having aides draft a report on the number of blacks appointed by his administration. He again declined to mediate, however, citing the need for police to determine their own personnel decisions. In the end, Ledbetter was the only casualty of the affair. Jacobs was never re-promoted and Ledbetter subsequently moved out of New Haven.

Despite the Jacobs affair, the mayor's relationship with the NAACP continued to run smoothly. Lee wrote to Jackie Robinson on behalf of the chapter asking him to come to the branch's annual fund-raiser. As usual, Lee's good will served two functions. The more benevolent objective he explained to Robinson:

> If this were simply a dinner alone, we would not press you to come as our speaker. However, this is part of an ambitious pro-gram for our neighborhood. It will include a coordinated ap-proach by the city, Yale University, industry, labor, retail busi-ness and the Dixwell Community Council to work on problems of health, job opportunity, housing, recreation, adult education, and family life, particularly for members of minority groups.[14]

The other purpose, of course, was to solidify Lee's political standing in the black community. Robinson agreed and after the dinner Lee at-tempted to continue their association, writing Robinson a warm letter of gratitude with the added invitation, "I'd like you to come to New Haven quietly and I will show you our whole program on relocation and inte-gration. I feel confident you will be impressed with it." On May 14, 1957, Robinson replied, "I got a thrill out of meeting a public official that got so much kick out of an accomplishment because it did something for his community." Nonetheless he declined Lee's invitation.[15]

Lee and the NAACP both gained political mileage from their associ-ation. But as the organization became more activist, responding to the shift in focus by the national NAACP in the late 1950s, the connection between the two began to frazzle. The most significant change in the New Haven branch took place with the election of James E. Gibbs as branch president in 1959. A native of New Haven, Gibbs had been active in the NAACP for five years, serving on the executive board of the branch for four years, organizing the local youth council of the NAACP, and in 1955 heading the branch's political action committee.[16] Gibbs was also a labor organizer employed by the Seamless Rubber Company and an active member of Local 338, United Rubber Workers of America. He was a union steward for four years and sat on the grievance committee, negotiating committee, and fair employment practices committee. A member of the Greater New Haven Industrial Union Council for three years, at the time of his election he was a delegate to the Greater New Haven Central Labor Council. Under Gibbs's leadership, the branch became for its time a radical organization.[17]

Gibbs's radicalism had a history in his involvement with other political groups, including the Communist Party. A confidential report by the New Haven police noted that in 1953 and 1954 Gibbs had been active in the Dixwell Avenue Branch of the Communist Party and in 1954 was a member of a cell consisting of six people whose purpose was to recruit black members. The police further suspected that Gibbs had been advised to join the NAACP by Simon Silverman, a prominent Connecticut Communist, convicted under the Smith Act in the early 1950s.[18]

Gibbs's flirtation with the Communist Party was likely a reflection of the relative inactivity of other organizations in and around New Haven in the early 1950s. The party took a strong stand on many issues, such as housing and labor, that the Dixwell Ministerial Alliance and the NAACP were not addressing. When the NAACP began to emerge nationally as a direct action protest group with Montgomery and Little Rock, Gibbs may have seen possibilities for the New Haven branch. "Gibbs was never openly active in the Communist Party," the New Haven police observed, and "at this point [when he joined the NAACP] he became completely inactive."[19]

As president of the branch, Gibbs immediately began to move the chapter in the direction of more substantive issues, including the housing and labor concerns that the Communist Party had taken on. This inevitably meant challenging the mayor. Gibbs was not as apt to take advantage of the mayoral committee as past chapter presidents. In clear defiance of the union between the NAACP mayoral committee and the Citizens Action Committee, he appointed several new committees to deal with a myriad of problems affecting blacks in New Haven and was quick to confront the mayor about his dealings with the branch.

Gibbs's activities alienated Lee's supporters within the branch and led to a very public rift with the Dixwell Ministerial Alliance early in 1959. In February, Branch Secretary Andrew Harris wrote to the national offices to update Gloster Current, national director of chapters, on the status of problems within the New Haven branch. Harris warned Current that local clergy were denouncing the members as radicals. In addition, Harris complained that Mayor Lee and the chief of police, McManus, were attempting to play the two groups against each other by staging a meeting to which they invited the Ministerial Alliance without the knowledge of the NAACP. Both the New Haven branch of the NAACP and the Dixwell Ministerial Alliance placed most of the blame for the incident on McManus and the president of the Board of Police Commissioners. In a joint statement the organizations declared, "We deplore such actions as detrimental to the best interest of our community, and we strongly urge that the necessary steps be taken to prevent such a reoccurrence." The two groups declared their mutual respect for each other, reaffirming "our united struggle for equal opportunity and equal protection under the laws for all the people of this community."[20]

In a subsequent letter to the national offices of the NAACP, Harris told Current that the incident had been "confined to our colored community" and that the NAACP would not respond in the press to the "very silly statements made by the clergy." The "members of the various churches," Harris reported, "were not kind in their task-taking of their ministers." Pressure from these members had brought about a conciliatory meeting between the Alliance and the NAACP that produced the joint press release. Harris concluded his letter with an assurance that the Ministerial Alliance would "never openly attack the Branch again" and that the NAACP "believed the matter closed."[21]

On March 10, 1959, Current responded, noting that "the organizations in the Negro community should be kept fully advised of our activities. It is not a bad policy to educate the clergy, although they would resent the term 'educate,' by meeting with them frequently and bringing them up to date on what is going on." Current thought it "unfortunate when any segment of the community has a disagreement with the NAACP over matters in which they should have a common interest." The ministers, he acknowledged, "are a potent force in any community and the NAACP could not exist without their aid."[22]

Harris was confident that the NAACP had minimized fallout from the situation, but in the months to come the New Haven branch of the NAACP would split over support of the mayor. Gibbs continued to agitate Lee supporters through his presidential activities. When Lee rejected several proposals made by the newly created branch delegation on housing, Gibbs dispatched an angry letter to the mayor on September 18, 1959. "Your answer to their request and your attitude towards them did not resemble that of a candidate seeking reelection, but of one who already has the Negro vote in his hip pocket," Gibbs complained. Six years of the Lee Administration had persuaded him "that the time has come to unseat the popular myth that Dick Lee is concerned about the Negroes' problems." Gibbs continued, "I also take this opportunity, Mr. Mayor, to terminate this you-tell-me-and-I'll-take-care-of-it relationship between us. We shall resume our tried and trusted ways of the past for they bring results."[23]

For Gibbs, tried and trusted ways meant applying pressure on the mayor to make lasting changes within New Haven. It also meant adopting direct action protest. The mayor worried about what impact the Gibbs presidency would have on the branch as a whole and what prospects the negative attention might have for the city as well. He was quick to alert his allies within the branch to watch over its president; nor was he beyond instructing his supporters to express their disapproval of Gibbs. In this manner Lee helped to deepen the rift in the local branch. One of his primary agents, at least initially, would be a young black law student named John Barber.

Gibbs's election coincided with John Barber's arrival from Detroit. He had been invited to apply to Yale Law School and was first introduced to Mayor Lee in 1958. Lee wrote a letter of recommendation for Barber describing him as a "very impressive chap" who "seems to be very sharp" and "someone I feel confident you would likely consider, and I wanted to send this note to endorse him to you."[24] Barber was similarly impressed with Lee and contacted the mayor the following week to express his "sincerest thanks" for Lee's endorsement. "Needless to say," Barber added, "I look forward to being able to put into practice the human values you exemplify in community service." Several months later Barber joined the New Haven branch of the NAACP and began reporting on the activities of the group to the mayor. He joined several older members of the branch who, remembering Lee's openness, constituted a faction within the NAACP favorable to Lee that greatly compromised the organization's effectiveness.[25]

During the preparation for the local NAACP's annual membership and fund-raising event, Freedom Fund Drive, Gibbs made Barber the fund's promotional director. Barber immediately approached Lee about writing a letter inviting Daisy Bates, president of the Little Rock Arkansas branch of the NAACP, to speak at the Freedom Fund dinner scheduled for October 19, 1959. Lee agreed and extended an invitation to Mrs. Bates, which she accepted. In the meantime, Gibbs was engineering a modest protest campaign aimed at getting the mayor to act on a long-standing demand of the NAACP that blacks be appointed to the New Haven Board of Education. He decided that one of the most effective ways to reach Lee would be through postcards to the mayor's office from citizens who supported the demand for a black board member.[26]

In the aftermath of the postcard campaign Barber wrote Lee in an attempt to distance himself from the branch's actions. In a letter dated September 11, 1959, he affirmed his loyalty to Lee, explaining, "If I had known what was developing I would have surely decided hands off for me." That would be, he claimed, because "I have too much to learn about many things to pop off ill considered demands and besides I am increasingly acquiring implicit faith in you which more and more precludes me allying with transient and subverting causes."[27] Speaking as a neophyte to his teacher, Barber exclaimed:

> My civic loyalties are with the Negro cause, the Democratic party
> and your political stature. . . . I think of you as a political hero

... and my acquired adulation of you is to a great extent independent of the fact that you have helped me in my academic and employment situations for which I am eternally grateful. I like you as the epitome of the liberal politician for what I consider your sincere interest in the progress of the long underprivileged of this community.[28]

And to his mentor Barber concluded:

If I sincerely believed my loyalties to my race, the party and you were conflicting, I would be beset by dilemmas which I am not sure how I would resolve. Perhaps, integrity would impel me to step one way, perhaps another. One factor in my choice in such a hypothetical situation would be my consideration of two occasions in which you counseled me on my youthful proclivity toward impetuousness and on the virtues of patience. I appreciated your considered opinion as in large measure correct and worthy of implementation in terms of its value.[29]

In the meantime, Gibbs followed up the postcard protest with an all-out assault on Lee's civil rights record. His vehicle was a biting editorial in the branch newsletter entitled, "Just a Little Mail."

Gibbs attacked Lee for refusing to place a black on the Board of Education: "It seems that for the past six years, since Mayor Lee has been in office, we have been trying to get a Negro on the Board of Education. During these six years we have pleaded, we have reasoned, we have worked and yes we have begged. But like the stone and mortar and concrete of the buildings that are new New Haven, Mayor Lee has been unmoved."[30]

Gibbs related the events of the September meeting between Lee and the NAACP, noting that, "This time the Mayor was furious . . . because more than 250 of you dropped the Mayor a card asking him to consider a Negro for the Board of Education." The mayor, Gibbs observed, had informed the branch that the selection of a member of the school board was a political issue and that "we Negroes haven't earned any appointments and . . . WE haven't worked hard enough for HIM." To this Gibbs responded, "Well now didn't he carry the Negro wards in 1953, 1955, and 1957 with a healthy majority? . . . In fact in 1957 the 19th and 22nd Wards were the only wards to overwhelmingly support his pet projects the Charter Reform."[31]

"So deep is our concern for the future of our children," Gibbs charged, "that a spontaneous movement has emerged within the Negro community to elevate a member of our race to the Board of Education." For this effort, "We may well be on the verge of fighting our Battle of Little Rock, in any event the New Haven NAACP is 1000% behind this movement." Gibbs concluded, "Coincidental as it may seem, the very woman who symbolizes the Negro's fight for Educational Equality will be our keynote speaker in just a few weeks. How will Mayor Lee appear to us standing there on the stage next to Daisy Bates of Little Rock?"[32]

Juxtaposed to the Gibbs editorial was a short article by John Barber on the upcoming mayoral election in New Haven entitled "Political Scene." Barber surveyed the field of candidates but subtly reminded voters of the branch's special relationship with Lee. He remarked, "personally this writer is going out and vote for . . . Oops, pardon me. I almost slipped up there and named my choice"; not really a slip since Barber had emerged as one of Lee's chief supporters within the branch. Despite the tenor of Barber's comments, he had cause to be concerned about the placement of his article in relation to Gibbs's editorial.[33]

On September 22, 1959, Barber sent Lee a Western Union telegram. Explaining that he had been out of town at the time the newsletter was published, he told the mayor that upon reading Gibbs's editorial he had resigned as Freedom Fund director. Barber called Gibbs's article "an outright and unjustified political slap. More importantly personally it was a slap in my face since I had in good faith turned to you in behalf of the organization for Ralph Bunche, for ads and to appear on the program with Mrs. Bates."[34] Barber ended with an apology for the branch: "I am sorry for the position we have placed you in through our president. I can imagine how you feel. I remain committed to the party and your candidacy to any extent you deem it worthwhile. I pray it is not too late to demonstrate such dedication."[35]

Barber's story was confirmed by David Altschuler, another aide to Lee who had joined the NAACP branch. On September 28 Altschuler mailed the mayor a copy of the newsletter. In an accompanying note he explained, "the attack on you is malicious and unwarranted, and of course its development was kept from John Barber or myself."[36]

After Barber's resignation the branch's Freedom Fund drive ended abruptly. This brought to the attention of Current the developing conflict in the local chapter. In reply to a special inquiry by Current concerning the drive, Branch Secretary Andrew Harris in December of 1959 sent a letter to Roy Wilkins, the executive director of the national organization.

As Harris conceived the problem, "A group of enthusiastic people, and some older ones, all members of the Branch became overzealous in their support of our Mayor Lee during the past year. Also, during this year the New Haven Branch has had reasons to inquire very closely into some of the policies of the Mayor."[37] Harris located the root of the disagreement in the effort of Lee's supporters to prevent the branch from taking any action or raising any issue that might embarrass the mayor during his reelection bid. In reaction to the branch administration's disagreement, Harris claimed, Lee's supporters had attempted to elect a slate of their group to head the local chapter in 1960. Harris believed the danger had passed: John Barber, the leader of this group, realized he had been "used" by the mayor. Harris explained, "He is very sincere in his desire to help our branch, and its policies but more than that he was influenced that the way to achieve progress was through close and quiet cooperation with the city administration."[38] Harris reported that with the help of the Reverend Edwin Edmonds, minister of the Dixwell Congregational Church, the whole situation had actually brought the branch together. Harris credited Edmonds with being a calming influence within the branch.

From North Carolina, where he was president of the Greensboro chapter of the NAACP, the Reverend Edmonds had moved to New Haven. He replaced Reverend Ledbetter as head of the Dixwell Congregational Church in 1959 and also became head of the Dixwell Ministerial Alliance. Having participated in civil rights protests in the South, Edmonds was initially viewed as a radical. He was much in favor of direct action and shared Gibbs's belief that any improvement in racial conditions would require change on the part of the mayor himself. As Edmonds was to recall:

> [Lee] had a scheme that any promotion on the police force had to take a two-part examination. Forty percent of its core was a written exam. Sixty percent was an examination by the Mayor orally and there was space enough in there to manipulate anyone's score. So we said we have to put pressure on you if we are going to have any officers or promotions in the police department.[39]

But like Barber, Edmonds eventually was taken with Lee, who he believed had a genuine interest in seeing the black community prosper. Lee, in Edmonds's later appraisal, was "not free of prejudice but . . . he was an astute politician, he saw the political worth of an amicable and productive agency with the Black community." Edmonds also came to think that the local branch often was too militant in dealing with a mayor and city government willing to communicate with them, a willingness Edmonds had not experienced in North Carolina. Edmonds remembers one instance:

> We had this negotiation session before nine o'clock and the Judge conceded all of our demands and we went back and told the group that we don't have to picket because we've gotten a settlement and all of our demands have been met . . . and one guy spoke up and said we can't do that. We already agreed to picket, missing entirely the purpose.[40]

According to Edmonds, Lee supported his idea of building a black middle class in New Haven. Yet personal conflict kept Edmonds and Barber apart.[41]

Quick to take advantage of Barber's offer of support, Lee in the meantime was beginning to solicit suggestions for dealing with the city's black leaders. In December of 1959, Mitchell Sviridoff, a native New Haven resident who was head of the state AFL-CIO and a Lee appointee to the New Haven Board of Education, sent the mayor a memorandum entitled "Memo on Problems of Leadership in the Negro Community." Sviridoff argued that black leadership could be divided into three categories, conservatives, moderates, and immoderates or direct actionists.

Once the dominant leaders in the black community, Sviridoff argued, conservatives included a wide range of personalities from "the apathetic, the obsequious, the compliant and the frightened" to "the highly rational but innately conformist or assimilationist personality." Sviridoff postulated that the conformist nature of the conservatives led many politicians to exaggerate their importance. "To rely on them today for practical assistance in coping with the potentially explosive social, economic and political problems of the Negro community would be an exercise in futility," he concluded.[42]

The moderates, including educators, ministers, professionals and intellectuals, were at least on the surface the dominant force at that time. The moderates, Sviridoff observed, "would appear to offer the kind of leadership with which municipal authorities could form an effective alliance for the solution of the seemingly ever-present and nagging problems of the Negro community." The moderates represented a leadership that was palatable to the sophisticated white community. But they could not be relied on in most crises. As Sviridoff explained, "In tough situations they seem to falter, hesitate, vacillate—and even run for cover." The remaining group was the reason why.[43]

The immoderates or direct actionists, as Sviridoff identified them, ranged from responsible and objective radicals to "extreme fanatical nationalists." The nature of the crisis or the way the white community responded determined which side a large centrist element within the group would take. "Though in numbers the direct actionists are considerably smaller than either of the other groups," Sviridoff concluded, "they all too frequently assume dominant leadership in the Negro community."[44]

Sviridoff identified three reasons for this. He argued that the black community harbored an insatiable appetite for progress or at least the appearance of progress, which made it more responsive to the radical voices who promised more returns than the moderates. Direct actionists, moreover, had been responsible for most of the more significant victories of civil rights. Further aiding their future was "the ineptitude in the white community."[45] Acknowledging that "irresponsible radical Negro leadership" was not an accident but often the product of white insensitivity, Sviridoff made several recommendations to Lee on how to avoid social unrest.

It was up to the city, the memorandum contended, to determine the differences between the "adjustment problems" of black migrants to New Haven and the experiences of other minority groups who may have settled in the city earlier. Politicians should resist the tendency to dismiss black complaints by measuring them against other ethnic groups. Instead, Sviridoff argued, the city should make every effort to "detect the sore spots and at least attempt to initiate positive programs and policies in consultation with a wide range of leadership from the Negro community." Sviridoff warned that the alternative was to wait for things to explode, "With the leadership inevitably passing into the waiting hands of the irresponsible."[46]

In a policy of openness to black needs and demands, however, the city would find only limited value in using political appointments or favors. While "such tactics may even contribute to the winning over to the city administration of some important community leaders . . . they may have the effect of neutralizing the potential of these same individuals for leadership."[47]

In a passage, duplicating the warning that Gibbs had made to Lee in the letter of September 18, Sviridoff predicted that politicians who placed too much faith on election day results and public opinion polls were practicing self-deception. Democratic politicians would be tempted to interpret black support "as reassuring evidence that nothing more need be done in the way of genuine and positive programming." The "natural identification of the Negro with the Democratic Party," Sviridoff observed, might invite Democratic politicians to ignore more moderate forms of protest. Black people therefore would be forced to resort to more radical means of exerting pressure that although "seemingly irresponsible, too often do seem to work."[48]

Recognizing that protest movements might lead city administrators in the direction of strengthening alliances with black moderates, Sviridoff insisted that maintaining communication with "responsible radicals" was important as well.

True, the responsible radical may fail to show proper appreciation for programs, or even for personal favors. His behavior may even border on downright discourtesy. To cut oneself off from him completely, however, is again to invite irresponsibility. We may indeed be rejecting a valuable divining rod for real or potential community discontent, as well as cutting off a possible source of positive and constructive ideas.[49]

Having just been through his ordeal with Gibbs, Lee responded to the Sviridoff memorandum, "I subscribe to everything there." In the first few months of 1960 Lee seemed to be putting part of Sviridoff's advice into practice by cultivating his relationship with Barber and Edmonds, and by attempting to anticipate issues affecting the black community.[50]

At the same time, Gibbs began to experience the fallout from his militancy. On June 15, 1960, Roy C. Jackson, the first vice president of the New England Regional Conference of the NAACP, received an anonymous letter recounting the citation of Gibbs during 1956 hearings before the House Un-American Activities Committee as a possible associate of the Negro Commission of the Communist Party. "In these days when we are engaged in an all important struggle for equality for members of our race, can we afford to continue to offer our enemies such a justifiable basis for criticizing our organization?" asked the writer, who proposed that Gibbs be removed by a "self-imposed house cleaning" rather than exposure from enemies of the NAACP.[51] The letter was the first in a series of events that effectively destroyed the NAACP as a viable organization in New Haven.

Jackson forwarded the letter to Gloster Current, who subsequently contacted Gibbs. Upon receiving the letter, Gibbs informed the national office that he had distributed copies to the branch executive committee. The committee, he explained, had concluded that the writer's failure to sign a name rendered the letter unimportant. Current responded a few days later thanking Gibbs for his response and agreeing to a meeting with him.[52]

While Lee's supporters were working to get rid of Gibbs from the inside, the mayor attempted to demonstrate his new sensitivity to the problems facing black people by proposing a controversial protest for the early spring. As Allan Talbot recorded the events, Lee had been given a draft of a speech that called for New Haven blacks to stage a sit-out and obstruct late afternoon traffic to demonstrate to homeward bound suburbanites the poor conditions in which urban blacks lived. The mayor's proposal served two purposes: to identify with the problems of urban blacks and to drum up support for urban renewal projects that would obliterate those conditions.[53]

Lee's speech evoked the desired response from the local radical element, in this case James Gibbs, who assured the mayor that, "The relationship between you and the branch can develop into a much stronger and healthier one, and I am sure this is what we both want, if you just deal with us directly on matters of importance." Lee was not prepared, however, for the backlash against his proposal from elements with no great interests at stake.[54]

Some of Lee's supporters may have made him nervous. Robert A. Haber, the president of Students for a Democratic Society, the youth department of the League for Industrial Democracy, wrote Lee, "Your suggestion of a sit out intrigues me. I wonder whether you can elaborate a little. We have been thinking of a demonstration and program to focus national attention on the deplorable situation in Deerfield, Illinois. Perhaps you might have some suggestions along that line." Within New Haven, Lee was contacted by William "Bill" Winnick who was identified by both CORE and the NAACP as a member of the Socialist Workers Party. Winnick wrote the mayor, "I see you are getting a lot of abuse about your courageous stand in connection with the sit out issue. . . . I want you to know that you have struck a very responsive chord with many people. You have my unqualified support in this issue. I congratulate you on your fine and vigorous stand."[55]

The opposition was formidable. Arleigh D. Richardson wrote:

As a former resident of New Haven, Conn., and a fervent admirer of Mayor Richard Lee's accomplishment . . . I am inexpressibly shocked at his suggestion to a group of youths that a sit out in the middle of the streets would be an effective and acceptable practice. These are strange words indeed from the man whose own police I have personally observed in a night stick attack upon students who were doing nothing more than standing on the sidewalk.[56]

Arthur Irwin, accusing the mayor of "buttering up the minority groups for their dubious political support," asked the mayor to "consider carefully the impact of a sit out on the tax payers of your community." Irwin concluded that the mayor seemed more a "left wing radical" than a "responsible, intelligent adult, with a great responsibility to the local and state communities."[57]

Attempting damage control, Lee distanced himself from his previous announcement and returned to the church where he had delivered the speech. There he promised to create an urban renewal program aimed at the slums within New Haven. Tempered by this experience, Lee made further use of his friends within the NAACP, Barber and Edmonds, to see to it that Gibbs was kept in check. Edmonds and Barber began reporting to the mayor at regular intervals on events in the chapter and marshaled support against what they termed Gibbs's abuse of power.

In November of 1960 eighteen members of the Dixwell Ministerial Alliance, including the Reverend Edmonds, signed a protest letter to the national offices charging Gibbs with bringing disgrace on the chapter. The issue this time was the Dewitt Jones Housing Case, a local cause célèbre involving a middle-class black couple attempting to purchase a home whom real estate agents had turned down. On November 4, 1960, Gibbs had distributed a letter criticizing Edmonds and the Dixwell

Church for not supporting the NAACP in the Jones case. In particular, Gibbs accused Edmonds of making a "concerted effort" to restrict information on NAACP activities and not allowing him to speak before the congregation to announce news relative to the NAACP.[58] The protest letter from the Alliance charged Gibbs with embarking on an "irresponsible and unauthorized public letter writing campaign which was the source of much embarrassment for the organization." The signers invited Current to attend a proposed meeting scheduled for November 17, 1960, as an official observer of the national offices.[59] Current responded personally to Edmonds and advised him that he would be present and that Gibbs had been apprised of his visit as well.

In reality, Edmonds was only pursuing a moderate course that he had used as head of the NAACP in Greensboro. While Edmonds was not opposed to direct action protest, he believed that in order for any protest to be effective it needed to speak directly to the issue and not simply function as a show of disapproval for elected officials. Having dealt with the intransigent government of Greensboro, Edmonds realized the importance of maintaining open lines of communications with the mayor. He was also quick to claim victory after protest demands had been met. Edmonds's style of leadership had brought him into direct conflict with the more proactive Gibbs.[60]

Barber, in the meanwhile, was motivated by an overwhelming loyalty to Lee largely growing out of the many political favors Lee had bestowed upon him. As Barber explained in a letter to the mayor, "This relationship has been one I've highly appreciated and at times been plainly awed by, that I, in my early twenties, while yet a student, and a Negro, should have had such camaraderie with the chief executive of a significant, and increasingly so, American municipality." Lee undoubtedly found it very easy to manipulate Barber with even the slightest hint of his disfavor. In one incident in February of 1961, during which Lee called Barber a racist for endorsing some of the actions of the local branch, Barber sent the mayor a three-page letter which he described as an "apologia, that is more in explanation and confession than anything else." Recounting, in an eagerness to prove his loyalty to Lee, the events of the postcard protest, Barber wrote:

> My stand earned for me the label of a vassal of Dick Lee . . . the censure was quite a bitter pill to swallow. In addition my law school grades plummeted downwards as a direct result of my over-involvement in politics that fall semester but I felt I was doing what integrity impelled of me in bucking Gibbs all the way. So, my greatest consolation rested in your reelection and the thought that I'd given what support I could to that endeavor and I would undoubtedly adopt the same course again if I found myself in the same posture.[61]

In 1961 Blyden Jackson, a young black nominated by the Republican Party as a candidate for alderman, withdrew from the race to organize a local chapter of CORE. Wishing to see direct action protests against unfair housing practices and other social ills in New Haven, Jackson sought to make the New Haven CORE the most radical group in New Haven. As one of his first acts in the presidency of the new CORE chapter, Jackson renewed Lee's call for a sit-out to dramatize poor housing conditions in New Haven. Gibbs endorsed Jackson's proposal which was much to his own taste, and further announced plans for the NAACP to participate in the CORE sit-out. Lee was horrified by the specter of his mistake coming back to haunt him. He began to put pressure on his contacts within the NAACP to oppose Gibbs's call. Edmonds and Gibbs were now pitted directly against each other.

Lee's supporters within the NAACP inundated Gloster Current with dozens of letters questioning the legality of Gibbs's actions. Current was also contacted directly by Lee, who telephoned the NAACP headquarters on September 18, 1961, the week before the protest was to take place. The conference call, which according to the NAACP typed transcripts of the conversation included Edmonds and Sviridoff, focused on the "James Gibbs problem." Sviridoff and Lee complained to Current that Gibbs was a radical who was proposing the sit-out only to embarrass the mayor and highlight problems that did not exist. During the conversation Lee reminded Current of the upcoming election for mayor and his record on civil rights.[62]

As a result, Current contacted Gibbs by telegram that afternoon. Dispensing with the usual pleasantries, he informed Gibbs that before any action could be taken the national office needed to be advised. Urging Gibbs to respond by telephone that evening, Current warned him of the potential consequences of an ill-conceived protest without a sound basis in fact. Current had placed the national office directly in the conflict between the mayor and the New Haven branch.[63]

The following evening the branch held a two-hour meeting, which the local press characterized as "stormy," to decide on possible postponement of the sit-out. "In the wake of shouted demands for action now, contrasting pleas for observance of NAACP procedure, and two challenged votes on a motion for further deliberation," the *New Haven Register* reported, the meeting finally ended with the provision that the protest would be reconsidered at another meeting scheduled for September 29. It was Edmonds who had succeeded in tabling the discussion of the proposed sit-out by calling for the submission of the proposal to the executive committee for further consideration.[64]

By now it was becoming clear to many within the branch that the Reverend Edmonds had struck a deal with Lee. In a confidential memo to the mayor the morning after the meeting, Lee aide Barry Passett wrote "It was obvious that your spokesman was Edmonds. He was sharp, brilliant and effective" Critiquing the performance of Lee's other "friends" Passett accused Barber of taking "the easy way out" by abstaining from the reverend's motion. He further reported that "Brewer was simply a dud and almost got himself in a great deal of difficulty" and that "Sam Dickinson tried to do right by you and publicly broke with Gibbs; but he acted like such a buffoon all night that he merely destroyed his own standing with the group." Betraying the politicized nature of Lee's interest in the matter, Passett recorded how the "Republicans, with one exception voted for Gibbs." But Passett also warned the mayor not to view the situation in purely political terms. As he explained, "The problem is that all of these people with the exception of the rich and the secure city employees—are angry about housing conditions, especially rent gauging, and expect something to be done." "They are not necessarily mad at you," Passett explained, "They do not however, feel the Dixwell Project is benefiting them and they have the strong feeling that they must do something active, like down South, to win support for their cause."[65]

Current, in the meantime, continued to try to make contact with Gibbs. In a letter dated September 20, he reminded Gibbs that the NAACP could "ill afford" to have the organization proceeding on some highly complex matters, such as in the field of housing, without advice from its housing secretary or possibly its legal authority. Current again strongly advised that Gibbs contact him or postpone the protest until more information was available.[66]

While he was attempting to contact Gibbs, Current continued to receive pressure from people within the chapter to have the branch president removed. On September 26, Gibbs finally replied to Current's letters insisting that reports of the proposed sit-out in the New Haven press were grossly exaggerated and that the New Haven branch had acted in accordance with organizational procedure. Gibbs explained that the proposed protest was "merely one small part of our Housing campaign to develop community awareness and support for our program." Concerned like Harris about undue influence from the mayor's office, Gibbs added, "Some people, politically motivated, have been attempting to discredit our housing campaign by attacking our sit out." Gibbs said that the sit-out would still take place that Saturday afternoon and offered Current an invitation to observe it.[67]

Current drafted a response to Gibbs and made arrangements to attend the planning meeting for the sit-out. But he rebuked the branch president: "We have engaged in direct action, such as sit outs, where legal remedies are not available or where duly constituted authorities fail, neglect or refuse to act. None of these factors are present here." At the meeting, Current delivered his statement, which received wide coverage in the local press. In addition, Current threatened to revoke the

New Haven branch's charter if it proceeded to carry on the protest. Minutes from the meeting reflect the growing tension and partisanship within the local NAACP, at which the national office repressed the will of the majority.[68]

Following the meeting, Current called for a session of the New Haven executive board for October 5, to consider the fate of President Gibbs, whom he clearly blamed for the volatile atmosphere in the local chapter. In official charges brought against Gibbs by the national office for conduct "inimical to the best interest of the National Association for the Advancement of Colored People," Current concluded:

> The entire attitude of the president reflects a disrespect for the organization which he supposedly represents and indifference to the most effective and orderly ways of taking advantage of the progress already made and of insuring community cooperation in future progress. Obviously he is more concerned with his own position and with colorful demonstrations and newsletters than action in keeping with the organization's reputation for reliance on lawful channels.[69]

On October 2, 1961, John Fernandez, president of the Negro American Labor Council of Connecticut, wrote to National NAACP Labor Secretary Herbert Hill. Fernandez complained about the national office's handling of the sit-out meeting, especially the manner in which Current had circumvented Gibbs's authority and the chapter's desire to protest: "At the present time many of us feel that the National NAACP has placed itself in the position in which many may be led to believe it is taking sides on local issues." Fernandez urged Hill to conduct a complete investigation of public housing in New Haven before deciding on whether Gibbs had acted improperly.[70]

Yet Lee's forces continued to push for Gibbs's expulsion. In a confidential memorandum, Current recorded that on October 3, 1961, Bishop C. H. Brewer, a Mr. Ullman, and John Barber had visited his office to insist that the chapter would survive only if Gibbs was no longer president.[71]

On October 5, the day that his fate was to be determined, Gibbs resigned but not before drafting a letter to Roy Wilkins, the NAACP national executive director, outlining his concerns for the future of the NAACP. Expressing his frustration with the way Current had handled the sit-out meeting, he accused the national offices of sending mixed messages. As Gibbs wrote, "At the Philadelphia Convention sit-outs and sit-ins were endorsed. Now one is told that endorsement was only for the South and not for the North. Further one is told that only with the support of a segment of the political community and segment of the white community could a direct-action program be carried out." That, Gibbs charged, contradicted the past policy of the national office of not putting itself behind a political party and would make the branch dependent on a portion of the political community—a portion, moreover, that had worked against a branch project. "It is necessary," Gibbs observed,

> to point to the growing disillusionment among intelligent Negroes in the community at the obstacles placed in the path of those who wish to protest discriminatory practices. Indeed many within the New Haven Branch have become so disillusioned with the response of the National Office that it becomes impossible to work within the framework of the NAACP.[72]

In his official report to Roy Wilkins on problems within the New Haven branch, Current betrayed much of the backward thinking that Gibbs complained about. As he explained,

> I am beginning to conclude that some of our northern branches are infiltrated and the line is calling for demonstrations and other protest activities, the success of which is questionable, but which stirs up confusion and brands the NAACP as an irresponsible organization. This has happened in San Francisco where the group picketed the Fairmont Hotel and in Los Angeles where a boycott has been called against the Los Angeles *Times* and the large hotels.

Current concluded, "I am planning to take strong action in every instance where this situation crops up."[73]

In the meanwhile, speculation about who was responsible for undermining Gibbs was rampant in the local chapter. That Edmonds was singled out as one of the people who had opposed Gibbs illustrates the perceptiveness of Sviridoff's memo. In the aftermath of Gibbs's public censure a controversial newsletter entitled *Bee's Sting Spark* attacked Edmonds for the "Sit-out sell out" and accused Current of high-handed tactics in dealing with the local chapter. The *Sting* reserved its strongest venom for Edmonds, who it argued had engineered the whole debacle. Prior to the removal of Gibbs, Edmonds had moved into a new home that critics dubbed "Mt. Carmel Plantation." Rumor circulated that Edmonds had purchased the home with money provided by Lee. In July, just a few months before the sit-out fiasco, Lee had invited Edmonds to attend the NAACP convention for July 7, all expenses paid, as a fraternal delegate of the City of New Haven. Many saw a direct connection between Edmonds's willingness to see Gibbs removed and what they termed his selling out to the mayor.[74]

The incident demonstrates the inadequacies of the NAACP as a protest organization rooted in the community. The national office was denying indigenous leaders the right to exercise meaningful protest specific to their locale. Even though both Current and the NAACP noted that the majority at the meeting of October 5 had supported Gibbs and some form of protest in New Haven, Current dismissed them as the "Gibbs clique." The NAACP was not the organization for new leaders and did not relate well to local issues. CORE promised to deliver where the NAACP had failed.

Gibbs joined CORE, which continued to push for a sit-out in New Haven. October 7, two days after his resignation, Gibbs participated in the first of a series of pickets staged by CORE to dramatize the plight of New Haven blacks. On October 17, CORE announced plans to stage a massive sit-out on Grand Avenue to protest housing discrimination.[75]

The NAACP, meanwhile, went through the motions of selecting a new president. In a highly charged election in December of 1961, the *New Haven Register* reported that the NAACP was a battleground divided between conservative, moderate, and extremist influences. The *Register* identified Sam Dixon, the acting president of the NAACP, as a conservative candidate. It labeled John Barber the moderates' choice and Walter Henderson, who was also a member of CORE, the militant selection. The personal feud between the two men working on Lee's behalf within the organization put Edmonds in Henderson's camp. In events leaving the local chapter of CORE in a shambles as well, CORE would later misinterpret Edmonds support.[76]

During the meeting to select the new president, Henderson and Barber bitterly attacked each other, Barber calling Henderson a "faceless man" propped up by Edmonds and Blyden Jackson. Referring to Barber's summer job with the Redevelopment Agency, Henderson observed that the "mayor is not paying my tuition." He implied that if elected Barber would take orders directly from the mayor. Barber noted the brevity of Henderson's association with the NAACP and charged that he was a pawn promoted up by Edmonds and CORE to control the NAACP. Although the pair tied, each receiving thirty-eight votes while Dixon got ten, Barber ultimately won the election, only to preside over the NAACP's further decline.[77]

Notes

1. Robert Austin Warner, *New Haven Negroes* (New York: Arno Press, 1969), 288.
2. Ibid., 288.
3. Reverend Edwin Edmonds, interview by author, tape recording, New Haven, Connecticut, 23 July 1997; Mr. John Daniels, interview by author, tape recording, New Haven, Connecticut, 25 July 1997; Allan R. Talbot, *Mayor's Game* (New York: Harper & Row, 1967), 11.
4. Talbot, 11.

5. Charles A. Hubbard, Branch Secretary, NAACP New Haven Branch Chapter, to Mayor Richard C. Lee, 17 February 1954, Richard C. Lee Papers RG 318 Series I Box 3 Folder 60, Manuscripts and Archives, Yale University Library.

6. Charles A. Hubbard, Branch Secretary, New Haven, NAACP, to Mayor Richard C. Lee, 17 February 1954; "Resolution Against the Excessive Use of Force within the New Haven Police Department," Executive Committee New Haven, Connecticut, Branch NAACP, to Chief Howard O. Young, Department of Police Services, New Haven, Connecticut, 14 January 1953, Richard C. Lee Papers RG 318 Series I Box 3 Folder 60, Manuscripts and Archives, Yale University Library.

7. Civil Liberties Committee, New Haven Branch NAACP, to Mayor Richard C. Lee, 8 March 1954, Richard C. Lee Papers RG 318 Series I Box 3 Folder 60, Manuscripts and Archives, Yale University Library.

8. Harold Fleming to Mayor Lee, 12 March 1954, Richard C. Lee Papers RG 318 Series I Box 3 Folder 60, Manuscripts and Archives, Yale University Library.

9. Charles A. Hubbard, Branch Secretary, NAACP New Haven Branch, to Mayor Richard C. Lee, 29 March 1954, Richard C. Lee Papers RG 318 Series I Box 3 Folder 60, Manuscripts and Archives, Yale University Library.

10. Mayor Richard C. Lee to Frank McManus, Re: Police incident 5/12/56/, 5 June 1956, Richard C. Lee Papers RG 318 Series I Box 9 Folder 235, Manuscripts and Archives, Yale University Library; Mayor Richard C. Lee to Bill Hamilton, 6 June 1956, Richard C. Lee Papers RG 318 Series I Box 9 Folder 235, Manuscripts and Archives, Yale University Library.

11. Edward Logue to Dr. Harold Fleming, 10 January 1955, Richard C. Lee Papers RG 318 Series I Box 6 Folder 153, Manuscripts and Archives, Yale University Library.

12. John Daniels interview.

13. Report by Bishop Brewer to Mayor Lee, 26 February 1957, Richard C. Lee Papers RG 318 Series I Box 113 Folder 2018, Manuscripts and Archives, Yale University Library.

14. Mayor Richard C. Lee to Mr. Jackie Robinson, Vice President Chock Full of Nuts Coffee, 2 April 1957, Richard C. Lee Papers RG 318 Series I Box 11 Folder 302, Manuscripts and Archives, Yale University Library.

15. Mayor Richard C. Lee to Mr. Jackie Robinson, Vice President Chock Full of Nuts, 9 May 1957; Jackie Robinson, Vice President Chock Full of Nuts Coffee, to the Honorable Richard C. Lee, 14 May 1957, Richard C. Lee Papers RG 318 Series I Box 11 Folder 302, Manuscripts and Archives, Yale University Library.

16. "Gibbs's heads 59 Slate," *NAACP Newsletter*, February 1959 contained in NAACP Papers Group III Box I 6, Manuscript Division, Library of Congress.

17. Confidential Police Report re: James E. Gibbs, dated [1961?] Richard C. Lee Papers RG 318 Series II Box 107 Folder 1911, Manuscripts and Archives, Yale University Library.

18. Ibid.

19. Ibid.

20. Andrew R. Harris, Secretary of the New Haven Branch, NAACP, to Gloster B. Current, National Director of Chapters, NAACP, 15 February 1959, NAACP Papers Group III Box C18, Manuscript Division, Library of Congress; News Release from New Haven Branch, NAACP, and Dixwell Ministerial Alliance, News Release date: 16 February 1959, NAACP Papers Group III Box C18, Manuscript Division, Library of Congress.

21. Andrew R. Harris, Secretary of the New Haven Branch, NAACP, to Gloster B. Current, National Director of Chapters, NAACP, 15 February 1959.

22. Gloster Current, National Director of Branches, NAACP, to Mr. Andrew R. Harris, Secretary of the New Haven Branch, NAACP, 10 March 1959, NAACP Papers Group III Box C18, Manuscript Division, Library of Congress.

23. James E. Gibbs, President of New Haven Branch, NAACP, to the Honorable Richard C. Lee, Mayor, City of New Haven, 18 September 1959, Richard C. Lee Papers RG 318 Series II Box 113 Folder 2016, Manuscripts and Archives, Yale University Library.

24. Mayor Richard C. Lee to Gene Rostau, 10 February 1958, Richard C. Lee Papers RG 318 Series II Box 113 Folder 2016, Manuscripts and Archives, Yale University Library.

25. John Barber to Mayor Richard C. Lee, 19 February 1958, Richard C. Lee Papers RG 318 Series II Box 113 Folder 2016, Manuscripts and Archives, Yale University Library.

26. *NAACP News*, 18 September 1959, contained in NAACP Papers Group III Box I 6, Manuscript Division, Library of Congress.

27. John Barber to the Honorable Richard C. Lee, 11 September 1959, Richard C. Lee Papers RG 318 Series II Box 113 Folder 2016, Manuscript and Archives, Yale University Library.

28. Ibid.

29. Ibid.

30. James E. Gibbs, "Just a Little Mail," *NAACP Newsletter*, February 1959, contained in NAACP Papers Group III Box I 6, Manuscript Division, Library of Congress.

31. Ibid.

32. Ibid.

33. John Barber, "Political Scene," *NAACP Newsletter*, February 1959, contained in NAACP Papers Group III Box I 6, Manuscript Division, Library of Congress.

34. John Barber to Richard C. Lee, via Western Union Telegram, 22 September 1959, Richard C. Lee Papers RG 318 Series II Box 113 Folder 2017, Manuscript and Archives, Yale University Library.

35. Ibid.

36. David A. Altschuler to Mayor Richard C. Lee, 18 September 1959, Richard C. Lee Papers RG 318 Series II Box 113 Folder 2017, Manuscript and Archives, Yale University Library.

37. Andrew R. Harris, Secretary of the New Haven Branch, NAACP, to Mr. Roy Wilkins, Executive Secretary of the NAACP, 13 December 1959, NAACP Papers Group III Box C18, Manuscript Division, Library of Congress.

38. Ibid.

39. Reverend Edwin Edmonds, interview by author, tape recording, New Haven Connecticut, 23 July 1997.

40. Ibid.

41. Ibid.

42. Mitchell Sviridoff to Mayor Richard C. Lee, Re: Memo on Problems of the Leadership in the Negro Community, 29 December 1959, Richard C. Lee Papers RG 318 Series II Box 113 Folder 2018, Manuscripts and Archives, Yale University Library; Fred Powledge also records the contents of the Sviridoff Memo in his book *Model City*. Powledge notes that while Mayor Lee had possessed the Sviridoff Memo since 1959 there was "no available record of his (Lee's) reaction to it." Powledge, 50. I found Lee's reaction in his personal papers. In reference to the memo, Lee wrote Sviridoff, "I subscribe to everything there. Parts of it, of course, resemble people I know." Richard C. Lee to Mitchell

Sviridoff, 29 December 1959, Richard C. Lee Papers RG 318 Series II Box 113 Folder 2018, Manuscripts and Archives, Yale University Library.

43. Mitchell Sviridoff to Mayor Richard C. Lee, Re: Memo on Problems of the Leadership in the Negro Community, 29 December 1959, Richard C. Lee Papers RG 318 Series II Box 113 Folder 2018, Manuscripts and Archives, Yale University Library; Powledge, 48.

44. Mitchell Sviridoff to Mayor Richard C. Lee, Re: Memo on Problems of the Leadership in the Negro Community, 29 December 1959; Powledge, 48.

45. Ibid.

46. Ibid.

47. Ibid.

48. Mitchell Sviridoff to Mayor Richard C. Lee, Re: Memo on Problems of the Leadership in the Negro Community, 29 December 1959; Powledge, 49.

49. Mitchell Sviridoff to Mayor Richard C. Lee, Re: Memo on Problems of the Leadership in the Negro Community, 29 December 1959; Powledge, 50.

50. Mayor Richard C. Lee to Mitchell Sviridoff, Re: Memo on Problems of the Leadership in the Negro Community, 29 December 1959, Richard C. Lee Papers RG 318 Series II Box 113 Folder 2018, Manuscripts and Archives, Yale University Library.

51. "Discouraged" to Mr. C. Roy Jackson, First Vice President of New England Regional Conference of the NAACP, 15 June 1960, NAACP Papers Group III Box C18, Manuscripts Division, Library of Congress; A Jimmy Gibbs is mentioned in the text of the Hearings before the Committee on Un-American Activities, New Haven, September 1956, U.S. Government Printing Office, Washington, D.C., 1956: 5607.

52. James E. Gibbs, President of the New Haven Branch, NAACP, to Mr. Gloster B. Current, National Director of Chapters, NAACP, 23 August 1960, NAACP Papers Group III Box C18, Manuscript Division, Library of Congress; Gloster B. Current, National Director of Chapters, NAACP, to James E. Gibbs, President of the New Haven Branch, NAACP, 29 August 1960, NAACP Papers Group III Box C18, Manuscript Division, Library of Congress.

53. Talbot, 170–171.

54. James E. Gibbs, President New Haven Branch of the NAACP, to Mayor Richard C. Lee, 7 August 1960, Richard C. Lee Papers RG 318 Series II Box 114 Folder 2040, Manuscript Division, Library of Congress.

55. Robert A. Haber, President of Students for a Democratic Society, to Mayor Richard C. Lee, 8 August 1960, Richard C. Lee Papers RG 318 Series II Box 114 Folder 2040, Manuscript Division, Library of Congress; William Winnick to Mayor Lee, 4 August 1960, Richard C. Lee Papers RG 318 Series II Box 114 Folder 2040, Manuscript Division, Library of Congress.

56. Arleigh D. Richardson, III, to Mayor Richard C. Lee, 6 August 1960, Richard C. Lee Papers RG 318 Series II Box 114 Folder 2040, Manuscript Division, Library of Congress.

57. Arthur E. Irwin to Mayor Richard C. Lee, 29 July 1960, Richard C. Lee Papers RG 318 Series II Box 114 Folder 2040, Manuscript Division, Library of Congress.

58. Open Letter addressed Dear Friend and Fellow Member of Dixwell Congregational Church: from James Gibbs, 4 November 1960, NAACP Papers Group III Box C18, Manuscript Division, Library of Congress.

59. Dixwell Congregational Church, New Haven, Connecticut, to Gloster Current, National Director of Chapters, NAACP, 9 November 1960, NAACP Papers Group III Box C18, Manuscript Division, Library of Congress.

60. Gloster B. Current, National Director of Chapters, NAACP, to Dr. Edwin R. Edmonds, 15 November 1960, NAACP Papers Group III Box C18, Manuscript Division, Library of Congress; Reverend Edwin Edmonds, interview by author, tape recording, New Haven, Connecticut, 23 July 1997.

61. John Barber to Dick Lee, 27 February 1961, Richard C. Lee Papers RG 318 Series II Box 113 Folder 2017, Manuscripts and Archives, Yale University Library.

62. Transcript of telephone conversation between Mayor Lee, Dr. Edmonds, and G. Current, Re: James Gibbs Problem, five page typed transcript, 18 September 1961, NAACP Papers Group III Box C292 Folder: New Haven, Connecticut Branch Problems 1961, Manuscript Division, Library of Congress.

63. Gloster B. Current to James Gibbs, via Western Union, 18 September 1961, NAACP Papers Group III Box C292 Folder: New Haven, Connecticut Branch Problems 1961, Manuscript Division, Library of Congress.

64. "NAACP Postpones Sit-Out Action After Stormy Two-Hour Meeting," *New Haven Register*, 19 September 1961, 1–2.

65. Barry Passett to Mayor Richard C. Lee, Re: Last night's NAACP meeting, 19 September 1961, Richard C. Lee Papers RG 318 Series I Box 35 Folder 771.

66. Gloster B. Current, National Director of Chapters, NAACP, to James E. Gibbs, President of the New Haven Branch, NAACP, 20 September 1961, NAACP Papers Group III Box C292 Folder: New Haven, Connecticut Branch Problems 1961, Manuscript Division, Library of Congress.

67. James E. Gibbs, President of the New Haven Branch, NAACP, to Gloster Current, National Director of Chapters, NAACP, 26 September 1961, NAACP Papers Group III Box C292 Folder: New Haven, Connecticut Branch Problems 1961, Manuscript Division, Library of Congress.

68. "Sit-Out Plan Is Blocked At City Meeting," *The New Haven Register*, 29 September 1961, 1–2.

69. Gloster B. Current, Official Charges, Findings of Fact and Conclusions, Re: James Gibbs, undated report, NAACP Papers Group III Box C292 Folder: New Haven, Connecticut Branch Problems 1961, Manuscript Division, Library of Congress.

70. John M. Fernandez, President of the Negro American Labor Council of Connecticut, to Herbert Hill, the National NAACP Labor Secretary, 2 October 1961, NAACP Papers Group III Box C292 Folder: New Haven, Connecticut Branch Problems 1961, Manuscript Division, Library of Congress.

71. Confidential Memorandum for the files New Haven (Gloster B. Current), 4 October 1961, NAACP Papers Group III Box C292 Folder: New Haven, Connecticut Branch Problems 1961, Manuscript Division, Library of Congress.

72. James Gibbs et al. to Roy Wilkins, 5 October 1961, NAACP Papers Group III Box C292 Folder: New Haven, Connecticut Branch Problems 1961, Manuscript Division, Library of Congress.

73. Gloster B. Current to Roy Wilkins, 29 September 1961, NAACP Papers Group III Box C292 Folder: New Haven, Connecticut Branch Problems 1961, Manuscript Division, Library of Congress.

74. Sam Carruthers, "Doc Ed Stung As Uncle Tom Par Excellence," *Bee's Sting Spark*, 10 October 1961, Vol. 1 Edition 4, contained in Richard C. Lee Papers RG 318 Box 44 Folder 922, Manuscript Division, Library of Congress.

75. "First Sit-Out Is Staged Along Dixwell Ave Curb," *New Haven Register*, 7 October 1961, page unknown, clippings file, local history collection, New Haven Public Library, New Haven, Connecticut; "CORE Pickets Stage March At City Hall," *New Haven Register*, 10 October 1961, page unknown, clippings file, local

history collection, New Haven Public Library, New Haven, Connecticut; "CORE to Picket Pavilion to Protest Housing," *New Haven Journal Courier*, 18 October 1961, page unknown, clippings file, local history collection, New Haven Public Library, New Haven, Connecticut.

76. "A Moderate And A Militant Tie In Vote For NAACP President," *New Haven Register*, December 1961, page unknown, clippings file, local history collection, New Haven Public Library, New Haven, Connecticut.

77. Ibid.

CHAPTER THREE

In 1962 Richard C. Lee
Was the Civil Rights Leader
in New Haven

The Black American knows intuitively that his time of acceptance depends less on his own efforts than on the conscience of
other ethnic groups who are affluent and secure and don't care
to look behind them.

> —Walter Cronkite,
> news commentator, 1969

The undesirable aspect of the affair is that the Negro . . . is
always kept on the outside and is used as a means to an end. To
obtain the meager consideration which he receives the Negro
must work clandestinely through the back door. It has been
unnecessary for the white man to change this procedure, for
until recent years he has generally found it possible to satisfy the
majority of Negroes with a few political positions earmarked
"Negro jobs" and to crush those who clamor for recognition.

> —Carter G. Woodson,
> *The Miseducation of the Negro*,
> 1933

One of the more curious and common features of most studies on New
Haven in the late 1960s was the low opinion they record of black civil
rights organizations in the city. Allan Talbot's study of Mayor Lee, for
instance, notes that Lee held very little respect for the "Negro political
leadership" in New Haven because he believed that "none of them could
deliver the political support that he could get for himself." Examining
the lack of activity by the NAACP and other civil rights groups in New
Haven after 1960, Fred Powledge concludes, "In 1962 Richard C. Lee
was the civil rights leader in New Haven, Connecticut." At election time

alone was his position challenged, Powledge notes, "and then the questioning was done ordinarily by a Republican candidate who merely reflected his party's near-zero understanding of the problems affecting Blacks and New Haven's poor."[1]

Powledge, like Talbot and Miller, was undoubtedly unaware of what was going on privately in New Haven, how Lee had worked to manipulate many of the civil rights organizations, how political infighting and also a good deal of incompetence made impossible a viable alternative to Lee or even a raised voice in objection to his programs. In addition, after 1962 Lee worked to create his own agency designed to handle many of the concerns of these marginal constituents which only further endeared him to them and precluded any charge that the mayor was completely insensitive to their needs.

By 1962 the NAACP was thoroughly infiltrated by the mayor's supporters, including the chapter president, John Barber. The Reverend Edwin Edmonds was appointed to serve on Lee's experimental poverty program. Only CORE remained outside of the mayor's web of control. Internal problems coupled with haphazard protest tactics employed by the group had driven down its membership. The sit-out arrests cooled some people's enthusiasm for CORE. Alphonso E. Tindall, the only black member of the Board of Education and the executive director of the Dixwell Community House, a local community center, came to the defense of the maverick group. CORE was a much younger group, he explained, not subject to the same concerns as New Haven's more established organizations. Tindall, who was also a member of the NAACP, observed, "Our value systems are different but the NAACP will pay for legal services and support that younger group. Those kids aren't fanatics you know. I couldn't afford to go to jail. But psychologically what they're doing is good."[2]

At the start of 1962, CORE continued to pursue direct action as a means of redressing its housing concerns. It's president, Blyden Jackson, led the assault. Of particular importance was a vote before the Board of Aldermen concerning the proposed fair housing ordinance. Despite the sit-outs and agitation of the year before, the Board of Aldermen voted in early February to reject the ordinance. CORE responded by staging a picket in front of city hall. Many considered the arrest of the protesters to be akin to the tactics being used in the South. Recognizing the potential represented by their arrests, the New Haven CORE appealed to Lee's old friend Jackie Robinson for support. On March 7, 1962, Robinson admonished the mayor by letter that, "New Haven and other northern cities should set the proper example."[3]

Lee responded on March 8, "We do have a civil rights problem in New Haven, so does every city in America," he noted. "There is one difference however, ours is not buried under the table. . . . You know my record. Without being immodest, I think I can say that I have done more in the field of Civil Rights than any Mayor in the United States. At this point I'm feeling a bit persecuted and fed up with shouting and demonstrations—just as I am with discrimination in housing." Lee offered, "Perhaps you might consider coming to New Haven to discuss the situation and you may be able to help us reach an understanding. I certainly would appreciate your help."[4]

Attempting to get more political mileage out of Robinson's interest, the New Haven *Core-lator*, the newsletter of the New Haven CORE, published in its March issue Robinson's letter along with an article on its demonstrations. The NAACP, under pressure to assist the CORE picketers, announced plans to join them if the aldermen refused to reconsider the fair housing bill.[5]

Again faced with the prospects of an all-out protest, Lee sent two representatives to meet with Jackie Robinson, who had arranged for the two parties to meet in Lexington, New York, at the offices of his company Chock Full of Nuts. Lee sent the Reverend Edmonds, who was fast becoming the mayor's troubleshooter on matters of race, and Richard Dowdy, the mayor's advisor on human relations.

Born in Pittsburgh, Pennsylvania, in 1925, Dowdy, similar to the Reverend Edmonds and John Barber, had attended Morehouse College as an undergraduate. He joined the Air Force shortly after completing his first year and served for two years mainly at Tuskegee toward the close of World War II. After his service expired he enrolled at Duquesne University near Pittsburgh where he obtained both a bachelors and masters degree in economics. From 1951 to 1959 he worked at the Urban League in Pittsburgh as director of a career counseling program for adults. He came to New Haven in 1959 as he recalls, "mainly to work with Ed Logue who at that time was the development director of the city." Instead Dowdy was offered a job as human relations advisor to the mayor.[6] He had gained Lee's attention with a memorandum dated December 1960, outlining his views on "the Negro and the Status of Race Relations in America."[7] Similar to Sviridoff, Dowdy argued that conservative elements in New Haven's black community could not be left to deal with the problems before New Haven blacks:

> If we assume that it is the middle class and upper classes which stimulate and direct the drive for status and ultimate uplift of the lower classes, can we reasonably look to the split and splinter Negro middle and upper groups in cities like New Haven to have any great impact on the giant problem of assimilating 90 percent without a team effort involving the larger resources of the total community—freely and thoughtfully extended.[8]

Edmonds clearly shared Dowdy's view. In an interview printed in the *New Haven Register* just three days before Robinson's letter to Lee,

Edmonds reemphasized that New Haven's blacks needed to build up a strong black middle class. As Edmonds explained, "For years the educated people have fled. New Haven has had to import its educated Negroes in recent years."[9]

Edmonds's efforts on behalf of Lee made him again the target of negative speculation. *The Open Gate News*, an independent newspaper in New Haven, observed that "many local members of CORE have expressed surprise that Reverend Edmonds had acted as a courier for Mayor Lee, particularly after the support given by CORE to the candidates for whom Reverend Edmonds had appealed to CORE for support in the NAACP elections last December."[10]

At the meeting in Robinson's Chock Full of Nuts office, Edmonds and Dowdy met with James Farmer, the executive director, and Richard Haley, the national director of chapters for CORE. A representative from the national offices of the NAACP was also present. Little was resolved, Edmonds and Dowdy denying that there was any need for a protest in New Haven and insisting that the CORE picketers had clearly violated the law. Not completely satisfied with Edmonds and Dowdy's explanation of events in New Haven, shortly after the conference in New York, Haley came to New Haven at the request of the national office to discuss with local members their problems with the city government. In advance of Haley's visit, Dowdy arranged for him to meet with "twenty non-Core people" in order to give him "a fairly good cross section of impressions of the local Core Chapters activities."[11] Despite Dowdy's efforts, Haley sided with the local chapter. Haley subsequently informed the branch that National CORE "saw no reason to enact any strong change in local policies."[12]

Just after this victory, though, a new problem emerged for the local chapter. On the evening of April 3, 1962, Jackson stumbled into the emergency room of the Grace-New Haven hospital with a gunshot wound in the upper chest. As medical personnel administered aid, Jackson told them he had been shot by three men after he refused to turn over his wallet. The *New Haven Journal Courier*, relying on Jackson's description of the assailants as "three shabbily dressed Negroes between the ages of 19 and 25" reported that the shooting had "no connection with Jackson's activities against segregation."[13] The day after the shooting the Executive Board of CORE sent a letter to the national offices confirming its faith in Jackson. But in the course of their investigation, police determined that the shooting had actually taken place at Jackson's apartment and that his wife, Carmel, had pulled the trigger. Jackson was driven to the hospital by Elinor Holmes and Inez Smith both Yale law students and CORE members. The two were later arrested for conspiracy to give false information to police. When police finished, four women and three men were charged in the shooting including Jackson and his wife, Jackson's sister, and several members of CORE. The revelation that it was Jackson's wife who had shot him shook the local chapter. While Norman Hill, assistant program director for the National CORE, said that there would be no inquiry into the incident, an editorial in the *Open Gate News* underscored the seriousness of the situation when it pondered what the future of CORE could be with Jackson still in the leadership.[14]

Dowdy, in the meantime, used the incident to raise the mayor's credibility with Jackie Robinson, National CORE, and the National NAACP. On April 5, 1962, he wrote Robinson on behalf of the mayor, "It is too bad the shooting occurred. Also, it will be lamentable if the lives of a few promising, though misguided young people are adversely affected. . . . But, life's lessons in accountability and responsibility sometimes have to be learned the hard way." As for Haley's visit, Dowdy remarked, "While I am glad Haley came, I am not fully convinced that his mind was open enough to actually 'see' what he could have seen as regards local CORE people and what they are doing."[15] On the same day Dowdy wrote Haley, "I suppose one can expect young people who are inexperienced and immature to make many mistakes. But when people, young or old, are acting in the role of leaders, they cannot afford the luxury of involving personal lives in ways that do damage to the very causes they claim to advance."[16]

Nearly a year after dispensing advice to CORE Dowdy found himself at the center of a much more serious situation in New Haven. The circumstances that surround the controversy help to demonstrate the politicized nature of Lee and people tied with city hall acting as civil rights stewards. As longtime NAACP member Earl Williams was to recall, Lee brought Dowdy into the mayor's office as a "blocker," someone to divert the attention of the black community away from pressing issues of civil rights. Williams described this as a pattern with Lee of using blacks in his administration to handle matters of race with Lee's interests first. There was little room for self-expression, a point to which Dowdy readily agrees. Early on in his tenure with the mayor's office Dowdy claims to have made a conscious decision to try and maintain a separate identity from the political dealings of the mayor but in the winter of 1963, at least from Lee's perspective, that no longer was possible. In February of that year three men, Harold Cloud, Harry Reed, and Lawrence Oliver, had been arrested for the rape and abduction of a white nurse as she walked home from the Grace-New Haven Hospital. The charges against Oliver were reduced but Cloud and Reed faced long prison sentences for their alleged involvement. The two were assigned a public defender named Richard Sperandeo who proceeded to provide a lackluster defense which drew sharp criticism from certain segments within the city. The case attracted the attention of the Yale Law School

Public Defenders Association and Criminal Law Professor Abraham Goldstein who contacted Dowdy. They asked the human relations advisor if he would help them interview witnesses in the black community who may have known of a prior relationship between one of the defendants and the nurse. Dowdy agreed and with a list of names provided by the professor did find a witness. After a good deal of persuasion Dowdy was able to convince the man, Willie Carr, that he should tell authorities what he knew, but Carr, who had a criminal record and feared retribution, subsequently told prosecutors that Dowdy had forced him to testify. The Cloud case became a public relations nightmare for both Dowdy and the mayor.[17]

Making matters worse from Lee's perspective was the involvement of a young black female CPI staffer, Jean Cahn. In Dowdy's recollections, Miss Cahn, who was a graduate of Yale Law School, wanted to ensure that the defendants received a fair trial. She made daily trips to the courthouse during the trial and offered the public defender advice on how to argue the case. When her activities became too high profile Dowdy was approached by Sviridoff to keep a lid on her. Her involvement along with that of Dowdy cast a dark shadow over the Lee Administration. The *New Haven Register* bitterly attacked the mayor for permitting Dowdy to become involved in what the state's attorney described as the rape of the victims reputation. Although Professor Goldstein ultimately came to Dowdy's defense, the Cloud case destroyed his ability to work effectively for the mayor. In the months following the Cloud case both Dowdy and Cahn were offered generous deals in which they were compensated for vacating their positions. Dowdy was admitted to Yale Law School where he continued to receive one half of his salary as human relations director for one year and was promised work with the city for the summer. Dowdy was later to observe that Sviridoff and Lee were more concerned with protecting the reputation of the mayor's office and his community programs than advancing the cause of black civil rights.[18]

The sit-out fiasco lowered the status of the NAACP, and the shooting of Jackson that of CORE, for civil rights advocacy in New Haven. Part of their decline is easily explained by the ultimate failure of their methods and the very public airing of their internal disagreements. Considerable blame must also be placed on Lee and his supporters within those organizations. John Barber, more than any other person, proved to be the most duplicitous in serving as an intermediary between the mayor and local chapter. In his new capacity of chapter president, Barber briefly retreated from his association with Lee but never too far to make himself unavailable if the mayor should desire his services.

In this period Barber was responsible for addressing at least one serious issue facing blacks in New Haven, the question of police protection. Barber charged that the New Haven police were only haphazardly enforcing antigambling laws in the New Haven slum areas. Police Chief McManus called him a liar. Barber seemed to make a hasty retreat when he refused to elaborate or provide the police with specifics concerning the gambling operation. Barber later contacted the FBI, however, which launched a full-scale investigation into the NAACP's charges against the city of New Haven.[19]

In June of 1963 Barber seemed to be moving further away from the mayor after he engineered an alliance between the NAACP and Raymond H. Paige, a political independent running to become the first black mayor of New Haven. Barber and Chapter Vice President Earl Williams agreed to head up Paige's campaign unit. In an article in the *Open Gate News* entitled "Will the Negroes Control?" Barber said that in 1963 blacks would control the voting power in New Haven. Expressing his unqualified support for Paige's candidacy, he further noted that even if the campaign was ultimately unsuccessful, the Independent Party could use its voting power as a weapon in demanding concessions from both parties.[20]

Barber's political independence was short-lived. In a letter to Lee dated August 1963, he undermined the effectiveness of the coalition by pledging his wholehearted support for Lee, even offering to sabotage the Paige campaign. Barber confessed to Lee, "I am writing this statement because I would like to say a few things to you which I would never be able to say face to face primarily because of an irrational, but unavoidable impediment—an overweening pride."[21] Barber explained:

At the outset I would like to make one bald and, perhaps, unbelievable statement which is this—I like you Dick—and I use the verb "like" advisedly because it's the only adjective in my inadequate vocabulary to convey a sentiment short of using another word which has too many syrupy, sycophantic, and sexual connotations and which leaves one uncomfortable in its use. The Ancient Greeks use to describe the sentiment more precisely with their term "philos" a brotherly kinship or regard or love.[22]

Barber continued:

I once expressed disaffection because I had heard you had referred to me as a racist, but I think that your comment, or at least the rumor, had rung the bell of a bitter truth. I had erected a personal wall against every white man I've come across as a result of the deep sensitivity to the accidents of history and the countless incidents of inhumanity perpetrated in the name of racial superiority. I just ascribed to every white man responsi-

bility for history's indignities. It was out of such "racism" that I
spurned the political and personal hand of friendship which you
offered. Even when I was close to the downtown scene I harbored fears for my integrity and worried about being caught in a
web of paternalism. Thus, I armed and rearmed myself with the
rejoinder that "this guy can't be for real."[23]

Barber confessed to seeking:

the Babylon of Black togetherness and sable politics, a sickening
Muslim like chimera for which I forsook all, status, school, personal well-being, etc. In retrospect I think of the Bible's prodigal
son who left his father's substance and home of familial camaraderie to chase the baubles of wine, women and song in the
strange and alluring city of Babylon only to end up in the mire
of a spent and wasted existence, friendless, penniless, feeding
with the swine. So one poet has said that he awoke one morning,
wallowing in the mud, barely able to glimpse the rising sun out
of the fog of yesterday's hangover and through blood redden
eyes. Then, it was that he came to himself and said "I will arise
and go to my father and will say unto him—I have sinned against
heaven and before thee and am no more worthy to be called thy
son: make me as one of thy hired servants . . . "[24]

He concluded:

Awaking now from my self-imposed captivity, I seek only a
chance and opportunity to function in your behalf and to "be
alive again" and "found." I have a desire to pitch my stake in
your camp this fall and afterwards so that whether you win, lose
or draw with Townsend at least I will not have facilitated the
greatest wrong to the New Haven Community and to my Soul.
To that end, I am committed to do all I can, to effectuate the
withdrawal of Paige or the subversion of his prospects either of
which I think can be brought about prior to the election. This is
not stated as part of any package dealing or bargaining. It's just
that I have a personal commitment to the ideals which you sym-
bolize and after too much heady wine and long slumber—I've
arisen and am going to try to make it home.[25]

Lee replied on August 20, 1963, "Dear John, Your letter struck a
warm chord in my heart. I want you aboard, and I would like to talk to
you whenever you have the time. Just call Barbra and come in."[26]

Paige ended up withdrawing and the independents threw their support to Lee. In November of 1963 Barber appointed to serve as honorary co-chairmen of the organization's annual Freedom Fund Drive none other than Mitchell Sviridoff, the new director of the mayor's anti-poverty program, Community Progress, Incorporated (CPI), and James L. Mitchell, director of the New Haven Human Relations Council.[27]

It may have been too late for Barber to pledge his undying support for Lee as the mayor had moved beyond playing politics with local black organizations and decided to strike out on his own. The result was CPI, one of the main reasons that many considered Lee the civil rights leader in New Haven after 1962.

Early on in the process of urban renewal, Lee had hoped to create an agency to deal with problems posed by housing relocation. In 1959, the mayor was holding meetings to determine what to do about a possible community backlash against the program. After the fiasco with the NAACP and CORE the mayor had plenty of motivation to avoid similar problems. Both William Lee Miller and Allan Talbot maintain that the result, CPI, was the mayor's effort to shape a comprehensive antipoverty program in New Haven. CPI would also serve as the mayor's own personal civil action group. As Talbot explains, CPI became the human renewal component of Mayor Lee's program. It also in many ways surpassed in its benefits to the community the efforts of black organizations that then existed in New Haven.

The CPI was financed in 1962 by a two and a half million dollar grant from the Ford Foundation. The grant was to last three years. Additional funding was dependent on the success of the agency in addressing problems of the poor. According to Miller, most of the elements of an extensive antipoverty program had existed in New Haven before the creation of the CPI. CPI primarily served as an umbrella organization centralizing the efforts of other local antipoverty agencies. It directed them toward a newly defined goal of eliminating poverty in New Haven. It also included provisions for programs in education, employment, and social services. CPI had deep pockets to finance the work of these agencies.[28]

Although CPI was not directly linked with the city government, it helped to set a national pattern for community action. Top CPI officials were sought by other cities to design similar programs to deal with the issues of poverty. As William Lee Miller observes:

New Haven's CPI has been a leader in the national effort to eliminate slums and poverty. It started early and has been successful, showing the way to others. All that talking and coffee drinking by bright young fellows seems to have resulted in something impressive. CPI has combined the possibility, at least, of a proud social effort with broad social support.[29]

By way of comparison, the Washington, D.C. Urban Renewal Commission betrayed from its inception the pitfalls of such a massive undertaking. Committed to overly ambitious standards that set a goal of "no slums in ten years," the District launched its own program in 1955. Just three years into the project, the District Urban Renewal Council branded itself a failure as the advisory component to the District's antislum efforts. Council members cited a "lack of leadership both within and without the council." A former council member who had resigned in 1957 called the body a "hodge podge of pressure groups, vested interests and personal ambitions." Reorganized in the winter of 1958 as the Urban Renewal Commission, the agency met with many of the same problems.

In 1965 the capital city recruited L. Thomas Appleby, the former director of the New Haven Redevelopment Agency, to head up its program in Washington. Philip Shandler, a reporter for the *Washington Evening Star*, pondered whether the District of Columbia could achieve the same success. In an article praising the architects of New Haven's program, Shandler observed that in little more than a decade 2,700 new units of development-linked housing had been created for New Haven's 140,000 residents. In Washington, six times as big, about 3,500 new units had been developed. In addition, 7,500 New Haven residents rehabilitated their homes at an average cost of $6,000 each. Washington, Shandler declared, was only beginning to consider the possibility of rehabilitation. "Can the lessons of New Haven," he questioned, "truly be applied to Washington, a much bigger city, with no strong Mayor, no city council responsive to the voters, no tradition of developmental unity?"[30] Appleby's successor in New Haven, Melvin J. Adams, told Shandler that "a lot depends on the man." Shandler interpreted "the man" to be Appleby. In reality it was Mayor Richard C. Lee. While CORE and the NAACP were constantly in need of funds, CPI had the political and economic backing to accomplish what other groups and leaders could only propose. Although Miller counted CPI in the tradition of such New Deal antipoverty measures as the PWA and the WPA, he pointed out that it was unique in being initiated by the city of New Haven. President Johnson's 1964 antipoverty program was the first federal address to poverty that was not induced by a national catastrophe such as the Great Depression. As Miller explained no one expected the federal government to take the lead against poverty. Miller commented, "certainly we have not hitherto expected that such a thing be done by the city government."[31] CPI was hailed as an innovative response to poverty in New Haven. It attacked each of the problems outlined by the city's black leaders in 1962.

Mrs. Millicent B. Tyson the African-American alderman from the 22nd ward, for example, had complained that inadequacy of job training was holding back New Haven's black population.[32] CPI was credited with creating several job-training programs during its first year including a culinary institute in which forty-five cooks and waiters were trained and placed. Seventeen of the graduates were nonwhite. In July of 1963, CPI was able to add that at the time the training facility boasted thirty cooks, eighteen of whom were classified as nonwhite. CPI also established a middle technical training program having fifty trainees, twenty-two of whom the organization classified as nonwhite.[33]

Backed by federal funds, CPI was able to promise both skills training and fair hiring practices. In 1962, John Fernandez, president of the Negro American Labor Council in Connecticut declared, "Give us jobs and we'll take care of our housing and educational problems." Likewise, at the height of the debate over the CORE sit-out, the New Haven CORE initiated a job search program at 21 Dixwell Avenue. The *Core-lator* advertised the branch's new function: "If you are looking for any sort of job, contact CORE first to insure that you will not be turned down for irrelevant reasons such as the color of your skin."[34] The CPI was also able to break down barriers in hiring by using the mayor's office to facilitate meetings with employers and labor groups. To guarantee results CPI's manpower director, George Bennett, invoked the name of the mayor.

In a memorandum dated August 19, 1963, for instance, Bennett informed Lee that after a meeting with the Contractors Association, "The contractors were told that you want action to show that the contractors and building trades are making real progress to open up hiring to all qualified individuals."[35] On August 20, 1963, Bennett reported that as a result of CPI's activities the masons agreed to take on several black apprentices, opening up new opportunities for blacks in the building trades. In the weeks that followed, Bennett with the help of the Reverend Edmonds and Vincent Sirabella, a labor specialist with the CPI, found more positions for roofing helpers, carpenters, and painters. Other building trades, he explained to Lee in late September of 1963, were opening for carpenters and electricians as CPI continued to "recruit, test, and refer candidates."[36]

Despite CPI's successes there were some major problems that kept it from making the kind of difference that Lee and others had anticipated. One was Mayor Lee's tendency to politicize the positions won by CPI. In many ways the program operated like his own personal fiefdom, providing jobs for loyal voters and friends of friends when what were needed were people with a solid background in education and social work. Many complained as well that the men farthest removed from the blight of poverty were being employed to help its victims. Of the nine member board of the CPI, three were selected by the mayor. The board also contained representatives from Yale, the Redevelopment Agency, the Board of Education, the Community Council, and the United Fund.

In the spring of 1965 the agency received another grant from the Ford Foundation for three more years of work totaling two million five hundred and fifty thousand dollars. CPI was receiving more than sixty percent of its funds from eight agencies in the federal government. By the end of 1965, CPI had received nearly ten million from the Ford Foundation, the federal government, and the city.[37]

In the battle for school integration, an example of the CPI's eclipse of the NAACP, the older organization was the first to act. The efforts, however, did not originate within the local chapter. In October of 1961, the general counsel for the NAACP, Robert Carter, sent out a memorandum advising northern and western branches to utilize the services of the national office in attacking de facto segregation.[38] During its annual meeting in 1962, the NAACP committed itself to challenging segregated schooling in the North and West. To this end, Miss June Shagaloff was placed in charge of coordinating branch efforts. In late 1962 the NAACP, under her direction, distributed a set of detailed guidelines for northern and western branches interested in pushing for desegregated schools. Connecticut was part of the NAACP's region II. The region's membership of more than ninety thousand, concentrated in New York, Pennsylvania, and New Jersey made it the largest in the country. In 1960 Gloster Current observed that "intense fieldwork could be done in CT." Stamford, Connecticut, was a model for June Shagaloff who then proceeded to move on to Bridgeport, Norwalk, and finally New Haven, where in 1963 public school enrollment was over sixty percent white, the rest black with a tiny Puerto Rican enrollment.[39]

On May 21, 1963, Mitchell Sviridoff sent the mayor a memorandum on the NAACP's plans to press for an end to de facto segregation in northern schools. Sviridoff informed the mayor, "I think it might be useful to have a discussion of this problem soon in terms of the New Haven strategy before it hits us like a lead balloon."[40] Following several formal complaints by the NAACP and CORE, as well as local residents, about the New Haven school system, the board had already arranged for public hearings for that spring. Discovering some overcrowding, the hearings revealed the more important finding of de facto school segregation in the neighborhood elementary schools and junior high schools. The arrival of Miss Shagaloff that summer heightened the board's concern[41] (see Table 3.1).

Armed with the information from the public hearings, the NAACP pushed for immediate integration of New Haven public schools. Miss Shagaloff, in conjunction with local civil rights leaders, asked the school board for a meeting in July of 1963 to answer several specific questions. The NAACP wanted know whether the board intended to integrate the schools, whether it had already adopted a plan of integration and if so

Table 3.1

Racial Distribution of Public School Children,
New Haven, 1963–1969

Year	White (%)	Black (%)	Puerto Rican (%)
1963	61.9	35.4	2.4
1964	57.5	39.2	2.7
1965	54.1	42.4	3.1
1966	50.9	44.8	3.8
1967	47.9	47.1	4.4
1968	43.6	49.9	6.1
1969	40.8	51.8	6.9

Source: "Racial Distribution in New Haven Public Schools," 1963–1969, Claudia Scott, Forecasting Local Government (Washington, D.C.: The Urban Institute, 1972), 17.

what timetable it was operating on and how many children would be involved. To underscore the seriousness of the situation, Miss Shagaloff added that if the board was not prepared to give an immediate and satisfactory response, the NAACP would support local civil rights groups in orchestrating a citywide protest for school integration with sit-downs, picketing, and stoppages of school construction.[42]

John Braslin, the president of the school board, responded that the board would give the matter its immediate attention and assured the NAACP that the board would develop an integration plan during the coming school year and implement it the following fall, September 1964. The board's response satisfied the NAACP. Two months later, the board adopted a resolution that called for a plan "to alleviate racial imbalance and to provide a greater intermingling of students of social and economic backgrounds."[43] To this end, it enlisted a team to collect data on student enrollment and the racial make-up of New Haven's public schools. In the meanwhile Lee's stock as a civil rights leader continued to rise. In September of 1963 he was criticized for saying that Alabama segregationist Governor George Wallace was officially unwelcome in New Haven. The governor had been invited by the Yale Political Union to address the student body, but the invitation took place only days after four little girls were murdered in the bombing of a black church during civil rights protests in Birmingham, Alabama. The highly publicized exchange between the two public officials deflected attention away from what was happening with regard to the school situation in New Haven.

As Talbot observed, "ironically, the furor over a segregationist governor from a Southern state had served to obscure the significance of a proposed integration plan in a Northern city."[44]

After adopting a plan which would include moderate busing, the board was astonished when elements of it were leaked to the press. On June 1, 1964, the week before the board was to announce its busing plan, resistance was growing. The mayor and the school board were overwhelmed by hostile calls and letters from lower- and middle-income white families opposed to busing. The situation was further exacerbated when Joseph Einhorn, a member of the advisory panel, shifted sides and emerged as the leader of the opposition to the board's plan.

The school board found itself in a difficult position. It decided that starting in June it would hold a series of six informational meetings in different parts of the city to gauge reaction. Allan Talbot believed that this would "give the plan full and . . . rational exposure to counteract rumors." The informational sessions were anything but peaceful and served to exacerbate tensions about the possibility of busing and integration. Talbot records the reaction of a black man who attended one of the meetings and responded, "I always knew they didn't like us, but tonight I learned they hate us."[45]

In leading his attack on the busing plan, Einhorn blamed Lee for pressing for integration and the CPI for secretly manipulating the strategy for achieving it. In the meanwhile, black people in Allan Talbot's view exercised a great deal of restraint in letting the white community fight over the integration of New Haven's public schools:

> While white families held private protest meetings guarded carefully by self-appointed vigilantes to keep outsiders away, the Negroes restricted their discussions to shops and living rooms, where there were angry discussions and, now and then, calls for militant counteraction. Publicly, however, the Negroes remained silent as the white community fought among themselves.[46]

The local branch of the NAACP remained only tangentially involved in the school battle. On February 11, 1964, Andrew Harris inquired into the progress of the school board's action on formulating a plan. He wrote, "We had hoped for a closer communication with the New Haven Board of Education in the formulation and designing of the plan. We feel also that very valuable time, has and is, passing and factually, we know nothing of its accomplishments."[47] So it was clear in many minds that Mayor Lee and the CPI were directing the show and that in the words of James E. Gibbs, Mayor Lee was definitely "friend to the Negro." This contributed to the decline of black organizations in New Haven.

By the mid-1960s, the NAACP and CORE were dormant organizations in most accounts of New Haven. In 1964 the NAACP was again under scrutiny by the national offices for a violation of election bylaws. Also in 1964, John Barber was replaced by Attorney Earl Williams, in whose tenure membership dropped by almost nine in ten. Williams's militant style put him at odds with the national offices whom he infuriated by inviting Nation of Islam minister Malcolm X to address a group in New Haven. Williams was replaced in December of 1965 by Dr. Carter Marshall, whose supporters Williams denounced as people "tied in with City Hall, or the Community Progress Inc." He publicly equated Marshall with the "sold out Uncle Tom's" of the Lee Administration. Under Marshall the NAACP ceased to be involved in protest activities and in the words of the Reverend Edmonds the organization underwent a period of dormancy that lasted until the mid-1970s. This would support Cleo Abraham's claim that between 1966 and 1969 the NAACP was only a paper organization.[48]

CORE meanwhile briefly re-emerged in 1965 with a smaller following but the same flair for the dramatic. It's only noteworthy activity after the pickets of 1961 and 1962 was picketing the home of Mayor Lee in 1965. Reflecting a general change in attitude, the New Haven *Journal Courier* responded with an editorial entitled "Let's Enforce the Law!" It charged that the mayor needed to get tough with local black organizations.

By 1965 it appeared that the mayor had succeeded in replacing civil rights groups with his own antipoverty program. These organizations were not only hamstrung by the mayor but by internal problems as well.

One obstacle to the local NAACP and CORE is that both were subject to direction by national offices. This was especially true of the NAACP, which sent mixed messages to its northern and southern branches concerning acceptable protest tactics. The NAACP and CORE were both subject to investigation by national officers who had the power to dismiss those chapters for violating policy and procedure. While CORE supported the work of its New Haven branch, the intervention of the national office of the NAACP in the Gibbs affair and in the fight for school integration seriously hampered indigenous protest initiatives in New Haven. If, as Gloster Current reports, this was a problem suffered by many of the NAACP's northern branches, then it is not surprising that the organization began to decline nationally in the early 1960s, to be surpassed by indigenous protest groups. This especially happened in the North, which bitterly resented and in some cases even resisted the entrance of national civil rights organizations in their affairs. These offices were more concerned about the national organization's image and reputation than about establishing quality indigenous leadership. As the letters concerning Gibbs in the NAACP and Winnick in CORE attest, both organizations were fearful of being infiltrated by leftist organizations. This provided enemies of the local branch with a sure weapon against them should they deviate from national policy.

The intimate relationship between Mayor Lee and the various black organizations working in and around New Haven also served to limit their effectiveness. Lee established a very paternalistic relationship with both the NAACP and the Dixwell Ministerial Alliance that made them less inclined to pursue issues beyond the mayor's office and effectively created a Lee lobby within both. Lee was able to accomplish this through political favors and appointments that made certain influential members beholden to him. Whenever someone crossed Lee, such as the Reverend Ledbetter, James Gibbs, and eventually John Barber, the mayor had a means of controlling them either through his supporters within the organization or through direct intervention. That Lee kept John Barber's very personal letters in his political files underscores the conclusion of the Reverend Edmonds that Lee was more "political than racist" and manipulated these groups to work on his behalf. Nonetheless his influence on these groups was one of the chief reasons for their decline.

Political infighting within these organizations further served to dampen interest and gave the appearance of disorganization. The factionalism which developed in the NAACP hurt the organization's efforts at addressing the real problems facing blacks within the city of New Haven. Leadership struggles and lesser contests for power and influence served to provide Lee with a greater wedge to exploit within the branch.

Finally the creation by the mayor of his own interest group, the Citizens Action Committee, helped to undermine the efforts of black organizations in New Haven by giving him the appearance of something those groups did not have, a popular base. Especially important is that Lee's antipoverty program, CPI, duplicated many of the functions of these early protest groups in finding jobs and financing programs for New Haven's poor blacks. A testimony to the effectiveness of CPI is that after 1960, Mayor Lee marshaled an even greater proportion of black votes. CPI, not the NAACP, began to be credited with producing important achievements, even the desegregation of New Haven's public schools, which had originated in protest by the NAACP.

By 1965 New Haven was crying out for indigenous black leadership. That would arrive in 1965 in the form of the Hill Parents Association.

Notes

1. Allan Talbot, *Mayor's Game* (New York: Harper and Row, 1967), 170; Fred Powledge, *Model City* (New York: Simon and Shuster, 1970), 63–64.

2. "New Haven's Negro Leaders Speak Out On Problems," *The New Haven Register*, 4 March 1962, 13.

3. Jackie Robinson to Mayor Richard C. Lee, 7 March 1962, Richard C. Lee Papers RG 318 Series I Box 50 Folder 1018, Manuscripts and Archives, Yale

University Library; On CORE protest and Fair Housing proposal see "NAACP Plans New Push for Housing Bill," *New Haven Register*, 7 February 1962, page unknown, clippings file, local history collection, New Haven Public Library, New Haven, Connecticut.

4. Mayor Richard C. Lee to Jackie Robinson, 7 March 1962, Richard C. Lee Papers RG 318 Series I Box 50 Folder 1018, Manuscripts and Archives, Yale University Library.

5. Jackie Robinson, "Dear Mayor Lee," reprinted in the *New Haven Corelator*, Vol. I No. 3, New Haven Connecticut, March 1962, Manuscript Division, Library of Congress; see also "NAACP Plans New Push for Housing Bill," *New Haven Register*, 7 February 1962, page unknown, clippings file, local history collection, New Haven Public Library, New Haven, Connecticut.

6. Richard Dowdy, interview by author, telephone tape recording, New Haven, Connecticut, 22 March 1999.

7. Dick Dowdy memo to Mayor Richard C. Lee, "The Negro in American Society, Some General Observations on Race Relations," 21 December 1960, Richard C. Lee Papers RG 318 Series I Box 35 Folder 771, Manuscripts and Archives, Yale University Library.

8. Ibid.

9. "New Haven's Negro Leaders Speak Out On Problems," *New Haven Register*, 4 March 1962, 13.

10. Editorial, "Will Jackson," *The Open Gate News*, New Haven, Connecticut, 12th edition, 4 May 1962, 4.

11. Richard S. Dowdy, Jr. to Jackie Robinson, 5 April 1962, Richard C. Lee Papers RG 318 Series I Box 50 Folder 1018, Manuscripts and Archives, Yale University Library.

12. "National CORE Stays Out Of Jackson Dispute," *The Open Gate News*, New Haven, Connecticut, 12th edition, 4 May 1962, 2.

13. "Blyden Jackson Shot By Man On Shelton Ave," *New Haven Journal Courier*, 3 April 1962, page unknown, clippings file, local history collection, New Haven Public Library, New Haven, Connecticut; "Seven Facing Charges In City Shooting," *New Haven Register*, 4 April 1962, page unknown, clippings file, local history collection, New Haven Public Library, New Haven, Connecticut.

14. "Blyden Jackson Shot By Man On Shelton Ave," *New Haven Journal Courier*, 3 April 1962; "Seven Facing Charges In City Shooting," *New Haven Register*, 4 April 1962; "CORE Leader Fined $25 For Cover Up In Shooting," *New Haven Register*, 24 April 1962, page unknown, clippings file, local history collection, New Haven Public Library, New Haven, Connecticut; "Wife Is Freed For Shooting CORE Leader," *New Haven Register*, 25 May 1962, page unknown, clippings file, local history collection, New Haven Public Library, New Haven, Connecticut.

15. Richard S. Dowdy, Jr. to Jackie Robinson, 5 April 1962.

16. Richard S. Dowdy, Jr. to Richard Haley, Field Director CORE, 5 April 1962, Richard C. Lee Papers RG 318 Series I Box 50 Folder 1018, Manuscripts and Archives, Yale University Library.

17. Earl Williams, interview by author, telephone tape recording, New Haven, Connecticut, 3 April 1999; Interview with Richard Dowdy; "A Sound Sentence—And A Serious Question," *New Haven Register*, 13 March 1963, page unknown, newspaper clippings Cloud Case, New Haven, 1963 from the files of Richard S. Dowdy; "Cloud, Reed Begin Prison Terms for Kidnaping, Attacking Nurse," *New Haven Journal Courier*, 13 March, 1963, page unknown, newspaper clippings Cloud Case, New Haven, 1963 from the files of Richard S. Dowdy; "Role in Cloud Trial Is Described By Dowdy, 18 March, 1963; "Silence Veils

Dowdy Action In Cloud Case," 20 March 1963, *New Haven Register*, 1, newspaper clippings Cloud Case, New Haven, 1963 from the files of Richard S. Dowdy; "Balanced Human Relations In The Mayors Office," *New Haven Register*, 22 March 1963, page unknown, newspaper clippings Cloud Case, New Haven, 1963 from the files of Richard S. Dowdy; "NAACP Levels Blast At Cloud Case Defense," *New Haven Register*, 26 March 1963, page unknown, newspaper clippings Cloud Case, New Haven, 1963 from the files of Richard S. Dowdy.

18. Ibid.

19. "NAACP Head Reported At FBI Meeting," *New Haven Register*, 10 October 1962, page unknown, clippings file, local history collection, New Haven Public Library, New Haven, Connecticut; "NAACP Police Charges Rejected Entirely," *New Haven Register*, 16 October 1962, page unknown, clippings file, local history collection, New Haven Public Library, New Haven, Connecticut; "NAACP Reported Perplexed Over Police Board Action," *New Haven Register*, 17 October 1962, page unknown, clippings file, local history collection, New Haven Public Library, New Haven, Connecticut; "NAACP Gives Promise To Document Its Charges," *New Haven Register*, 23 October 1962, page unknown, clippings file, local history collection, New Haven Public Library, New Haven, Connecticut; "Crime Laxity Alleged At Hearing But Police Offer Data On Arrests," *New Haven Journal Courier*, 10 November 1962, page unknown, clippings file, local history collection, New Haven Public Library, New Haven, Connecticut.

20. "Will the Negroes Control?" *The Open Gate News*, 21 June–5 July 1963, contained in Richard C. Lee Papers RG 318 Series II Box 113 Folder 2017, Manuscripts and Archives, Yale University Library.

21. John Barber to Mayor Lee, August 1963, Richard C. Lee Papers RG 318 Series II Box 113 Folder 2017, Manuscripts and Archives, Yale University Library.

22. Ibid.

23. Ibid.

24. Ibid.

25. Ibid.

26. Richard C. Lee to John Barber, 20 August 1963, Richard C. Lee Papers RG 318 Series II Box 113 Folder 2017, Manuscripts and Archives, Yale University Library.

27. "Honorary Chairmen Of Drive," *New Haven Journal Courier*, 7 November 1963, page unknown, clippings file, local history collection, New Haven Public Library, New Haven, Connecticut.

28. William Lee Miller, *The Fifteenth Ward and the Great Society* (Boston: Houghton Mifflin, 1966), 222.

29. Ibid.

30. Philip Shandler, "New Haven Urban Renewal Sets Pace For Nation," *Washington Evening Star*, 17 November 1965, section B, page unknown, clippings file, Washingtoniana Collection, Martin Luther King Public Library, Washington, D.C.; On Urban Renewal in the District of Columbia see George Beveridge, "Finley Raps Agencies As Renewal Plan Drags," *Washington Evening Star*, 9 January 1959, page unknown, clippings file, Washingtoniana Collection, Martin Luther King Public Library, Washington, D.C.; James G. Deane, "Renewal Council Admits Failure, Suggest Death," *Washington Evening Star*, 14 February 1958, page unknown, clippings file, Washingtoniana Collection, Martin Luther King Public Library, Washington, D.C.; "Mrs. Riggs Angrily Quits Urban Renewal Council," *Washington Evening Star*, 13 November 1957, page unknown, clippings file, Washingtoniana Collection, Martin Luther King Public Library, Washington, D.C.; As it turned out Appleby did not meet with the same success in D.C. Part of the problem was the earlier failures of the DC Urban Renewal

Council. After the city undertook to rehabilitate the Shaw neighborhood in 1966, Appleby's program drew sharp criticism from a local minister who explained, "This community's tragic experience with an urban renewal effort . . . which did not provide housing and adequate and humane relocation services remains painfully etched in the minds of many residents of the area." Robert J. Lewis, "Shaw Renewal Project Will Be City's Biggest," *Washington Evening Star*, 8 April 1966, A-6.

31. William Lee Miller, 222.

32. Millicent Tyson's comments recorded in "New Haven's Negro Leaders Speak Out On Problems," *New Haven Register*, 4 March 1962, 13.

33. CPI, Equal Opportunities Program, Employment statistics, July 1963, Richard C. Lee Papers RG 318 Series I Box 56 Folder 1125, Manuscripts and Archives, Yale University Library.

34. John Fernandez's comments recorded in "New Haven's Negro Leaders Speak Out On Problems," *New Haven Register*, 4 March 1962, 13; on CORE see "New Office At 21 Dixwell Taking Job Applications," *New Haven Core-lator*, Vol. I, No. 3, New Haven, Connecticut, March 1962.

35. George Bennett memo to Mayor Richard C. Lee, Re: Building Trades–Contractors, 19 August 1963, Richard C. Lee Papers RG 318 Series I Box 56 Folder 1125, Manuscripts and Archives, Yale University Library.

36. George Bennett memorandum to Mayor Richard C. Lee, Re: Building Trades–Contractors, 19 August 1963; George Bennett memorandum to Mayor Richard C. Lee, Re: Building Trades-Contractors, 24 September 1963, Richard C. Lee Papers RG 318 Series I Box 56 Folder 1125, Manuscripts and Archives, Yale University Library.

37. Ibid., 223.

38. Robert Carter, General Counsel of NAACP, memo to Northern Branches, NAACP, NAACP Papers Group III Box A99 Folder: Desegregation Schools, Connecticut 1956–1965, Manuscript Division, Library of Congress.

39. Gloster Current, Director of Branches, to Executive Secretary, NAACP, 12 August 1960, Group III Box A99 Folder: Desegregation Schools, Connecticut 1956–1965, Manuscript Division, Library of Congress.

40. Mike Sviridoff to Dick Lee, 21 May 1963, Richard C. Lee Papers RG 318 Series I Box 56 Folder 1125, Manuscript and Archives, Yale University Library.

41. Talbot, 189–191.

42. Ibid., 190.

43. Ibid., 191.

44. Ibid., 195.

45. Ibid., 195.

46. Ibid., 202.

47. Andrew R. Harris, Vice Chairman, NAACP Educational Committee, to Mr. John E. Braslin, President New Haven Board of Education, 11 February 1964, Richard C. Lee Papers RG 318 Series I Box 66 Folder 1279, Manuscripts and Archives, Yale University Library.

48. Earl Williams interview; Charles J. Hines, "NAACP Faction Lashes Leadership—Cites Big Drop in Membership," *New Haven Register*, 31 August 1964, page unknown, clippings file, local history collection, New Haven Public Library, New Haven, Connecticut; Kenneth Matthews, "NAACP Sets Probe Into Unit Here," *New Haven Journal Courier*, 27 August 1964, page unknown, clippings file, local history collection, New Haven Public Library, New Haven, Connecticut; Kenneth Matthews, "Marshall New Head Of NAACP," *New Haven Journal Courier*, 9 December 1964, page unknown, clippings file, local history collection, New Haven Public Library, New Haven, Connecticut; Reverend Edwin Edmonds interview.

CHAPTER FOUR
A New Day in Babylon

Rights are not won on paper. They are won only by those who make their voices heard—by activist and militants. Silence never won rights. They are not handed down from above; they are forced by pressure from below.

—Roger Baldwin,
Brandeis University
publication, 1969

The Hill Parents Association or HPA, began after a group of concerned parents living in the Hill section of New Haven criticized the Prince Street Elementary School. Even before the creation of the HPA, many parents had complained about problems ranging from the lack of material supplies such as books and paper to the physical condition of the school. Most of their objections, however, went unheeded before Rosemarie Harris became involved. The community organization that came in good part of the efforts of Rosemarie and Fred Harris would soon eclipse the CPI and the NAACP.

Mrs. Harris had first become aware of the problem after she attended an event at the school in the spring of 1965. She was appalled by the substandard physical condition of the school. She was more shocked when she contacted city hall and discovered that among dozens of complaints logged against the school, many had never received a formal reply. Her anger piqued when she learned that the school was rationing certain essential commodities such as issuing coarse hand towel paper to students in lieu of toilet tissue. Many of the students developed sores and rashes including her own children. Mrs. Harris and her husband, Fred, called for a public meeting about the situation in the school.[1]

During the meeting, the Harrises were encouraged by the community's response. Fred Harris was further surprised to see a number of people from Yale University and even several teachers from the Prince Street School in attendance. He was to recall that this gave him a sense that the entire community wanted to get involved. At the meeting, the group quickly drew up a list of demands, addressing chiefly the need for physical repairs in the school. The parents insisted on small but tangible improvements such as better toilet paper for students and a fresh coat of paint for the school. After settling on a list, the group decided to picket in front of the school to increase public awareness about conditions in Hill. The group also adopted the name the Hill Parents Association.[2]

What truly distinguished the HPA from other organizations at the time was its decision to pursue a remedy independently of any dialogue with the CPI or the mayor. The CPI, since its creation back in 1962, had received national accolades as the model for community improvement. Mayor Lee had also projected the image of being open to working with the neighborhoods for improvement. Despite this, the HPA pursued a militant direct action protest of a kind previously unknown in New Haven. The HPA was not looking for leadership from the CPI but dictating the types of improvements that it wanted to see in the Prince Street School. This put it at contraries to the NAACP, which, having made a great uproar over the substandard nature of segregated schools in New Haven, then passively allowed the city to dictate the terms of integration. No provision among the HPA's demands drove this point home more than the call for a black principal at the Prince Street School.

The HPA decided, as part of its discussion of what needed to be improved, that the white principal of the Prince Street School should be dismissed. The HPA's gripes with the principal were not based solely on race. The principal had a reputation for alcohol abuse. He also tended to ignore the complaints of parents, who in turn blamed him for the substandard condition of the school. The HPA argued that the community should have a role in determining who should run the schools. Despite all the talk of citizen participation in New Haven, this was a new concept. It was being dictated from the residents to city hall and not the other way around.

The protest by the HPA, as Fred Powledge was to present it, suggests the black power militancy soon to sweep the nation. Fred Harris notes that for years the black leadership that emerged in New Haven had quickly been coopted by the white leadership. As Powledge explains, "a black who broke the surface and was obviously skilled, or articulate or both, had little difficulty getting a job in CPI or the Redevelopment Agency, where his value as a potential dissenter, of course, would be quickly wiped out." Harris remembers:

New Haven is such a conservative town, the only thing here was the NAACP and CORE, and CORE had sort of petered out; it had a lot of white people in it. And this kept away a lot of blacks. After HPA got started, this was a new kind of thing. It was the first real militant black organization that was saying the things that black people really wanted to say. Whites were working with us, and trying to help in any way they could help, but it was under our leadership, which was a completely different type from what CORE and the NAACP had been.[3]

The HPA, Harris reports, became known as the organization that was really making black people move.

The HPA was different from CORE and the NAACP also in being a community organization drawing both its leadership and membership from a neighborhood and reflecting for a time the interest of the people residing there. This provided the participants with a unity of purpose and a knowledge of issues that both older bodies in trying to deal with the whole city found elusive. The HPA, moreover, could not be blamed on outside influences within New Haven. Its leaders lived in the community in which they served.

In social and economic background as well, the HPA differed from the NAACP and CORE. The NAACP was made up of predominately middle-class blacks oriented toward politics. This was characteristic of most local chapters of the organization. While CORE had a less affluent membership and addressed many of the issues relative to the inner city, its push and appeal was for the city government to do something about those conditions. When CORE began to move in the direction of community-based programs with its jobs initiative in 1962, problems within the local chapter prevented the continuation of the group's efforts.

A further advantage of the HPA was that it did not have to answer to any national office on policy. The issues were generated by the Hill community. This allowed the HPA to set its own agenda. Unlike the NAACP, the HPA opened its membership to the entire community by charging a modest membership fee. It also never refused to help those in need who were not members.

For all of these reasons, the HPA picket proved remarkably successful. Whenever CORE had attempted such an approach the mayor and later the CPI had been able to point to conditions elsewhere in the city as proof of their work. Remarking on the effectiveness of the CPI in destroying local sentiment, Harris adds, "You'd be surprised how many people who had to deal with [shitty] conditions like the school believed things weren't so bad because city agencies said they weren't." With the spotlight squarely on the Hill, however, there was no escaping the seriousness of conditions at Prince Street. The day after the protest, city workers arrived at the school to apply a fresh coat of paint and complete other minor repairs. The issue of replacing the white principal was not so quickly resolved.

In an effort to avert additional protests, the mayor and school board suggested that the black principal of the Abraham Lincoln School in Newhallville fulfill both positions on a part-time basis. The HPA responded that only a full-time replacement would be acceptable. This was by far the most significant of the parents' demands and eventually the city government gave in. George Harris was appointed as the new principal of the Prince Street school. "At the time this made us happy," Fred Harris reflects. "We weren't really hip then to the gap between a lot of black professionals and the people."[4]

After the success of the protest, Fred Harris and Willie Counsel decided to keep the organization going. As Harris recalls, "I guess none of us knew what we were getting into or what the HPA would become." In the months following the Prince Street picket, the HPA merged with another community organization known as the Hill Neighborhood Union run by a local activist named Ronald Johnson. The Hill Neighborhood Union had emerged a few months before the Prince Street School protest. It was financed by a private philanthropic organization known as the Aaron Norman Fund, which specifically prohibited organizations under its sponsorship from collaborating with any "organizations having broad public support."[5]

The HPA's merger with the Hill Neighborhood Union coincided with the interest of Mayor Lee. Lee considered the efforts of the Hill Neighborhood Union damaging to the CPI and in competition with it.

On July 26, 1965, the mayor wrote the special agent in charge of the New Haven FBI, Charles Weeks, requesting "any information" on the Hill Neighborhood Union and its sponsoring organization the Aaron Norman Fund. Lee wanted to know whether either organization was being investigated or appeared on the attorney general's list of subversive organizations. On the same day, Lee alerted the Ford Foundation of the existence of the Hill Neighborhood Union and enclosed a memorandum that, he claimed, revealed the group to be causing problems. Lee explained, "By and large, the leadership is made up of Yale undergraduate students. To the best of my knowledge, there is no responsible adult guidance." Lee asked whether the Ford Foundation had any information on the Aaron Norman Fund.[6]

James Coogan, who had been sent by Lee to investigate the HNU, reported to the mayor that the organization was made up of "four or five white men, one girl and two or three Negro men, all of college age, who live in a rather dirty building at 35 Arch Street" and serves about a dozen children ages seven to twelve. The leaders of the HNU told investigators that they "would not align themselves with the Hill Community Council, Hill Recreation Committee or other established neighborhood civic group."[7]

The HPA obviously did not fall into any of those categories and so a merger between the two organizations was not suspect. The HPA initially focused on spreading the word about the Prince Street School incident and the neglect of residents of the Hill by Mayor Lee and urban renewal. At the time, according to Harris's recollections, he was still optimistic that if white people knew about conditions in the Hill, "they wouldn't allow them to continue." When it tried to persuade city officials to pay more attention to the Hill, in fact, the HPA met with more hostility than success. This resistance, coupled with the merger with the Hill Neighborhood Union, greatly expanded the HPA's activities.[8]

One source of support was the American Independent Movement (AIM). This was a predominantly white radical organization that had long been established in New Haven. AIM contributed funds to the HPA that went to pay the rent on a small office in the heart of the Hill and provided small salaries for Johnson, Counsel, and Harris. Otherwise the HPA remained independent of AIM in all other areas. The organization largely operated on a shoestring budget.[9]

The HPA quickly earned a reputation for troubleshooting. People from the Hill who were not used to having someone speak for their interest began to bring their problems to Harris. As a result, Harris became involved in such problems as teen violence and the lack of antipoverty programs.[10]

The HPA's work in the Hill greatly increased the visibility of the organization. In the summer of 1966, AIM approached Harris about running as an independent for state representative. When Harris agreed, thereby further increasing his own notoriety and that of the HPA, AIM hired Cordell Reagan of Freedom Singers fame, to help manage the campaign. Reagan helped Harris to reach a wider audience within New Haven. Although the results were not always positive, people were learning a great deal more about problems in the Hill. Harris was approached during the campaign by one of Mayor Lee's representatives about the possibility of running for some office as a Democrat. Harris's refusal further alienated him and the HPA from city hall.[11]

The local media almost completely ignored Harris's candidacy and refused to deal with issues raised by the HPA. In addition, Harris was criticized by many middle-class blacks for challenging a Democratic candidate. He was verbally abused by whites on the campaign trail. While campaigning in one predominately Italian neighborhood adjacent to the Hill, he was greeted with flying tomatoes from a group of elderly Italian women who hurled insults, hissed, and demanded that he go back where he belonged on the Hill. Yet, Harris maintained his conviction that he would be judged on the strength of his platform.[12]

Harris learned an important lesson about money and politics in New Haven. After spying a pair of young men that he knew driving blacks to vote for the Democratic Party on election day, Harris concluded that he was up against more than the image of New Haven as a model city, or the ignorance of the people. Money could also corrupt. "When they said, 'Listen Freddie, they pay me $30 for one day to just do this driving'— what was I going to say? This is how the man really fucks with you. Money. People in the streets are receptive to new ideas, but when there is money out there, they are going to grab it."[13]

The campaign taught Harris a great deal about citywide issues. "We ran it," he explains, "just like the day-to-day workings of the HPA going into people's homes, talking about the problems. And trying to eliminate the individual problems of the people who had them, which was most of the people." Harris and the HPA became intensely aware of the difficulties associated with poverty that were becoming evident at the same time Martin Luther King wrote his book *Where Do We Go from Here: Chaos or Community?* Shortly after the campaign, the HPA began to concentrate on statewide welfare reform and entered the planning stages for a march on the state capitol in Hartford.[14]

The welfare strike turned out to be a great success in gaining attention for the HPA. Frightened by the plans for the march, the Welfare Department had attempted to dissuade the HPA from carrying out the protest, which ended when the picketers were arrested and charged with breach of the peace.[15] The press coverage increased the membership of the HPA and its influence in the Hill.[16] More residents began to seek the support of Harris and the HPA. "The publicity we received" he recalls, "indicated that we were going to deal with the community's problems and stand up to the man. I think this was important to a lot of folks and brought them to HPA, because after the welfare stuff a lot more people started coming into the office with their problems."[17]

The city began to focus considerable attention on the HPA. The mayor and the Redevelopment Agency, in particular, were alarmed at its work, which they believed was a threat to the public good. After the welfare incident the media and the mayor began to inquire about who belonged to the HPA. The HPA refused to supply entire membership lists, citing the need to protect its people from harassment. Harris would observe that the focus on membership lists also marked basic differences in ideology:

We believe that membership in organizations is no indication of community sentiment. The whole idea is just a way for insensitive white people to deal with a neighborhood. They want to say that unless you have a large membership you don't represent the people. But in a neighborhood like the Hill, that's silly. People here just don't join organizations, that's just a fact. We knew when people supported us and when they didn't.[18]

At the same time that the city was closely scrutinizing the HPA, the group was gearing up for an attack on the city for the problems in the Hill. Central to its assault was the conduct of the CPI, which Harris argues had "never done much for the people in the Hill."

One disagreement with the CPI was over funding. The HPA wanted the CPI to grant it access to some of the federal money being pumped into New Haven. That way it could create its own community programs. "We told them at a meeting that we weren't children and they didn't have to take care of our money for us. We wanted neighborhoods to receive direct funding." Harris concludes, "People in the Hill certainly weren't getting the money and an awful lot of it never seemed to leave downtown. The CPI told us to write up some programs and they might fund us."

At the time of HPA's verbal assault on the city, the CPI was having serious internal troubles. The organization had earned a reputation for coopting dissenters. Fred Harris complained that it often took young militants and made them into apologists for the city government. At his insistence, the board of the CPI was enlarged in the fall of 1965 and that winter. It grew to sixteen, with the intention of encouraging more participation by the poor. The new board members were to be chosen from and by the residents of the seven areas served by the CPI.[19] The new board members demanded that the CPI reflect the people it served.

In February of 1966, a group of CPI employees known as the Negro CPI Staff Concerns and Action Committee petitioned the executive director, Mitchell Sviridoff, to fill the position of manpower director with a black candidate. The dissidents pointed out that of ninety-five persons employed in policy making positions in CPI only five were black. In a follow-up memo to the director, the group contended that CPI, as a body created to deal with the problems of the poor and minorities, "should be in the vanguard of organizations of working to upgrade Negroes for high-level job openings and to training lower-level employees who demonstrate high potential to prepare them to take advantage of opportunities for upward movement when they occur." A black director would possess

the knowledge and insight gained only through the experience of being a Negro which the committee strongly feels would aid him in initiating programs and the conducting of such programs to meet the needs of the unemployed Negro (who are in the majority) and therefore expedite his entrance into the employment field. Thus, accomplishing the ultimate goal of the Manpower Division.[20]

Lee, in the meanwhile, was becoming increasingly frustrated with the CPI. It was not only failing to meet the needs of the people, but making him look bad as well. Instead of increasing community participation, Lee tried to bring the organization under tighter control. A letter late in the fall of 1966 from Mayor Lee to Larry Spitz, the newly appointed head of CPI, indicates the level to which Lee saw the CPI as an extension of himself. On the morning of November 14, 1966 he had driven past the CPI neighborhood offices in the Hill just after 9:00 a.m., only to find the offices closed and a man standing outside, apparently in search of assistance or a job. "That is no way to run a neighborhood office as far as I am concerned," Lee wrote Spitz, "and almost the first thing I think ought to be done in CPI is to bring the neighborhood offices closer to the main function." The CPI offices did not function as "separate autonomies," but were "important jurisdictions which are . . . so to speak adjuncts of your office and City Hall—indeed my office," and "people judge me, believe it or not, by the way your staff performs in the neighborhood." Lee concluded, "If we can't begin on the right level and have these offices open on time, where in Heavens name are we going to begin?"[21]

It was this attitude that brought some workers within the CPI to begin to question the organization's commitment to citizen participation. Peter Almond, a white CPI staffer, questioned why the CPI took such an adversarial position with Fred Harris since the type of organizing that he and the HPA were doing was what the CPI had been created to accomplish. Almond complained that few city officials were discussing citizen participation in the same way that neighborhood people envisioned the concept. For the officials it was always a question of getting people from the community involved in what CPI was doing. "They were asking how do you get people involved? How do you get people to a meeting you've called?" Too often they were answering these questions in the same way William Lee Miller did when he quoted the comments of one middle-class black politician who remarked, "You can't get those people . . . out for anything, you'd have to blast them out."[22]

The HPA had a much different conception of community organizing. It measured strength not in terms of voter turnout, but in getting out and working among the people. The HPA spent a great deal of time organizing people in the community. "These people didn't think they had to come to a meeting and wait an hour or two to say their few remarks because they already told us," Harris observes. Although HPA wanted to increase its actual membership, it realized that "membership is really a middle-class thing and poor people don't show their allegiance by joining groups. We knew how strong or weak we were."[23]

By the spring of 1967 the HPA considered itself to be very strong. As a direct result of the organization's activities, the Hill was identified as a prime trouble area in desperate need of assistance. A public report entitled "Ideas for the Hill Neighborhood Program," highlighted a number of problems in the Hill. Some of the more staggering statistics included an infant mortality of 35.5 for a thousand births, the highest in the city. The rate of premature births was fourteen for a thousand compared with just 9.3 for the entire city. The accidental death rate in the Hill was an astonishing 69.2 against 39.0 for the city as a whole.[24] The crime rate in the Hill was among the highest in the city and the Hill had the greatest number of youth at risk. While the neighborhood population represented about fifteen percent of the city's total, close to a quarter of all juvenile court referrals and twelve percent of the jail inmates came from the Hill. Of the city's twenty parks, which contained a total of 1,862 acres of land, only one was in the Hill, and it contained seven acres. In the four-year period ending in 1966, the number of cases of Aid to Dependent Children rose by sixty percent in the neighborhood. Unemployment in the Hill was nearly twice that for the city as a whole. Yet, at a time when the Hill was crying out for imaginative programs, Lee focused on the potential for violence represented by these problems.[25]

By the summer of 1967 the nation had undergone a second rash of civil disturbances in urban areas. Throughout the spring of 1967 a number of cities erupted in rapid succession, beginning with Jackson, Mississippi, and Houston, Texas, in early May and reaching a fever pitch in June and July in Newark, New Jersey, Phoenix, Arizona, Dayton, Ohio, and Detroit, Michigan. While Lee remained publicly silent on the violence in other cities, in May of 1967 he had sent Richard Belford, the executive director of the New Haven Commission on Equal Opportunities, and John C. Daniels, his deputy director, to attend a National Conference on Community Values sponsored by the City of New York Commission on Human Rights. In a subsequent memo to the mayor, Belford and Daniels outlined what the city needed to do in order to prevent a violent disturbance in New Haven.[26]

In a follow-up memo, the mayor distilled the Belford and Daniels communique down into short-term goals to prevent summer unrest, including new street lights, a refuse clean up program, and a summer employment program. Among long-term goals, the mayor placed professionalization of the police. Proceeding from the mayor's memo, Belford and Daniels on May 19 contacted Charles Randall of the New Haven Chamber of Commerce in hopes of persuading the Chamber to open up summer employment opportunities for ghetto teenagers.[27]

On May 23 Ralph M. Goglia, director of the Community Schools in New Haven, sent a memo to the mayor with program plans for the summer. He proposed having community school staff working in all seven of the New Haven neighborhoods so that public schools could remain open and active during the summer. He also called for establishing day camps, work programs, and extended day activities all under the leadership of "indigenous community relations workers" and providing adult basic education.[28]

Utilizing the talents of several Yale law students who had been working with the HPA for the summer, Harris, Johnson, and Belton meanwhile sat down to create the imaginative summer programming CPI lacked. The process was new to Harris and the other members of the HPA. Harris allowed people from the community to view the draft of the proposal and welcomed suggestions from anyone.

On July 10, 1967, the HPA submitted a proposal for a summer project called "Operation Breakthrough," a program conceived by Curtis Belton to "give the unemployed guys in the street some money." Belton hoped to use Operation Breakthrough as a means of reaching people in the Hill who were often overlooked by the CPI: young toughs, former criminals, and people who had been laid off from other jobs. The basic idea was to give them a sense of belonging to the community by working within the community and getting paid for it.[29] The job service was central to Operation Breakthrough in providing the labor force for the proposals set forth by the HPA. In order to fund Operation Breakthrough, Belton appealed to Mayor Lee and CPI for temporary money. Belton and the HPA pitched the idea as a summer program designed to keep people off the streets. Operation Breakthrough was designed as a full-year program, however, and the HPA was not appealing to the city alone. After the summer, Belton said, applications would be made to private foundations for funds. Before the program received its summer grant, Curtis Belton and Ronnie Johnson, assistant director of Operation Breakthrough, set up an office and began contacting landlords about maintenance contracts and seeking clients for minority moving services.[30]

In addition to the job service, the HPA proposed converting into a park a vacant lot donated by a neighborhood businessman. The park, located on Congress Avenue across from the HPA office, would be open thirteen hours a day Monday through Friday and seven hours on Saturday and Sunday. The long hours, Belton argued, would provide "a safe and supervised play area for the many neighborhood kids. Fifteen paid workers, operating in two shifts, one full-time and one part-time, would run the park.[31]

The HPA also asked for assistance in funding a day camp for kids from the Hill. The donation of three acres of land in the suburbs enabled the day camp to get underway. The HPA postulated an enrollment of as many as two hundred children. "These are the kids other camp programs don't reach, because of lack of knowledge that such programs exist, lack of finances, or both," the proposal observed. To rectify this situation, the HPA explained, its camp would be cost free and provide two snacks and one hot meal daily. Having initiated most of these programs before submitting its proposal to CPI, the HPA reported that "the first day of camp proved highly successful with 89 children attending."[32]

The HPA included an adult education program which included provisions for standard courses along with courses in black American history and English to Spanish-speaking people. It emphasized job skills such as typing and shorthand. The adult education classes were not built on the same model as the programs run by CPI. "It is believed," the HPA argued, "that professionals in the education field are inclined to teach according to traditional classroom standards and that by using nonprofessional volunteers, a more flexible situation will be achieved."

In a general commentary on its objectives, the HPA urged its readers to "look beyond the programs themselves to the significance of the total involvement of the people. Here for the first time a group of people have the opportunity and the responsibility to run a program themselves."[33]

The HPA, which was asking for $34,000 was fairly confident that the city government would offer something. After reviewing the HPA proposal, the CPI informed Belton, Harris, and the HPA that it was prepared to provide a total of $6,000 for the entire program. According to Harris, "When people found this out they were mad. A lot of guys had thought about summer work and they weren't up for no junk from CPI."[34] Harris and the HPA called a meeting with the CPI. "Although CPI said it didn't have the money," Harris remembers, "no one really believed them. We thought the meeting went well. There were some important liberals in the group and we thought they could convince CPI to reconsider. Maybe because of this, we were upset when the word came up from downtown that nothing could be done about what we wanted."[35]

Several days after the meeting the offices of the CPI were firebombed by unknown assailants. In the aftermath of the attack, Mayor Lee and CPI Director Larry Spitz called for a meeting with Harris, Johnson, and Counsel. Harris recalls that Mayor Lee ran the meeting and offered the HPA what Harris describes as a "sort of deal." As Harris explained, "He told us that he'd found the $34,000 for us. He said that in return for it we should make sure there was no trouble this summer." Although surprised by the mayor's offer, Harris concluded, "We weren't going to tell him we didn't control people in the entire city and didn't even control people in the Hill. I don't know what he thought. So we told him we didn't think there was going to be trouble. We weren't going to cause any, but we couldn't speak for everyone."[36]

Despite all of this preparation, the summer of 1967 began with several minor disturbances. Most consisted of rock- and bottle-throwing incidents. Some were more serious. On July 19, 1967 for instance, there was an altercation at Congress and White streets after a white ice-cream truck driver chased someone whom he suspected of throwing rocks at his truck. The driver was followed by what police described as a "group of Negroes," who began throwing rocks at the driver. By the time police arrived to escort the driver out of the Hill, officers reported, "bottles began falling from above." Several police cruisers were struck. Officers found a large crowd in front of the offices of the Hill Parents Association. The crowd dispersed after Harris intervened, but another disturbance broke out several hours later after another ice-cream truck entered the Hill. Questioned by police, Fred Harris explained that he believed the incident to be the result of a group of teenagers not connected to the HPA.[37]

Police found Harris's explanation unsatisfactory. In the weeks leading up to the riot the police had become increasingly hostile toward the HPA. Exactly a month after the incident at Congress and White streets, Harris again found himself in the center of a maelstrom in the Hill. As he and the HPA worked to quell what developed into a full-fledged riot, they came face-to-face with police officers who hardly appreciated their effort. The riot demonstrated how divergent opinions had grown in New Haven about the success of urban renewal. It also showed the lack of tolerance by city officials for dissent as New Haven stumbled into bad publicity for the first time.

Notes

1. Fred Harris, interview by author, telephone tape recording, 9 April 1999; Richard Balzer, *Street Time: Text Based on Conversations with Fred Harris* (New York: Grossman Publishers, 1972), 11–12; Fred Powledge, *Model City* (New York: Simon and Shuster, 1970), 152–153.

2. Interview with Fred Harris; Balzer, 11–12.

3. Interview with Fred Harris; Powledge, 155–156.

4. Balzer, 12.

5. Ibid., 12; Mayor Richard C. Lee to Paul Ylvisakek, Ford Foundation, 26 July 1965, Richard C. Lee Papers RG 318 Series II Box 110 Folder 1972, Manuscripts and Archives, Yale University Library.

6. Mayor Richard C. Lee to Charles E. Weeks, SAC New Haven, FBI, 26 July 1965, RG 318 Series II Box 110 Folder 197, Manuscripts and Archives, Yale University Library; Mayor Richard C. Lee to Paul Ylvisakek, Ford Foundation, 26 July 1965.

7. James Coogan to Dennis Rezendes, Memorandum, Re: Meeting of Park Supervisors with Hill Neighborhood Union, 8 July 1965, Richard C. Lee Papers RG 318 Series II Box 110 Folder 1972, Manuscripts and Archives, Yale University Library.

8. Balzer, 14.

9. Ibid.

10. Balzer, 16–17; Powledge, 155–157.

11. Ibid.

12. Ibid.

13. Ibid.

14. Ibid.

15. Ibid.

16. Balzer, 17–20.

17. Ibid., 23.

18. Ibid., 21.

19. Balzer, 21; William Lee Miller, *The Fifteenth Ward and the Great Society* (Boston: Riverside Press, 1966), 223.

20. Negro CPI Staff Concerns and Action Committee, "Concerns of Negro Staff Members" submitted to Mitchell Sviridoff, Executive Director Community Progress, Inc, 18 March 1966, Richard C. Lee Papers RG 318 Box 78 Folder 1452, Manuscripts and Archives, Yale University Library.

21. Dick Lee, Memorandum to Larry Spitz, 14 November 1966, Richard C. Lee Papers RG 318 Box 78 Folder 1452, Manuscripts and Archives, Yale University Library.

22. Powledge, 158; Miller, 69.

23. Balzer, 21.

24. "Ideas for the Hill Model Neighborhood Program," authors not listed, April 1967, contained in Powledge, 162.

25. Ibid., 162.

26. For information on riots of 1967 see US Riot Commission, *Report of the National Advisory on Civil Disorders* (New York: Bantam, 1968); Reverend Sidney Lovett, Chairman, Richard Belford, Executive Director, and John C. Daniels, Deputy Director Commission on Equal Opportunities, to Mayor Richard C. Lee, Re: Potential Summer Unrest, May 1967, Richard C. Lee Papers RG 318 Series II Box 114 Folder 2032, Manuscripts and Archives, Yale University Library.

27. Draft of undated unsigned memo from Mayor Richard C. Lee, Richard C. Lee Papers RG 318 Series II Box 114 Folder 2032; Richard Belford, Executive Director and John C. Daniels, Deputy Director of New Haven, Connecticut, Commission on Equal Opportunities, to Charles Randall, New Haven Chamber of Commerce, Richard C. Lee Papers RG 318 Series II Box 114 Folder 2032, Manuscripts and Archives, Yale University Library.

28. Ralph M. Goglia, Director of Community Schools to Richard C. Lee, Mayor of New Haven, CT and John A. Santini, Superintendent of New Haven, CT Public Schools, Re: Program Plans for the Summer, 23 May 1967, Richard C. Lee Papers RG 318 Series II Box 114 Folder 2032, Manuscripts and Archives, Yale University Library.

29. Hill Parents Association Summer Project Proposal, 10 July 1967, Richard C. Lee Papers RG 318 Series II Box 114 Folder 2032, Manuscripts and Archives, Yale University Library.

30. Ibid.

31. Ibid.

32. Ibid.

33. Ibid.

34. Balzer, 25.

35. Ibid., 25.

36. Ibid., 26.

37. Sgt. S. Tiddei, Office of the First Precinct, report to Francis V. McManus, Chief of Police, Subject: Disturbance at Congress-White streets, 19 July 1967, Richard C. Lee Papers RG 318 Series I Box 114 Folder 2032, Manuscripts and Archives, Yale University Library.

CHAPTER FIVE

There Is a Riot Going On

White racism is still the curse of America. We've lost the war to the Negro trying to keep him invisible. He's burning our cities, and we must begin to pay indemnities due him.

> —Henry Golden,
> author, 1969

If everyone who is oppressed were involved, the Government would fall in a couple of days. It's only a question of arousing people to a point of wrath. Many complacent regimes thought they would be in power eternally—and awoke one morning to find themselves up against the wall. I expect that to happen in the United States in my lifetime.

> —Eldridge Cleaver,
> Minister of Information,
> Black Panther Party, 1969

On Saturday, August 19, 1967, Lee's worse fears came to pass. The Hill exploded in racial violence. Just after twilight a Hispanic youth, Julio Diaz, was shot by the white owner of Tony's Snack Bar, a convenience store located on Congress Avenue, the main traffic artery through the Hill neighborhood. Less than half an hour later, police received accounts of sporadic window breaking along Congress Avenue, large crowds gathered in the area. Incidents of looting followed shortly thereafter. Law enforcement officials who arrived on the scene were greeted with jeers. Officers later reported being pelted with rocks and bottles. Despite efforts by the HPA to keep the peace, police used tear gas in an attempt to break up an especially rowdy and vocal group of residents. By the time word reached Mayor Lee chaos ruled the streets.[1]

The animosity of the crowd toward police in the Hill came as little surprise to Fred Harris. Roughly two months before the riot the HPA had drafted a report on the status of New Haven police services. Complaining that "the problem of adequacy of current police protection ranked with police misconduct as the most serious sore points in police community relations," the report noted that "When calls for help are registered, it is all too frequent that police respond too slowly or not at all. . . . When they do come, they arrive with many more men and cars than are necessary . . . brandishing guns and adding to the confusion." In his meetings with Belford and Daniels during the spring of 1967 Mayor Lee had expressed similar concerns about the police. During the riot, the New Haven police acted according to script. After the violence escalated Saturday evening, Police Chief McManus ordered his men in full riot gear into the affected areas. The police presence further exacerbated tensions in the Hill and the violence spread to three of the city's other low income sections: Newhallville, Fairhaven, and Dixwell.[2]

While angry residents registered their discontent at the system by rock throwing and looting, the mayor initially worked with the HPA to quell the violence. On Saturday evening, Lee agreed to allow Fred Harris and the HPA to distribute brooms. But, when Chief McManus's officers refused to allow the city trucks carrying the brooms into the Hill, Lee called in the state police adding to the volatility. On Sunday, he met with Harris and the HPA along with representatives of the clergy, the Redevelopment Agency, and the CPI. The mayor promised to keep the police presence inconspicuous. By late Sunday afternoon, he nonetheless had imposed a citywide curfew. He then turned the suppression of the riot over to the police.

Following continued violence against black and Puerto Rican residents, Fred Harris lambasted the police department on Monday evening for its poor handling of the situation. As he explained to reporters, "The guys that are suppose to be in charge look like they're the worst racists around." Despite appeals from constituents to decrease the police role the mayor, on Tuesday, August 22, extended the curfew and granted police full authority to deal with rioters. "I wish there were some way of getting across to the people in the neighborhood," he complained, "that the police and fire departments represent law and order and are the first line of defense for all people." Lee ignored signs that the police were part of the problem. Fred Harris observed that "there is no trust in Lee or the police" and charged that one way to end the hostilities was for police to stop using rifles, police dogs, and tear gas on rioters. An anonymous black woman confirmed Harris's thoughts when she told *Progressive Architecture*, "I think the violence should stop, especially by the police. The violence of the people is only against property; the violence of the police is against people."[3]

For four days the New Haven police assaulted Hill residents battling imaginary snipers in the shadows. In the process they permanently shat-

Toward the end of his last term as mayor, Richard Lee faced increasing criticism for the rise in crime in New Haven. He responded by appointing James Ahern, a one-time community outreach spokesman, liaison for the police in the Hill neighborhood. *(Reprinted with the permission of Manuscripts and Archives, Yale University Library)*

tered the image of New Haven as the nation's model city. State and federal investigators, reporters, and social scientists who had once flocked to New Haven to ask what was right now focused on what went wrong. In seeking the answers to those questions they discovered the deep-seated problems first exposed by the HPA.[4]

The most puzzling aspect of the New Haven riot for investigators was the city's poor response. Where were all of the innovative poverty programs? What had become of human renewal? The visitors quickly found that New Haven's riot was not unlike disturbances in other urban areas. The igniting event had served as a catalyst for building tensions over poorly administered police and social services. The widely circulating rumors of a disturbance, the poor initial response of the police to calm the situation, and the lack of leadership from city hall to adopt innovative approaches for dealing with the violence all allowed the riot to spread.[5]

Although the disturbance initially involved a Hispanic youth, the police sought out Fred Harris as a calming influence. In the months leading up to the riot Harris and the HPA had been working to organize the growing Hispanic population in New Haven. Harris would later tell reporter Gail Sheehy in 1971, that he was persuaded to enter the affected area after police informed him that "Puerto Rican mothers and babies" were in danger. Within hours of arriving on the scene, police snipers were gunning for him. As he and Willie Counsel attempted to distribute brooms through the affected neighborhoods, in Harris's account, several shots whizzed past his head. Harris and Counsel temporarily retreated to offices of the HPA, where they were informed by the police community liaison, James Ahern, that they had the support of the police. Upon Harris returning to the streets however, "Three cops grabbed me. They pinned my arms behind my back. Another one started kicking me . . . in the groin."[6]

Throughout 1968, New Haven's city fathers sought to minimize the damage of the city's riot. It was referred to as a nonracial disturbance perpetrated by a few miscreants not representative of New Haven's mostly peaceful minority population. The federal government disagreed. In its report to the President the National Advisory Commission on Civil Disorders concluded that the 1967 disturbance had been "serious." At least part of the problem identified by the Commission was the police. In support of its conclusion, the Commission noted the attitude of the HPA, which characterized New Haven's police review board as "worthless."[7]

Later, Mayor Lee and others would claim that the HPA had threatened the city with the possibility of urban unrest if it was not granted funds for their community programs. This gave rise to the belief that the mayor himself had helped cause the disturbance by attempting to cultivate allies among minority groups. The *Connecticut Herald*, for instance, blamed the riot partly on Connecticut's "muddle-headed liberals and free spenders." The *Herald* editor, William Loeb, queried, "Just how much more Mayor Lee and his administration can do short of inviting the minority leaders to meet him at a time in Macy's window is a moot point."[8]

Loeb, like many others, placed most of the responsibility for the riot on "the violent segment of minority groups." During the riot white citizens' groups had reacted strongly to the violence in the Hill. Police were overcome with offers from such groups, which volunteered to help restore order. In one instance reported in, *Progressive Architecture*, a white man brandishing a shotgun appeared on Congress Avenue and told police, "I'll help you kill the niggers." Loeb concluded, however, that the primary causes of the riot were not rooted in New Haven but were national in origin, "young know-nothings called to rebellion by the revolting pronouncements of H. Rap Brown, Stokely Carmichael, and Martin Luther King." They "do not want to be helped by whites," Loeb lamented, "for then they would no longer have even the present slender excuse for rioting, stealing and otherwise breaking the law."[9]

Melvin Adams, the redevelopment director, was far more critical of the New Haven black community whom he blamed for the riot. He noted that despite efforts by his agency to consult with the people in slated renewal areas these efforts were often met with apathy. "Call it Black power or anything else," he concluded, "but what it means is that the Negro in America is finally proud of himself." Electing like Lee to deal with leaders rather than the people, Adams argued that while the city should strive to listen to the people, it must identify the people who spoke for them. This was one of the fundamental problems in Lee's agreement with the HPA. Lee believed that working with the HPA would guarantee that no trouble would occur in New Haven. Yet, the US Commission on Civil Disorders observed that in New Haven "well intentioned programs designed to respond to the needs of ghetto residents were not worked out and implemented sufficiently in cooperation with the intended beneficiaries."[10]

This was a problem of the new, efficient bureaucratic programs which Lee implemented. As Fred Harris and the HPA moved from dealing with the School Board to the State Board of Welfare to the Executive Board of the CPI they encountered the crux of the problem identified by Max Ways in "The Deeper Shame of the Cities." As Ways conceptualized it, "The lowly citizen had been told this is a democracy; but police departments that ran themselves, school systems that ran themselves, did not seem to fit what he had been told. The antisepsis of bureaucratic municipal government killed a lot of inefficiency and corruption; it also killed too, a lot of connective tissue and nerve ganglia that had previously united citizen and city."[11]

This feeling of unconnectedness was evident in the many telegrams which flooded the mayor's office during the riot. The mayor received numerous letters from residents. Some supported the efforts of the HPA to bring the violence under control; others affirmed the actions of the mayor. Both asked a fundamental question, who was in control? For instance on August 22, 1967, William Jesse Bradley wired the mayor, "You are still one of the most popular mayors in the United States regardless of the recent unrest in our city. The HPA officials don't speak for the Negro majority of New Haven. We would like for you to go to the areas and speak to the people. They will still listen to you." Estelle Feldman, likewise wired Lee, "May I say you have done as fine job during these trying times it has been suggested to me and I pass on to you that your appearance in the restless neighborhoods may indicate to the people that your interest in them is deep and lasting." Finally, Joseph P. Bartlett, president of the Human Relations Council of Greater New Haven, assured the mayor, "You are still New Haven's most popular mayor and would instill confidence by your presence in various neighborhoods during these troubled times."[12]

Lee also received a number of telegrams from those affirming the work of the HPA in the Hill and asking him to bring the New Haven police under control. Dr. and Mrs. R. J. Propsky, for instance, informed the mayor, "Understand from first hand reports that police in the Hill are acting in such a way as to aggravate violence. Please use your influence to reverse this trend." At the same time, Mr. and Mrs. Harris Stone chastised Lee for not acting sooner. In a wire to the mayor's office they advised Lee that they were, "appalled by police brutality and arrest of Fred Harris. Urge continued consideration of real problems not blind action and programs which aggravate situation. Believe HPA activities indicate solution and deserve further support." In a similar manner, Robert Cook, of Court Street, wired the mayor, "Suggest you take immediate steps to bring police under control stop arresting Fred Harris was a dumb move. You should have all the evidence you need that the Model City has not touched the real problems of the people."[13]

Despite these appeals, *Progressive Architecture* observed that in 1968 Mayor Lee had little control over what the police did. Underscoring the findings of Max Ways, the article noted that this problem "seems to exist in urban governments, and perhaps the national government." Lee and Police Chief McManus, failed to maintain communications during the disturbance. In many cases Lee merely rubber-stamped actions taken by the police in their efforts to control the rioting. This left many asking who was in control in New Haven. It also caused many people, like Cook, to question why human renewal had not prevented the riot in the first place?[14]

Cook's comments were particularly searing considering the role Lee had envisioned for the CPI. CPI was supposed to deal with the real problems of the people. In its annual report to the Ford Foundation, however, the CPI blamed the riot on the youth. As CPI observed, "Some of the disadvantaged are too young to know about the progress that's been made or too burned up to care. They live in the here and now." The report cited evidence to indicate that these youthful elements had caused the four nights of disorder that broke out in New Haven on August 19, 1967. Paradoxically, the CPI claimed that "the loudest voices of protest are mostly directed at City Hall and CPI. But the fact is that City Hall and CPI are the chief militants in the inner city crisis."[15]

Showing some humility for its decision to grant the HPA funds, CPI officials tried to explain their blunder by playing up their well-intentioned motives. Citing the need for more innovative approaches to community problems, CPI also worked in an appeal for more funding as they introduced a new plan for the fall of 1967. Nonetheless, the CPI assured the Ford Foundation, "In this experiment in self-determination and self-help, no neighborhood group will receive substantial funds until it has demonstrated its capacity to run programs which meet the most urgent needs of residents of the areas they serve."[16]

Although many people agreed with the CPI and Loeb and blamed the violence which erupted on young blacks, the police disagreed. In a confidential study conducted after the riot, Police Lt. James Ahern and others determined that what occurred was "neither a teenage disturbance, nor was it overwhelmingly a Negro or a white one." The police report determined that while the initial incidents on the first days "appear to have involved Negroes mainly, this was definitely not true of the continuation and prolongation of the disturbance, during which large numbers of whites were involved." Police found that white groups contained a larger proportion of teenagers and older men including many drunks who participated in the violence.[17] The New Haven Police concluded, "As such, it may be said that these disturbances occupy a middle ground in the topology of these episodes. They are not a show put on by teenagers for 'kicks,' neither are they a rebellion against the system and everything pertaining to it."[18]

In an interview following the riot, Richard Beldford, chairman of the city's Commission on Equal Opportunities, observed that in his opinion some strong, progressive mayors like New Haven's Richard C. Lee had accomplished much at the expense of "grassroots resentment." Belford noted that, "We've been telling people what we think they should have, not asking them, and now they won't take it." Despite Lee's impressive record on urban renewal, Belford explained that one of the reasons for the resentment was that "people in the slums are continuing to live in the slums." Underscoring the findings of a decade earlier, Belford noted that not enough low-rent housing had been created and Negro unemployment remained at about eight percent, twice the white rate.[19]

In September of 1967, Belford resigned his position as executive director of the Commission on Equal Opportunities citing irreconcilable differences with the manner in which the organization was being run. According to Belford, Lee wanted both the Commission and the CPI to operate on a noncontroversial basis. Belford charged that there were statements from city hall which strongly indicated that the mayor would not allow dissent. As Belford explained, "Our first and only loyalty lay in maintaining the mayor's image in the community and that everything had to be geared toward that kind of activity."[20]

Mayor Lee and the Redevelopment Agency responded to these complaints by reiterating that massive low-rent housing projects would run counter to everything they had attempted to accomplish in New Haven. The development of scattered housing for the poor, although slow, was a much better alternative. Shifting part of the blame back on the community, they noted that much moderate-cost housing had been constructed, taking the pressure off low-rent units. They also contended that thousands of job opportunities have been created, but retraining people to fill these positions was also a slow process and interest from the people low. As for police service, they noted that it was also slowly being improved and that the Hill was slated to be the first of several neighborhoods to house neighborhood complaint review centers.[21]

In the aftermath of the riot, Fred Harris placed the blame squarely on the police. As he explained, "the cops are racists," adding that they often harassed and sometimes assaulted blacks without provocation. Harris has observed that in New Haven in 1967 there were no black policemen above the rank of patrolman. Ten years earlier, it will be recalled, after the only black of higher rank than patrolman was arrested in an incident of domestic violence, Chief Francis McManus had demoted him.[22]

Despite the mayor's fears, the riot did not dampen interest in New Haven. Leroy Jones, commissioner of the State Department of Community Affairs, predicted that the riot would not "interrupt the successful continuation of the entire program." Jones added that "the State of Connecticut through my Department of Community Affairs recognizes the importance of programs like those being carried out in New Haven." The state, Jones pointed out, had appropriated an additional $45 million for both urban renewal and human renewal programs, including many bold and innovative approaches. "We believe in New Haven," he told the press. "It has been successful and will be even more successful in the future."[23]

Embarrassed by the riot and the bad publicity which it brought, Lee pursued a different course in dealing with the HPA. In his column, Loeb offered Lee some advice: "The demands made on Mayor Lee by the rioters last week were insulting. He was entirely justified in telling them to go to hell. It's an attitude he might well consider adopting on a more permanent basis." Loeb's comments neatly summarize the mayor's future involvement with black groups in New Haven. Funding for the HPA's Operation Breakthrough was not continued into the fall. In addition, the New Haven police moved aggressively against the HPA.[24]

According to Harris, "It became clear in the next several months that CPI, the police, and the city were determined to get the HPA. . . . The city officials never liked us too much anyway, but they tolerated us when they thought we could keep things cool. When things blew, our only value to them disappeared." Betraying his own insecurities, Harris explained, "Some people might think this is some paranoid reaction to things that happened." Robert Bowles, executive director of the Urban League, was much more straightforward in his analysis. As he told *Progressive Architecture* in January of 1968, the city's efforts to silence the HPA amounted to a "break HPA" movement centered on discrediting the organization's leadership.[25]

That was not mere theory. Prompted by the mayor, the New Haven police initiated a harassment campaign against the organization that utilized electronic surveillance, informants, and agent provocateurs. The New Haven police submitted to the FBI's resident agency in New Haven the names of HPA leader Fred Harris and those of other members of the HPA. A subsequent memo from the Special Agent in Charge (SAC) of New Haven to the director of the FBI characterized the HPA as a "Black militant organization" most of whose leaders had "long criminal records . . . frequently arrested by the local police." The culmination of this campaign was the incarceration of key leaders of the HPA on charges of misuse of public funds, and an alleged bomb plot directed against city officials.[26]

Harris and the HPA were undaunted but not fully aware of the forces mounting against them. After the riot they became much more vocal in their criticism of Mayor Lee and the CPI.

John Barber meanwhile had relocated to Hartford where he was again involved in political organizing. He was on his way in a career that would give him a significant role as an advisor to such important black leaders as Dr. Martin Luther King, the Reverend Jesse Jackson, and Atlanta Mayor Maynard Jackson. George Edwards, a former member of the HPA, characterized Barber as ruthless in pursuit of power and explained that Barber believed that black people should pursue the same. As Edwards recalls, Barber "would double cross everyone, Barber would leave everyone holding the bag." By the time of his death in 1979, Edwards observes Barber had earned the reputation of a brilliant campaign organizer. In 1967 he made a brief return to New Haven politics, this time at a meeting held by the HPA on October 3 at the Winchester School, where he was introduced as the head of the Hartford Black Caucus.[27]

Edward Grant of the Union of Indigent People set the tone of the meeting when he refused to accept the city's version that the HPA had instigated the violence. As he told the audience, "We're calm people—everybody carries matches."[28] Barber joined with Fred Harris and the HPA in denouncing the CPI. Barber called for New Haven blacks to "lash out tomorrow" and "take over the CPI offices." He was followed on the podium by Harris, who criticized New Haven's poverty program for "failing to meet the needs of the people." Harris charged that instead of encouraging grassroots organizations CPI "bought off the grass roots Black leaders, gave them shirts and keeps them so near you can't even talk to them."[29]

Harris and Barber were mildly challenged by a CPI neighborhood worker, Maurice Sykes, who had been one of the sponsors of the CPI Negro Staff Concerns Action Committee. Sykes proposed that much of the confusion over poverty programs did not grow out of New Haven but was due to the intentional design of Congress. He urged that instead of focusing on the head of the CPI alone the black men, "put pressure where it belongs" on the CPI workers, who bore even greater responsibility since it was "our job to keep those programs honest."[30]

After Sykes, Harris returned to the podium. He called for the abolition of the CPI because it constituted a "rubber stamp for the mayor." He wanted it replaced by a Black Council. According to Harris, such a council would administer funds for local neighborhood projects. Harris's call for such a council would be realized but only after his arrest cast a stormy shadow over the HPA.

Three weeks after the meeting, on October 26, 1967, Fred Harris was arrested for possession of marijuana and stolen goods. In what was later described by supporters of Harris as a "gestapo type" of assault, police entered his apartment in a predawn raid. Police claimed to have found track marks on Harris's arm. The stolen goods turned out to be a typewriter that had been given to him during a birthday party some weeks earlier.[31]

On November 2, 1967, a week after Harris's arrest, a meeting of black women organized by Joan Thornell, Shirley Penn, Dorothy Warren, Rosemarie Harris, and Gail Lathrop was held at Lee High School. The leaders, recognizing that the city had targeted the HPA, insisted that "We represent no organization. . . . We represent ourselves and our own personal experiences."[32]

The women identified welfare, education, and housing as in desperate need of improvement and criticized the mayor and urban renewal for exacerbating many of these problems. Shirley Penn declared that Lee, "hasn't done anything for his Black brothers and sisters." Dorothy Warren also blamed the middle-class black woman who is "like the stained glass windows in her church; her soul is stained glass—flashing red, blue, yellow any color to please . . . she is not touched by the racial upheaval." Rose Harris urged black women to get together and demand curriculum reform that was relevant to the children of the poor.[33] Gail Lathrop identified state welfare policies as a continuing problem for black women. To supplement their monthly allotments she said, many poor women were forced into prostitution. She also implored the audience to support the HPA because "it has helped a lot of Black people; they need you now."[34]

After Harris's arrest, the HPA received overwhelming support from activists who shared the feelings of Belford and Powledge that the New Haven city government was repressing legitimate dissent. The raid occurred just days before Lee was reelected to his eighth term and according to Harris caused many blacks to question Lee's sincerity in dealing with the HPA. Worse from Lee's perspective was the growing number of white liberals retreating from his camp. On November 5, a predominantly white group known as the Coalition of Concerned Citizens, members of the intellectual community from Yale who were less radical than AIM, met at Lee High School to adopt resolutions against what they believed was growing repression. The coalition had formed as a direct result of Fred Harris's arrest on narcotics possession. In its founding document, members declared themselves, "United in their concern about the unchecked continuation of injustice and inequality in this city and . . . committed to action in order to change these conditions."[35] At the meeting, the CCC adopted several resolutions highlighting their own fears about the manner in which city hall dealt with political protest. Like the words of Joan Thornell and Gail Lathrop, the charter of the CCC would prove prophetic.

Sometime in November of 1967, George Edwards recalls, HPA had been approached by a mysterious benefactor who told them he could deliver explosives for a modest fee. Edwards found the membership far too enthusiastic about the proposed arrangement. One of these members was Ronald Johnson.[36] Following his arrest, Harris and Willie Counsel decided to serve out their sentences stemming from the state welfare protest back in 1966. While they were away, Harris noted that the police began to focus on Ronald Johnson. The day before Christmas Eve of 1967, police arrested five men in a motel who were found to be in possession of explosive materials. The *New Haven Journal-Courier* reported that the men were part of a plot designed to "break the back of law and order" in New Haven through the liquidation of certain police officials and the destruction of the city's police station, several schools and banks, and "many other public buildings."[37]

Questioned about the arrests, Chief Francis V. McManus characterized the investigation leading to the raid as, "The most far reaching conducted during my tenure of office." It had begun in November he said, and was conducted by local and state police, in conjunction with the state's attorney's office and the Alcohol Tobacco and Firearms unit of the Internal Revenue Service adding that the involvement of weapons such as the small machine guns and the large supply of dynamite found at the motel had also brought in federal agents.

The greatest trouble the bombing plot brought for the HPA was the apprehension of Ronald Johnson, twenty-five years old, whom the *New Haven Register* identified as the organizer of Operation Breakthrough. Damaging as well was the arrest of Curtis Belton, also twenty-five, and a former employee of the CPI.[38] During the trial of Johnson in 1968, the undercover agent who had initiated the discussions with the HPA about the purchase of explosives testified that Fred Harris had directed the negotiations from his jail cell. To the FBI's agitators list of 1967 the Bureau added information on Harris and other members of the HPA. An FBI memorandum from February of 1969, identified the HPA as a

> Black militant organization located in the Hill Section of New Haven. This organization has been the recipient of public funds in the past and is continually attempting to obtain additional public funds. Individuals active in the HPA are all active in the

Hill Neighborhood Corporation which is financed by a $105,000 Model Cities Program grant from the Department of Housing and Urban Development.[39]

Despite the legal troubles for the HPA, the organization continued to grow in influence. In January of 1968 it helped to reactivate the Black Coalition, an alliance of black groups that had banded together after the riot in 1967. The HPA approached Yale University President Kingman Brewster about contributing funds to the HPA. In Fred Harris's recollection, "About ten of us went into his office . . . we started the meeting real hard, calling the man all kinds of names. Then we started discussing what the university had and hadn't done." Although Brewster told the HPA that the University could not give money directly to any one neighborhood group, the following day Harris was contacted by Hank Parker, the head of Heritage Hall, a black arts organization in New Haven, who informed him that Brewster had called Heritage Hall and expressed interest in giving money to the Black Coalition. As a result the Black Coalition moved to the forefront of black civil rights organizations in New Haven.[40]

In February of 1968 a Yale sociologist, Dr. Louis Goldstein, conducted a survey of black teenagers in New Haven. Goldstein reported that a majority of the teens surveyed identified Fred Harris as one of the most influential black leaders they knew, even ahead of such national figures as Stokeley Carmichael and Martin Luther King. The Reverend Edmonds of the Dixwell Ministerial Alliance admitted that the HPA had grown in influence. After the assassination of Dr. King in April of 1968, Edmonds helped to organize a rally on the New Haven Green to commemorate Dr. King's life. According to Edmonds, Ronald Johnson and others from the HPA were invited to participate and used the platform as a forum to call for more violence. Edmonds recalls:

I couldn't keep quiet and I said this is not Martin Luther King's philosophy and to retaliate in kind was a contradiction of what he stood for and I called on the crowd to be calm but that took a lot of guts on my part as I look back on it because I had contradicted Ronnie and Fred Harris but I was more moderate I guess compared to Ronnie and Fred.[41]

Despite it's influence, the HPA soon realized that it was being excluded from a lead position within the Black Coalition. As Harris explains:

For a while the coalition listened a lot to us because they knew that the whole thing probably would not have come about if it weren't for us. But Brewster and all the others didn't want to deal with HPA. They knew we were talking about real community problems, problems the community cared about. So they had to find some responsible leaders who could talk about the same problems but whom they could deal with. That was the Black Coalition.[42]

Not long after the Black Coalition received funding from Yale, political infighting threatened to destroy the group. "There were a lot of middle class Black people and some poor Blacks," Harris observes. "Although the middle class always professed the same ends as the poor Blacks, they didn't share their ideas on means. The middle class won out after the money started coming in."[43] And as a flood of grants went to New Haven for projects to aid the black community in 1968, the HPA found itself pinched out. Knowing it would not receive direct funding, Harris says, the group continued to apply pressure to local governmental agencies, and so they too chose to finance the programs of the more moderate organizations that, at least on paper, had programs similar to those of the HPA.[44] In the meanwhile the HPA suffered continued police harassment for its militancy.

As usual, Lee looked to the federal government for assistance. It did not fail to deliver. In November of 1967, President Lyndon Baines Johnson announced a new crime fighting initiative that would help shape New Haven's future. As President Johnson explained, "Crime is a local problem and must be solved by local authorities. But the Federal Government can help to train better police forces and give them modern equipment to stem the rising tide of organized crime, to stop the illegal flow of narcotics, to keep lethal weapons out of the wrong hands, guarantee the right of privacy of every American citizen."[45]

Presented with alternatives such as community policing or skills training many police forces ended up promoting the idea that the money would be better spent on new technology and equipment for prevention and detection. The offer of hardware such as new patrol cars and mobile crime units from the federal government seemed far more appealing than the lofty notions of community policing that had become popular just before the rash of long hot summers between 1965 and 1968. In San Francisco, California, officer Dante Anderotti spearheaded one of the most comprehensive community relations programs in the nation. By the time he left that program in 1967, he had come up against the very root of the problem. As he explained:

The police in general look upon community relations as something of minor importance. They regard it as something forced upon them by the Negroes, not as something they want to do in their hearts. They want to be efficient. You can get technically efficient as hell, but if you are not effective with people you might as well close up shop. Our war was with the police department. We were never successful in getting the message down to the foot soldier: that community relations is the most important job.[46]

Anderotti continued:

I sincerely believe that policemen are hung up on this law-and-order bit. They forget the law part. Too many of them regard the law as something that they impose upon the people and not as something that protects the people's rights. Too many policemen feel they have to show they are the boss on the street. Instead of trying to communicate with the Negro, to make him feel that the law is for him too, they are busy espousing the thin blue line theory, the idea that they stand between you and chaos. The system itself contributes to the cynicism, the feeling of isolation, that many policemen have.[47]

Anderotti's departure coincided with the riot in New Haven in the summer of 1967 and what might be classified as a decline of interest in community policing. City officials were not the only culprits in producing the law-and-order mentality. An increasing crime rate, absence of decent pay, and black militancy directed at the police contributed to police frustration. Many police departments were quick to take advantage of the idea of the police as an efficient technocracy. The movement toward professionalization of the police actually increased problems within the department and heightened tensions between civilians and police. But by the late 1960s the professionalization of the police was a goal of every major metropolitan center. New Haven was no exception.

By 1967, it was clear to Lee as well as many others that the department McManus headed was no longer capable of effective policing. The riots of 1967 drove that point home, but New Haven residents had logged many complaints against the police. The local branch of the NAACP was particularly concerned about police community relations. The organization had first approached Lee in the early 1950s about better training of police. In the early 1960s the organization sought the intervention of the FBI to investigate police corruption in New Haven. As late as the winter of 1968 police disregard for civil liberties and new concepts of law enforcement served to further alienate the department from the steadily increasing black and student population. A survey conducted in the later months of 1968 revealed that a majority of city residents were not satisfied with police services. Many complained that the police were slow to respond to calls. Others charged that the police did not interact with the community.[48]

The basic problem was that the department did not reflect the racial makeup of the New Haven community. Despite a steady increase that migration and white exodus brought to the share of New Haven's blacks, until 1968 not one of New Haven's thirty-one nonwhite policemen, out of a total of 446, had been allowed to rise above the rank of a patrolman. Local officials had little if any appreciation for these demographic shifts. As a former Lee aide has recorded, very few public agencies kept racial records, even fewer perceived or at least identified any special "Negro problems": it had been "a period of public innocence, when the civil rights storm was a mere speck on the horizon, when civil rights progress throughout the nation was largely the product of political benevolence."[49] Now Lee was reasoning that the answer to better riot prevention was to be found not in community liaisons and citizens' action groups that would have included reconsidering the racial composition of the police—but in the technical professionalization of the force.[50]

The idea of professionalizing the police had its roots in the Progressive era, early in the century. At the time, major functions of the police had included strikebreaking and ward politics for city bosses. In 1908, August Vollmer at the University of California at Berkeley created the first program in police training, looking to a new police force whose primary goal would be crime prevention and detection. This meant the separation of the police departments from politics. It also called for application of the scientific method to crime detection. A result was in the new process of fingerprinting, an essential weapon of a new efficient urban police force.[51]

By the 1960s the issues had changed somewhat but the basic premise was the same. In high crime areas such as Los Angeles, the professionalization of the police took the form of cleaning up corruption. The concept was not without flaws. As Chapman College Professor Robert Slayton has observed in his study of the LAPD in the late 1950s and early 1960s, controlling corruption was only one small step toward professionalization. Too often civil administrators assumed that ending corruption was synonymous with professionalization. At the same time the LAPD was cleaning house, it continued a tradition of brutality and insensitivity to community needs that further alienated the department from the public. Criticism like that offered by Roy Wilkins and the NAACP in 1961 addressed the failure of this approach to professionalization. In New York City, to the contrary, the idea of professionalization engendered old fears about the union between the police department and city hall. When John Lindsay was elected mayor in 1965, one of his first battles was over the degree of control he could exercise over the police department. Lindsay's campaign promises, to bring the police under greater regulation, struck an unresponsive chord with many of his constituents. Confronted with cries of "keep city hands off the police" Lindsay was forced to retreat.[52]

Given a choice, many metropolitan police departments, including New Haven's, abandoned or scaled back community liaisons in favor of new hardware. They often ended up inviting more trouble, further alienating the police from the communities they served. In New Haven this meant police wiretapping, which in effect was the neo-progressives' fingerprinting. A voice over the telephone was the most reliable witness to a crime. The method also threatened civil liberties. As Max Ways conceptualizes the problem in "The Deeper Shame of the Cities," the relationship between government and governed was sacrificed on the altar of bureaucratic efficiency.[53]

In July of 1968 calls by Hispanic leaders for a better working relationship with the police underscored a growing Hispanic population problem in New Haven as well. Marcos M. Ocasio, a Hispanic community leader, sent a petition calling for a program to establish a better rapport between the police and "the citizens he protects." Ocasio observed that "as a Puerto Rican, I am particularly concerned about the language barrier that exists between the Spanish-speaking residents and the city's administrators."[54]

While blacks felt the increasing heavy-handedness of New Haven's police force, many people like Loeb interpreted the riots as a sign that the mayor had given in to the demands of black militants. The liberal response of groups such as AIM and the Coalition of Concerned Citizens came at a time when more conservative elements began to clamor for law and order.

A letter among the many pouring into the mayor's office in 1968 insisting that New Haven was becoming a haven for lawlessness is from Albert Kugell:

> The crime in itself does not disturb me. There will always be crime and criminals . . . what did disturb me was the attitude of the police, who, apprised of the occurrence, in effect told my brother to go home and forget about it. The implication was definitely since the crime was committed by Negroes nothing could be done about it. What good the gleaming facade of this beautiful new city? What reason to live here? Or to work here? or to seek an education, or entertainment, or any of the normal human requirements and desires? Are we now living in a society which condones the committing of a crime simply because the color of the criminals skin is Black? Or are we committed to a program of appeasement to Black skinned people so that they will not create an incident, or perpetrate a riot, nor foster revolution. If so the officials of our various governments, municipal, state, or national, should be reminded that appeasement is never an answer. Munich, back in pre–World War II days certainly proved this.[55]

Kugell's sentiments were echoed a few months later in May of 1968 by a Mrs. Joyce Longo. "When the next election comes up," she wrote the mayor, "I intend to listen and vote for the man who says appeasing the law breaker is not in effect the way to establish law and order. This country does not owe a debt to any race so anyone breaking the law should be punished accordingly."[56] Mrs. Pauline Kennedy, the head of a community center for the elderly, complained that "the colored men come in and out to use the men's room and they are either drunk or doped up." In a postscript Mrs. Kennedy wrote, "They may throw a bomb and set the place on fire. What will you do then?"[57]

At the same time the mayor was drawing criticism, his CPI was being bashed. Critics complained that the CPI was largely a front for the mayor's redevelopment schemes and charged that the programs did not meet the needs of the community. After the riot the CPI created several new programs to help keep teens off the street. Robert Berry, in a letter dated August 6, 1968, remarked upon many of the problems associated with the new community programs. Berry, who lived next door to one of the city's new recreation centers, spoke of the vandalism and crime which came with redevelopment and human renewal: "Right from the start of the place being made over into a recreation center I have had trouble with the so-called CPI kids." Berry maintained that there was little adult supervision and that the children in the program were allowed to run wild in the neighborhood. Citing his longtime residence in the neighborhood Berry concluded that the new CPI center left him no alternative but to move from a city no longer fit for law-abiding citizens.[58]

The increasing frustration with crime was summed up by Mrs. Claire Myers Owens who sent the mayor a letter in late 1968. She detailed for the mayor her own battles with crime and lawlessness in New Haven, recounting, for instance, a group of young boys whom had thrown a street sign through her dining room window. "Dear Mayor Lee," she pleaded, "Can't you do anything to bring law and order to New Haven? . . . The streets are no longer safe when citizens no longer feel safe in their homes. Should not something more drastic be done?"[59]

When McManus tendered his resignation in March of 1968, Lee found himself in a position to appoint a new chief. James Ahern seemed an ideal choice. He had been the community relations officer in New Haven since 1964. In the three years prior to the riot he had worked closely with Fred Harris and the HPA and was respected in the community. Harris would tell reporter Gail Sheehy that one reason for the worsening of conditions under the new chief was that the HPA had trained him:

> As a police liaison he'd ask to come down and talk to our group. We allowed it because back in 1964 we thought we were slick,

letting the police know exactly where we stood. Ahern would sit there discussing positions and asking how the police could create a better image to make us think he was really sincere. My guys treated him as just another guy. We cursed him out, blew his mind a little. Meanwhile, Ahern was digging our style. How we did things and what guys were what. . . .[60]

Touted as a progressive policeman of the future for his innovative ideas on law enforcement, Ahern advocated many of the suggestions made by the 1967 Kerner commission, including professionalization of the police. His nationwide reputation for keeping New Haven cool during demonstrations in support of the Panthers in 1970 was to make him seem a wise choice. In reality, Ahern merely sank law enforcement to a new and illegal level.[61]

Born and raised in New Haven, Ahern in joining the department in 1954 had followed his older brother Stephen, who was an up and coming New Haven detective. Ahern attended night school and received a degree in business administration in 1965. Meanwhile his equally ambitious brother Stephen had attained the rank of Chief Inspector, boasting one of the most impressive arrest records in the history of the New Haven police department. Stephen's success was due in large part to his

A celebrated symbol of police efficiency in the late 1960s, James Ahern's tenure as chief of the New Haven police saw the department's illegal wiretapping apparatus expanded to include political dissenters like the Hill Parents Association and the Black Panthers. Like many of the other "enlightened" bureaucrats of New Haven, Ahern masked antiquated thinking with the language of science and sociology. *(Reprinted with the permission of Manuscripts and Archives, Yale University Library)*

association with Richard Sulman, a Yale student majoring in electrical engineering. Sulman had first met Ahern in 1958 when he sold the officer two electronic listening devices. Their relationship continued over the years. In 1964, Stephen, with the assistance of a friend at the Southern New England Telephone Company, acquired additional wiretapping equipment. He installed it in a spare bedroom of his apartment. The machine provided a printout of the numbers dialed on the tapped telephones, allowing Ahern to collect positive intelligence including the names of organized crime heads involved in New Haven gambling operations and other facets of organized crime. To ensure that his work remained secret, Ahern adopted the FBI method of attaching his taps to the main frame at the Southern New England Telephone Company, the central switching point within the telephone company.[62]

Stephen Ahern's electronic surveillance helped to propel his career. In 1966 he was recruited to head a newly formed squad, the Special Services Unit. As a result he relocated his wiretapping equipment to police headquarters and selected several of his most trusted men to monitor it. One year later, after James was appointed Chief, Stephen widened the department's wiretapping capabilities. He acquired three new wiretap machines and expanded his squad so that the new equipment could be monitored around the clock.[63]

While James Ahern spoke well of new methods of police work like community policing and dismissed FBI gimmicks such as wiretapping, Stephen regularly traded information from his illegal taps with the FBI. Sergeant Walter P. O'Connor, an intelligence officer until the summer of 1969, testified that in 1969 or 1970 the telephone wiretaps were expanded from the criminal underworld to leftists and black militant organizations. According to Attorney John L. Williams, "They tapped everybody and anybody. They tapped their girlfriends, candidates running against the mayor, a lot of Yale ex-students and faculty, bookmakers, a lot of respectable business people, members of the communist party, a lot of lawyers, judges and prosecutors."[64]

New Haven's police expenditures over a period of fifteen years reveal the expanding operation. In 1959 when Stephen Ahern first purchased the wiretap equipment from Sulman, New Haven had spent a total of $6,700 on nonpersonnel expenditures in detectives, intelligence, and narcotics. In 1968, the year after Ahern took office and Lyndon Johnson pledged the support of the federal government, that number increased to $9,000. This was easily explained by changing demographics and the aftereffects of the riot. But the following year, according to O'Connor, when the wiretaps were expanded to radical groups, the department spent $80,800 on nonpersonnel equipment. Most of this was dedicated to surveillance and the new wiretap command center in New Haven police headquarters.[65]

At the same time that New Haven was building its arsenal of telephonic surveillance, Congress broadened the permissible scope of federal wiretapping. Prior to the passage of the 1968 Omnibus Crime Control Act, wiretapping had been a violation of the Federal Communications Act and Connecticut state law. The 1968 legislation specifically authorized federal agents to wiretap in criminal cases if they obtained warrants. They could also gather intelligence under the auspices of national security interests. The states enacted their own legislation outlining the scope of state wiretap operations under court order. Municipal police departments, however, were specifically banned from wiretapping unless they obtained a warrant. This law made it a felony to install unauthorized taps and added a civil remedy of money damages to the victims of taps carried out in violation of the law.[66]

Despite the limitation on municipal police departments, New Haven's intelligence buildup occurred at a time when the abuse of civil liberties seemed to have the permission and encouragement of the federal government. The national preoccupation with law and order coincided with a Republican victory in the presidential election of 1968. The Republican candidate Richard Nixon exploited the issue into a solid campaign effort. Citing what he called the divisive nature of civil rights legislation and the permissiveness and judicial activism of the Supreme Court, Nixon pledged to restore order to the riot-torn cities of the nation. Elected a minority President, with only forty-three percent of the vote, Nixon hoped to build his constituency by following what Republicans termed the "Southern strategy." It appealed to disaffected white voters by lessening the emphasis on civil rights and opposing busing to achieve school integration. It also supported the efforts of law enforcement to bring dissidents under control.

After Ahern was named Chief, the New Haven police force continued to move aggressively against the HPA. George Edwards, for instance, was targeted by local police for his militant stand on community participation and his call for blacks to support businesses owned by African Americans. At the height of the riot Edwards's fiery rhetoric earned him a spot on the FBI's agitators list. Twice arrested in 1967, Edwards faced a variety of charges that ranged from carrying a dangerous weapon and breach of the peace to inciting injury to person or property, and inciting to riot. The New Haven police, by ruthlessly targeting the leadership of the HPA, was sending a strong message: no militants in the model city.[67]

By the winter of 1968 the HPA began to decline as a potent influence within New Haven. Political infighting, lack of support, and the New Haven police department's continuous harassment of the organization all served to diminish its effectiveness. By its shift from working outside of the political framework before Operation Breakthrough to demanding monetary assistance from the city, the HPA also hurt itself. City money tied it to the local government and made it responsible to city hall. Mayor Lee and the New Haven police held the HPA accountable for failing to maintain peace in the summer of 1967.

One of the HPA's greatest accomplishments was its emphasis on community participation. Its pressure on the mayor and the CPI ultimately exposed the search for order lurking just behind the facade of progressive thinking in New Haven. In 1968 Richard Lee was no longer considered the civil rights leader in New Haven. After a record eight terms, in the course of which it was perceived as the liberal beacon for New Haven politics, the Lee Administration was taking on the characteristics of the law-and-order mentality that was overtaking the liberal Kennedy and Johnson years. The mayor was witnessing the collapse of his dream all around him. Lee began giving way his own personal influence to the reliability of dirty tricks, informants, and electronic surveillance. It was this situation that the BPP encountered when it arrived in New Haven in the winter of 1969.

Taking advantage of President Johnson's pledge of assistance, and President Nixon's emphasis on maintaining the law, the New Haven police department continued its illegal surveillance. In 1969, the New Haven wiretap operation would be directed against the Black Panther Party as it organized a chapter in the city. The New Haven Police were supported by the FBI, especially Director J. Edgar Hoover, who condemned the BPP as the "number one threat" to the nation's internal security. The Nixon Administration followed suit and New Haven emerged as a front line in the battle between Panthers and police. A memo of January 17, 1970, from Nixon's aide H. R. Halderman underscored the new fixation on the BPP:

> The President feels it is extremely important that Mitchell et al. get the word out to Congressmen and other leaders on what the Black Panthers actually stand for. He was concerned by the secret report that most Blacks support the Black Panthers, and feels that this could only be the case if the Blacks were not aware of what the Panthers were really trying to do.[68]

In the winter of 1969, New Haven found out what the Panthers were trying to do.

Notes

1. On the riots, see Peter M. Green and Ruth A. Cheney, "Urban Planning and Urban Revolt: As Case Study," *Progressive Architecture*, January 1968, 131–145; US Riot Commission, *Report of the National Advisory Commission on Civil*

Disorders (New York: Bantam, 1968); Cleo Abraham, *Protests and Expedients in Response to Failures in Urban Education: A Study of New Haven. 1950–1970* (Ph.D. diss., University of Massachusetts, 1971), 2–6.

2. "In Search of Fair and Adequate Law Enforcement," Report of the Hill-Dwight Citizens Commission on Police Community Relations, June 1967, 12–13, contained in US Riot Commission, 308.

3. Comments of Mayor Lee, Fred Harris, and anonymous black woman recorded in Peter M. Green and Ruth A. Cheney, 131–145.

4. Powledge, 108–142; Balzer, 11; Peter M. Green and Ruth A. Cheney, 131–145; Abraham, 2–6.

5. US Riot Commission, 286.

6. Fred Harris's comments reported in Gail Sheehy, *Panthermania* (New York: Harper and Row, 1971), 89–91; Peter M. Green and Ruth A. Cheney, 132–133; Abraham, 2–6.

7. "In Search of Fair and Adequate Law Enforcement," Report of the Hill-Dwight Citizens Commission on Police Community Relations, June 1967, 12–13, contained in US Riot Commission, 310; Peter M. Green and Ruth A. Cheney, 145; Powledge, 131–133.

8. William Loeb, "A Lesson In Ingratitude," *The Connecticut Sunday Herald*, 27 August 1967, 22.

9. Ibid., 22.

10. Melvin Adams comments recorded in Philip Shandler, "New Haven Looks Again," *Washington Evening Star*, 4 September 1967, A-8.; US Riot Commission, 286.

11. Max Ways, "The Deeper Shame of the Cities," in *The Negro and the City* (New York: Time-Life Books, 1968), 25.

12. William Jesse Bradley and son Edward to Mayor Richard C. Lee, via Western Union Telegram, 22 August 1967, Richard C. Lee Papers RG 318 Series I Box 87 Folder 1570, Manuscripts and Archives, Yale University Library; Estelle E. Feldman to Mayor Richard C. Lee, via Western Union Telegram, 22 August 1967, Richard C. Lee Papers RG 318 Series I Box 87 Folder 1570, Manuscripts and Archives, Yale University Library; Joseph P. Bartlett, President Human Relations Council of Greater New Haven, to Mayor Richard C. Lee, via Western Union Telegram, 22 August 1967, Richard C. Lee Papers RG 318 Series I Box 87 Folder 1570, Manuscripts and Archives, Yale University Library.

13. Dr. and Mrs. R. J. Propsky to Mayor Richard C. Lee, via Western Union Telegram, 20 August 1967, Richard C. Lee Papers RG 318 Series I Box 87 Folder 1570, Manuscripts and Archives, Yale University Library; Mr. and Mrs. Harris Stone to Mayor Richard C. Lee, via Western Union Telegram, 20 August 1967, Richard C. Lee Papers RG 318 Series I Box 87 Folder 1570, Manuscripts and Archives, Yale University Library; Robert Cook to Mayor Richard C. Lee, via Western Union Telegram, 20 August 1967, Richard C. Lee Papers RG 318 Series I Box 87 Folder 1570, Manuscripts and Archives, Yale University Library.

14. Peter M. Green and Ruth S. Cheney, 143; Samuel Kaplan, "More Stately Mansions," *The Nation*, 24 May 1971, 663. In 1970 a limited study conducted to assess the level and quality of police service in New Haven found the department wanting supervisory and managerial education and modernization of policies and practices. While the study found public attitudes toward police to be generally favorable, in incidents involving a high degree of interpersonal contact between citizens and police, police received low marks. The survey itself suffered from its own generality. Investigators chose to classify persons only by socioeconomic characteristics, age, education, and relationship with police. Conspic-

uous by its absence was the question of race. Raymond T. Galvin, "Survey of Public Attitudes Toward Police Services," unpublished study, New Haven, Connecticut, 1970, quoted in Martin L. Piccirillo, *Organizational and Personal Dimensions of the New Haven Department of Police Service* (Ph.D. diss., Fordham University, 1973), 44.

15. *Community Progress Incorporated, The Human Story: 1967*, quoted in Powledge, 172.

16. Ibid., 172.

17. Confidential New Haven Disturbance Arrest Study, 20 September 1967, Richard C. Lee Papers RG 318 Series I Box 114 Folder 2032, Manuscripts and Archives, Yale University Library.

18. Ibid.

19. Philip Shandler, A-8.

20. Powledge, 181.

21. Philip Shandler, A-8.

22. Ibid.

23. Statement of Leroy Jones, Commissioner of the State of Connecticut Department of Community Affairs, Richard C. Lee Papers RG 318 Box 144 Folder 2032, Manuscripts and Archives, Yale University Library.

24. William Loeb, 22.

25. Balzer, 38; Peter M. Green and Ruth A. Cheney, 143.

26. FBI Memo from SAC, New Haven to Director of FBI, 17 February 1969, File number 100-448006, Subject (BPP), Freedom of Information Act Reading Room, FBI Headquarters, Washington, D.C.

27. At his funeral, the Reverend Jackson would credit Barber's principles for his cutthroat style. Jackson related one incident in which, "after Maynard was elected and John was not clear on some of Maynard's positions, John marched on him." Jackson justified Barber's actions explaining, "He loved us, but his integrity obligated him to be who John was." Jackson's eulogy reprinted in Inez Cole Barber, *Rememberances of John Barber* (published by Inez Cole Barber, 1981) 162–163; Interview with Earl Williams, Interview with Richard Dowdy; George Edwards, interview by author, telephone tape recording, Silver Spring, MD, 18 August 1997.

28. Stephen Hand, "Black Men Attack CPI," *New Haven Journal Courier*, 3 October 1967, 1.

29. Ibid.

30. Ibid.

31. Ibid.; Powledge, 193–194; SAC, New Haven to Director of FBI, 17 February 1969.

32. William Betsch, "Angry Negro Women Decry, Threaten, Pledge," *New Haven Journal Courier*, 2 November 1967, 4.

33. Ibid.

34. Ibid., 4–5.

35. Powledge, 193–194.

36. Ibid.

37. Associated Press, "Plot to Kill Police Officials, 'Break Back of Law' Laid to 5 in New Haven," *The Washington Evening Star*, 25 December 1967, A12.

38. Ibid.

39. SAC, New Haven to Director of FBI, 17 February 1969.

40. Powledge, 206.

41. Reverend Edwin Edmonds, interview by author, tape recording, New Haven, CT, 24 July 1997.

42. Balzer, 45.

43. Ibid., 45–46.

44. Ibid.

45. Statement by the President on the Message on Crime in America, 6 February 1967, reprinted in *Public Papers of the Presidents of the United States Lyndon B. Johnson 1967 Book I January 1 to June 30, 1967* (US Government printing office, Washington, D.C., 1968), 145.

46. *The Negro and the City*, 124.

47. Ibid., 124–125.

48. Raymond T. Galvin, "Survey of Public Attitudes Toward Police Services," in Martin L. Piccirillo, *Organizational and Personal Dimensions of the New Haven Police Service*, 44; Powledge, 128–131.

49. Talbot, 166.

50. Mr. Michael P. Koskoff, interview by author, Bridgeport, CT, 5 May 1995; George Edwards's interview; Powledge, 128.

51. Sidney L. Haring, *Policing a Class Society: The Experience of American Cities, 1865–1915* (New Jersey: Rutgers University Press, 1983); David R. Johnson, *Law Enforcement: A History* (Saint Louis: Forum Press, 1981).

52. Max Ways, "The Deeper Shame of the Cities," in *The Negro and the City*, 25.

53. Ibid.

54. Marcos Ocasio to Mayor Richard Lee, 10 July 1968, Richard C. Lee Papers RG 318 Box 96 Folder 1712, Manuscripts and Archives, Yale University Library.

55. Albert Kugell to Mayor Richard Lee, 28 March 1968, Richard C. Lee Papers RG 318 Box 96 Folder 1712, Manuscripts and Archives, Yale University Library.

56. Mrs. Joyce Longo to Mayor Richard Lee, 21 May 1968, Richard C. Lee Papers RG 318 Box 96 Folder 1712, Manuscripts and Archives, Yale University Library.

57. Mrs. Pauline Kennedy to Mayor Richard Lee, 19 August 1968, Richard C. Lee Papers RG 318 Box 96 Folder 1712, Manuscripts and Archives, Yale University Library.

58. Robert Berry to Mayor Lee, 6 August 1968, Richard C. Lee Papers RG 318 Box 96 Folder 1712, Manuscripts and Archives, Yale University Library.

59. Mrs. H. Thurston Owens to Mayor Richard Lee, 16 October 1968, Richard C. Lee Papers RG 318 Box 96 Folder 1712, Manuscripts and Archives, Yale University Library.

60. Sheehy, 87.

61. Robert O. Boorstin, "James Ahern Dies; Expert on Police," *New York Times*, 3 March 1986, Obituary; Andrew Holding, "The Wiring of New Haven," *The Nation*, 7 June 1980, 668; Carole and Paul Bass, "A City Bugged," *Connecticut Magazine*, September 1984, 75–82; Herman Shwartz, "The Intrusive Ears of the Law," *The Nation*, 16 July 1995, 722; Jamie Workman, "Suspicion and Paranoia: The Secrets of the May Day Security Machine," *The New Journal*, 2 February 1990, 39.

62. Ibid.

63. Ibid.

64. Andrew Houlding, 668–669; for Ahern's view on Federal wiretapping see James Ahern, *Police in Trouble* (New York: Hawthorn, 1972); Jamie Workman, 39–40.

65. "Police Department Expenditures, New Haven, 1955–1969, New Haven

City Budgets, 1955–1969," reprinted in Claudia Scott, *Forecasting Local Government* (Washington: Urban Institute, 1972), 25.

66. Andrew Houlding, 668–669; Jamie Workman, 39–40; J. N. Silverman, "Wiretap Case Jolts New Haven," *Washington Star*, 16 October 1971, page unknown, clippings file, Washingtoniana collection, Martin Luther King Public Library, Washington, D.C.

67. Balzer, 11–12; Powledge, 152–153.

68. H. R. Halderman to Mr. Klein, 17 January 1970, contained in *From: The President Richard Nixon's Secret Files*, Bruce Oudes, ed. (New York: Harper and Row, 1989), 89.

CHAPTER SIX
Enter the Black Panthers

In 1966 New Haven was being touted as America's model city for its innovative solutions to poverty and slums; Oakland was scarcely noticed. Oakland lacked a dynamic political personality like Richard C. Lee, who, as chief architect of New Haven's revival, deserves much of the credit for New Haven's physical regeneration, and by extension much of the blame for the social problems his programs accentuated. New Haven benefited from the presence of Yale University. New Haven's black population was increasing but at a rate much slower than that of Oakland. The National Committee on Civil Disorders postulated that Oakland was one of eleven cities that would be half black by 1983. Nonetheless the Commission noted that this relative youth of population in central cities and the drain of white children into private schools would likely give New Haven's public schools a black majority in 1985.[1]

Jane Jacobs, in her classic study of American cities, observed of Oakland that "the worst and most extensive slum problem is an area of some two hundred blocks of detached, one to two family houses which can hardly be called dense enough to qualify as real city densities at all." In laymen's terms, Oakland suffered from poor city planning that created slums. It is an example of the frequent confusion between high density and overcrowding.[2]

Jane Jacobs explained:

> We are much more apt to find overcrowding at low densities than at high densities. Nor does slum clearance as practiced in our cities usually have anything to do with solving the problem of overcrowding. Instead, slum clearance and renewal typically add to the problem. When old buildings are replaced with new projects, the dwelling densities are often made lower than they were, so there are fewer dwellings in a district than before.[3]

Mrs. Jacobs concluded that even if the same dwelling densities were replaced or even raised, fewer people could be accommodated than were replaced and the result would be overcrowding in some other area, "especially if colored people, who can find few areas in which to live, have been displaced." Thus, in New Haven the principal housing problem was overcrowding as blacks concentrated in the Hill the last refuge from urban renewal. In Oakland lack of opportunity accounted for most problems.[4]

One of the principal complaints in New Haven as in Oakland was the treatment of blacks by the police. As Fred Powledge conceived the problem, archaic laws in New Haven accounted for the majority of problems between blacks and police. According to Powledge, college students as well as white teenagers as much as blacks were the victims of antiquated charges such as "Lascivious Carriage," "Being in Manifest Danger of Falling into Habits of Vice," and "Found Intoxicated." After investigating an incident in December of 1965 in which a group of white and black teenagers was beaten and harassed by police during a James Brown concert, the New Haven Commission on Equal Opportunities found that the New Haven police had acted excessively.[5]

While Oakland's black community, having swelled like New Haven's by the mass migration from the South beginning in the 1940s, experienced similar problems, its response differed from that of black New Haven. National civil rights organizations like the NAACP and CORE were active in Oakland. But the city's own indigenous protest group, unlike the HPA, quickly turned so militant as to become a national phenomena, the Black Panther Party for Self-Defense.

Huey Newton and Bobby Seale, the founders of the Black Panther Party were both products of the World War II black migration. Newton was born in Oak Grove, Louisiana, on February 17, 1942. He was one of seven children. His family moved to California after his father found war-related work in Oakland. After graduating from high school in Berkeley, California, Newton began taking classes at Oakland's two-year Merritt Junior College. It was while attending Merritt that Newton first became acquainted with Bobby Seale. Born in Dallas, Texas, on October 22, 1936, Seale had moved to California after the war. He attended Oakland High School, and served three years in the Air Force, before being discharged in 1958 for improper conduct. In September of 1961, Seale also enrolled at Merritt Junior College. He and Newton met in 1962, after Seale heard Newton speak at a rally for the campus Afro-American Association.[6]

It was through the Afro-American Association that Seale and Newton eventually became friends and collaborators on the Soul Students' Advisory Council (SSAC). Through SSAC, Newton and Seale hoped, campus organizations could get involved in community projects. They also wanted the group to take a more militant stance on matters affecting the black community, especially police misconduct, and even suggested as a symbolic act the carrying of loaded firearms.[7]

Newton and Seale quickly discovered that there was little support at Merrit for such initiatives. The pair began to question the purpose of student groups that failed to produce any meaningful change in the community. Newton and Seale left SSAC and during the summer of 1966 began discussing the possibility of creating a new organization. Disappointed in their first experience with collegiate groups, they planned to draw their membership from inner-city youth and adults who had been ignored by civil rights groups but were disproportionately the victims of the effects of racism, police brutality, and discrimination.[8]

By mid-October of 1966 Newton and Seale had put together the program for their new organization. They defined their movement in a ten-point program. Articulated for the most part by Newton, with suggestions from Seale, the program called for full employment for black people, an immediate end to police brutality and murder of black people, and the assumption of power by the black community to control its future. As Bobby Seale recalls, "We summed it up: We wanted land, bread, housing and education, clothing, justice, and peace. Then we flipped a coin to be chairman. I won."[9]

The first five points of the BPP program greatly resembled the early demands of the HPA. The HPA wanted freedom to determine the destiny of the black community in New Haven; this meant control of the schools. It also pushed for full employment by demanding a share of antipoverty money to institute its own schooling and training programs. George Edwards of the HPA was singled out in 1968 for his calls for New Haven blacks to patronize black businesses. This was also the third point of the Panthers program. James Gibbs of the NAACP and Blyden Jackson of CORE might have written the fourth point, which demanded "decent housing fit for human beings." The fifth point, "education for our people that teaches us our history and our role in present-day society," corresponds exactly with the proposal for black history classes as part of the HPA's Operation Breakthrough.

The last five points of the ten-point program, however, clearly separated the HPA from the BPP. The BPP was addressing a new set of issues that hitherto had been ignored in New Haven.

Researchers uncovering some troubling statistics about New Haven in the late 1960s found, for example, that the tax base was shrinking. By Fred Powledge's observation almost one third of all property in New Haven was tax exempt, a good portion of that tied to Yale University. At the same time, city expenditures were growing. In 1969, Mayor Lee was forced to ask the Board of Aldermen for a budget of approximately $53 million, more than six million higher than that of the year before. As New Haven's poorest communities suffered from continued displacement from urban renewal the city's welfare caseload increased as well. A study commissioned by the State of Connecticut Commission on

Civil Rights found that Connecticut's situation was not "untypical." Paraphrasing Whitney Young of the Urban League, the Commission observed:

> By 1975, 85 percent of all Negro citizens will live in major urban centers, mainly in the North . . . and unless some way can be found for housing them adequately—especially in connection with urban renewal, slum clearance, and superhighway construction, which will further dislocate them—they face the specter of being more segregated, not less segregated, in the unattractive areas of the cities which remain educationally, culturally and socially substandard.[10]

While the overall birthrate fell, the number of illegitimate births increased. As the standard of living rose in the state as a whole, the gulf between rich and poor was widening. One report concluded that "the 40 percent overall increase in real income masks the continuing discrepancies between income groups. Thus, while 35 percent of the population will be earning more than $10,000 per year (compared with 15 percent in 1959), 24 percent of New Haven families will be earning less than 5,000 (compared with 38 percent in 1959)."

As a result of these changes, by 1969 the BPP would find a welcome audience among New Haven blacks. The shift from civil rights to Black Power, the riot, and the campaign against the HPA only partly account for the BPP's appeal. A change in the focus of the BPP itself also contributed. The Black Panther Party was addressing many of the same issues that had begun to manifest themselves in New Haven and many other major cities in the late 1960s. Newton and Seale invigorated their movement too by recruiting the estranged ghetto youth Huey Newton called the "brothers off the block." The BPP hoped they would be the foundation of a new revolutionary army. In *Dark Ghetto*, Kenneth B. Clark describes this group as social pariahs who prey on other ghetto residents as well as rival gangs. One government report identified them as having a "propensity for antisocial behavior," a condition which Clark associates with their alienation from larger "societal values."[11]

In the literature of the BPP, Newton is portrayed as a product of the same ghetto forces. Seale's *Seize the Time* presents a portrait of Newton that elevated him as a legend among Oakland gangs for his bravado and violent behavior. What ultimately set Newton apart from his contemporaries, the work asserts, was his refusal to engage in any activity that "terrorized other members of the Black community." As a result, many of the "pimps and hustlers and righteous gangsters on the block" grew to respect Newton.[12] Newton and Seale hoped to politicize ghetto youth with the same type of social bandit mentality. Declares *Seize the Time*,

"Huey P. Newton knew that once you organize the brother he ran with, he fought with, he fought against, who fought harder than they fought him, once you organize those brothers you get revolutionaries who are way too much."[13]

Utilizing the offices of a local community poverty program as a base, Newton and Seale began to implement their platform. Their first order of business was to educate the community on the BPP's objectives. This included distributing leaflets and speaking on street corners to all who would listen. They had limited success at this. By late November, Newton and Seale decided that it was time to initiate article seven of the Party Program. This called for armed patrols to observe the police in the black community.[14]

Newton and Seale had carefully examined California law. They discovered it was legal for any citizen to have possession of a loaded weapon, as long as it was unconcealed. The BPP, armed with this knowledge, moved into open confrontation with the police. For Newton and many others, the police were the most visible sign of oppression in black neighborhoods. As Newton was to explain:

> The police, not only in the Oakland community but throughout the Black communities in the country, were really the government. We had more contact with the police than we did the city council. The police were universally disliked. . . . The police were impolite and they were fast to kill a Black man for minor offenses, such as Black youth stealing automobiles. They would shoot them in the back and so forth.[15]

Gene Marine, in *The Black Panthers*, notes that from an early age Newton had been a "cop hater." He was constantly involved in the everyday struggle faced by most ghetto dwellers against the police. This portrait of Newton tends to support the view of Hugh Pearson and others that the BPP's early focus on the police was somewhat of a personal vendetta for Newton. Oakland and Los Angeles were notorious for police brutality. As early as 1961, Roy Wilkins, the executive director of the NAACP had made headlines when he denounced the Los Angeles police as "next to those in Birmingham, Alabama in the treatment of Black citizens." During a speech at a rally on October 6, 1961, Wilkins spoke of the recurring beatings, shootings, and cold-blooded killings by Los Angeles police officers: "The Negro citizens have great difficulty in getting at this evil because the system in Los Angeles makes the Chief of Police almost completely independent of the Mayor and elected officials." Wilkins concluded, "This system allows the Police Department to be the judge and jury of its own personnel without having to pay attention to the public."[16]

The armed patrols were running smoothly by mid-December and met with the general approval of the community. Although many were cautious about the BPP's tactics, few would deny the impact they had on the police. The success of the armed patrols expanded the reputation of the BPP in the later months of 1966. By January 1, 1967, Seale and Newton were able to set up the first official headquarters of the Black Panther Party for Self-Defense. In the first three weeks of January alone, the BPP recruited twenty-five new members.[17]

Recognizing the favorable effect the armed patrols were having on its reputation, the BPP expanded this activity in the early months of 1967. In order to supply its growing membership with weapons, Seale and Newton sold copies of Mao Zedong's *Red Book* on the Berkeley campus of the University of California. English translations of the *Red Book* were scarce at that time. Newton and Seale obtained their copies from a small Chinese bookstore in San Francisco at thirty cents a copy and sold them at a dollar a piece. They soon had enough money to provide almost every party member with a weapon.[18]

This is important because it shows that the BPP tried to remain financially independent and generate funds through legitimate sources. In its formative period the BPP, recognizing the effect that solicited funds had on other civil rights groups, tried to find other sources of money. This meant not accepting grants or donations from white groups or government agencies, the kind of funding that weakened the effectiveness of the HPA. The policy of the BPP did not preclude members, however, from exploiting whites for the benefit of the Party, as in selling the *Red Book*. Future events would eventually move the BPP in the direction of accepting outside contributions. This ultimately undermined the Party's militancy and compromised its independent voice within the community.

Before receiving weapons, all Panthers had to go through a period of political education and training. During this period Newton and Seale were able to indoctrinate BPP recruits with BPP ideology. The Party also provided its new members with instruction on the proper care and use of firearms and some legal training. Newton, who had attended law school for a semester, insisted that each BPP patrol take along a law book and a copy of Legal First Aid, a printed list of thirteen basic legal and constitutional rights.[19]

In its first year of existence, violent confrontations with police brought the BPP the most notoriety. Two events in particular focused attention on Newton and the BPP. The first, which concerned the widow of Malcolm X, Mrs. Betty Shabazz, helped to make the BPP somewhat of an urban legend in Oakland. The second involved California's governor Ronald Reagan and the California legislature, which thrust the BPP into the national spotlight.

The first incident originated in an invitation by Eldridge Cleaver, author of *Soul On Ice* and then assistant editor at *Ramparts* magazine, to Mrs. Shabazz to be the keynote speaker at a memorial service and three-day program designed to resurrect her slain husband's defunct group, the Organization of African Unity. Cleaver, who at the time also ran a community group called Black House, invited several area groups to participate in the program, among them the Oakland BPP. After the preliminary planning meeting for the event, the BPP was selected to provide an honor guard for the speaker during her stay in San Francisco.[20]

On the day of her arrival, the BPP escorted her from the airport fully armed. Shortly thereafter close to thirty police officers arrived outside of the *Ramparts* magazine offices, where the BPP had taken her to be interviewed by Cleaver. The police surrounded the building, creating conditions for a standoff with the armed Panthers inside. When the BPP finally ushered Mrs. Shabazz from the building, an altercation occurred between Newton and the police.[21]

According to Cleaver, who witnessed the exchange from the steps of the Ramparts building, Newton was bringing up the rear of the Panthers exiting the building when he was blocked by a police officer who ordered Newton to stop pointing his gun. Newton, ignoring calls to keep cool, stepped up to the policeman and said, "What's the matter, got an itchy finger?" When the policeman did not answer, Newton reportedly taunted him saying, "You want to draw your gun?" The other officers were pleading with the policeman to back off. The result was a standoff between Newton and the officer. In Cleaver's rendering, he was staring into Huey's eyes, measuring him up. "O.K.," Newton said, "You big fat racist pig, draw your gun." When there was no move, Newton pumped a round of ammunition into the chamber of the shotgun and sneered, "Draw it, you cowardly dog! I'm waiting." After several moments the police officer lowered his head, and Newton walked off triumphantly.[22]

Whether or not Cleaver accurately reported the exchange, something had happened that impressed him. This incident further served to embarrass the local police, making them look ineffective against the BPP. It bolstered anti-Panther sentiment already growing in the department. It also led to discussions by lawmakers about amending California law to prohibit the carrying of weapons. These discussions led to the second incident.[23]

In response to escalating confrontations between the BPP and police, Representative Donald Mulford of Oakland introduced a bill "prohibiting the carrying of firearms on one's person or in a vehicle in any public place or on any public street." Mulford's proposal was well received and floor discussion of this legislation was scheduled for Monday, May 2, 1967. Reading about the proposed Mulford act in the newspaper,

Newton drafted a response and gave it to Bobby Seale to read at the state capitol in Sacramento.[24]

On May 2, a group of thirty Panthers, twenty-four men and six women, led by Chairman Seale, traveled to Sacramento to register the BPP's protest against the Mulford bill. Once inside the capitol, Seale and his companions, misled by reporters anxious for a story, mistakenly disrupted a session of the California legislature, for which Seale and five other Panthers would later be arrested.[25]

The specter of armed black men and women entering a session of the California legislature had an immediate impact on the BPP's image. Newton and Seale had taken a calculated risk in staging the BPP's protest of the Mulford bill. That risk had both good and bad consequences for the organization.

The BPP gained national attention. It commanded a forum that guaranteed the maximum media coverage and provided Newton and Seale with the opportunity to reach a broader audience. The story made the front pages of every major daily in the state and the major television networks. BPP membership markedly increased. If the exploits of Newton had not been able to convince people that the Black Panthers were more than a street gang, Sacramento proved that the BPP was serious and political. Within a few months, branches had been established in southern California, Tennessee, Georgia, New York, and Michigan. Hundreds of black ghetto youth were attracted to the Party and its programs. In response Newton and Seale shortened the name of their group to the Black Panther Party, because, according to Huey P. Newton, they wanted to make it clear that the Party was recognized as a "political" organization and not merely a paramilitary group or organization of bodyguards."[26]

The BPP's display at Sacramento also resulted, however, in the passage of even tougher gun-control legislation than had first been proposed. In July of 1967, the California legislature ratified the Mulford Act, making it illegal to carry loaded firearms on one's person or in a public place. The incident initiated a campaign of hysteria against the BPP on a nationwide scale. In the spring of 1967 California state and local law enforcement agencies stepped up their surveillance of the Party. The Federal Bureau of Investigation also took note of the BPP at this time.

In the opinion of Huey Newton, the Party had grown much too rapidly and too many members were more enthusiastic about "guns and berets" than about the BPP's community programs.[27] In response the BPP leadership banned the public display of all weapons, and called for a halt to the armed patrol of the police. This had dual consequences as well. The armed police patrols had brought the BPP the most attention. Once they were forbidden, Newton and Seale were free to develop other ideas in the BPP ten-point program. Community organizing efforts came to the forefront of the Panthers' activities. One of these was a newspaper to present the BPP's programs to the community. The first, which appeared in April of 1967, questioned the circumstances surrounding the death of a young black robbery suspect who the Panthers claimed had been shot in the back by police. The BPP thus proved that even in the absence of patrolling it could be the watchdog of the police.[28]

The BPP soon found that the BPP newspaper could be a popular recruiting tool. The Panthers could present their side of problems in Oakland independently of the conventional press. The addition of Eldridge Cleaver to the BPP greatly enhanced the newspaper's notoriety as well. Cleaver was named BPP Minister of Information and in this capacity lent his writing talents to pamphlets and to the newspaper which defined and advertised a number of the Party's important community programs. These fell roughly into the broad categories of public safety, such as protesting police brutality; political education, that included organizing against rent eviction; and economic outreach, of which an instance would be informing welfare recipients of their legal rights.[29]

Even the police noted the shift. As California Chief Deputy Attorney General Charles O'Brien has recalled:

> The Panthers seemed to be in deliberate, open, provocative confrontation with police departments. In their early periods they used revolutionary language, provocative language and seemed to be deliberately seeking to confront established authority particularly police authority. But then we observed . . . they seemed to have a social side, a concept of doing something beyond these angry confrontations.[30]

But although the BPP had ended the armed patrols, it continued to use provocative language toward the police. During the last weekend in June of 1967, for instance, the Panthers held rallies in Oakland and nearby Richmond County, which were covered by the *New York Times Magazine*. Sol Stern, a reporter for the *New York Times Magazine* covering the BPP, described a portion of Bobby Seale's speech:

> Graphically, Seale describes how a couple of bloods can surprise cops on their coffee break. The Negroes march up to the cop and then they shoot him down voom, voom, with a 12-gauge shotgun. That, says Seale, would be an example of righteous power. No more praying and bootlicking. No more singing We shall overcome. The only way you're going to overcome is to apply righteous power.[31]

The same article quoted the Oakland chief of police, Robert Preston: "It's not the police but society that should be concerned with groups such as this." When pressed he confided, "They have on occasion harassed the police and made some efforts to stir up animosity against us, but they are not deserving of any special treatment. They have made ridiculous assertions which don't deserve to be dignified by anyone commenting on them."[32]

But Officer Richard Jensen of the Oakland police force remembers being advised by his superior officers to take precautions against the "armed and violent" BPP. Stern's article records hostile comments by several of Preston's officers. One officer suggested, "Maybe those guys ought to pick their best gunman and we pick ours and then have an old-fashioned shoot it out."[33]

At the same time that the BPP was gaining wide notoriety and press coverage, the arrests from the protest against the Mulford bill threatened to break that momentum. Many of the new members were transitory and the core membership still remained relatively small. In fact, much of the growth between August and October of 1967 can be attributed to the recruitment of Stokley Carmichael as the prime minister of the BPP. It was Carmichael who had first used the black panther as the symbol, adopting it as a third party for blacks in Loundes County, Alabama. In 1967, Carmichael attempted to organize a Los Angles chapter of his own Black Panther Party. Newton took the opportunity to draft Carmichael as BPP prime minister and also made him field marshal for the eastern half of the nation. This was a significant development for the BPP.[34]

Increased surveillance of the Party in the spring of 1967 included lists of BPP automobiles and photographs of BPP leaders posted in police stations all over Oakland and surrounding counties. The police continued to harass the BPP membership. The disappearance of armed BPP patrols allowed the police to boldly pursue arrests of Panthers on a variety of offenses: weapons charges, minor traffic violations, and even spitting on the sidewalks. Panthers were invariably detained as long as the law allowed. "After Sacramento, the Establishment in California had succeeded in dissipating the strength of the Party by arrests, bail, and constant pressure," one Panther commented. "That is how they work, not to destroy overnight, but by the process of attrition."[35]

In late August most of the BPP members arrested in the Mulford protest, including Chairman Seale, elected to serve out their short jail terms.[36] The Party suffered a continued drop in membership. In October of 1967 Huey Newton was arrested for the murder of an Oakland police officer and the wounding of another. Although the circumstances of the shooting were questionable, Newton was indicted and sent to prison to await trial. The arrest of Newton sustained the decline in Party membership. But it would also be a catalyst for the rejuvenation, growth, and development of the BPP.[37]

The BPP, during its first year of existence, had been largely a local organization concerned with local problems. While recognizing police brutality as a national problem the Panthers focused particularly on Oakland, California. Thus, in its formative period the BPP exhibited many of the characteristics of a community-based activist organization. Though the ten-point program looked to goals Newton and Seale hoped to obtain for the black people in the United States, they put all of their programs to work in Oakland and Los Angeles.

Whether local or national the Panthers from the beginning pushed for the creation of autonomous black communities. While this was far from an original idea in 1966, the manner in which the BPP hoped to make it a reality distinguished it from other organizations at the time. The Panthers oriented their group to black ghetto youth from the North. This was a significant departure from the southern civil rights model of organizations like the Student Non-Violent Coordinating Committee, in which black middle-class college students predominated. The BPP, moreover, was willing to take up arms to protect itself. The Party fixed its attention on issues that directly affected the people on a community level. And, the BPP attempted to remain financially independent. In the later months of 1967 and in 1968, the Party would change sharply. The incarceration of its two theoreticians threw the leadership to individuals who did not always share the vision of Newton and Seale.[38]

If not for the efforts of Eldridge Cleaver, the arrest of Newton could have been the end of the BPP. It was during this time that Cleaver moved to the forefront of the BPP leadership and helped to forge the BPP into a national organization.

The police by their careless handling of the Newton case unwittingly helped to propel the BPP to greater status. As Newton awaited trial, he became an international cause célèbre. During extensive interviews with the press, he outlined for a larger audience the basic principles of the Party.

Cleaver, in the meanwhile, consulted Newton to fashion a coalition designed to increase the membership and notoriety of the BPP. In late 1967 and early 1968 the BPP engineered an alliance with the Student Non-Violent Coordinating Committee. It served the purpose of increasing membership, giving the BPP access to sorely needed equipment, and making available what the leadership thought were SNCC's greater organizational skills. The BPP figured that since SNCC was moving north and west where it had not developed a solid base of support it needed the Panthers as well.[39] The BPP now also courted support from white radical groups. Especially notable was the support of the Students for a Democratic Society which gravitated toward the BPP for its opposition to the war in Vietnam.

In portraying its incarcerated leaders as black political prisoners, and in Cleaver's nomination for President of the United States by the

Peace and Freedom Party, a predominately white dissident student organization, the BPP began to move away from community-based work and toward national issues. As a result, in the opinion of Huey P. Newton "the party grew much too rapidly" and new chapters formed without the same grounding in community that the original Oakland Panther Party had enjoyed.[40]

The alliance between SNCC and the BPP turned out to be short-lived. A significant number of SNCC members were suspicious of the BPP. The Party, on the other hand, overestimated both SNCC's national appeal and its organizational skills. While the Panthers were able to utilize the celebrity of SNCC and especially its former chairman Stokley Carmichael, they soon found deep divisions within SNCC that made an effective alliance impossible. Carmichael, moreover, under whose tenure SNCC had ejected all of its white members in 1966, was unhappy over the alliance of the BPP with the Peace and Freedom Party and its acceptance of marxism. Other black nationalists criticized the BPP's association with SDS, reminding the Panthers of their warning against depending on whites for black liberation.[41]

Despite these problems, by the spring of 1968 the Black Panther Party had shifted from a relatively localized operation to a national organization. One investigation by the House of Representatives Committee on Internal Security calculated that Party membership was between 1,500 and 2,000 members in as many as twenty-five chapters across the nation. The Panthers reached their peak membership in December of 1968, only a few months before the emergence of the New Haven chapter.[42] Yet at its moment of apparent success, the Party went through an abrupt shift such as endemic to organizations of the left. Rejecting Cleaver's agenda, it returned to its earlier concentration on community service programs.[43]

By the end of 1968 both of the issues that had largely defined the Black Panther Party had been resolved. Huey P. Newton was convicted of manslaughter for the shooting of Officer John Frey. Eldridge Cleaver, meanwhile, had left the country after being implicated in a shoot-out with police that left one Panther dead. In this period, David Hilliard emerged as the Party's chief organizer. Hilliard and Seale hoped to return some order to the BPP, which was experiencing a period of rapid growth with little oversight from the national headquarters. BPP chapters popped up all over the United States from Seattle, Washington, to Washington, D.C. This made it impossible to accurately estimate the Party's membership. The BPP often set its own numbers well above the two thousand identified by Congress. Membership counts, however, were the least of the BPP's worries. While certain chapters chose to follow the example of the Oakland and Los Angeles chapters of the BPP, for the most part many adopted the BPP banner but few of its principles.

Some chapters produced excellent community leaders like Fred Hampton in Chicago; others brought unfavorable attention to the BPP for getting involved in questionable dealings and using the Party as a front for criminal activity. Some chapters that claimed to be part of the Black Panther Party had no connection to its national offices. In addition, the BPP became involved in several highly publicized conflicts with local gangs. In Chicago the Black Stone Rangers emerged as the BPP's chief nemesis. In Oakland the cultural nationalists led by Ronald Karenga's "US" organization provided the opposition.[44]

Attempting to better its image among the people, the BPP adopted a new program. The new theme of serving the people was represented as harmonious with the expectations to bring "power to the people in the eventual showdown with the racist power structure." Nowhere was a politically confrontational community involvement more evident than in New Haven, where the BPP entered the fray between the mayor and black militants.[45]

The return to an ethos of community involvement, though now sharpened with a combative local politics, was first introduced by Panther Chairman Bobby Seale in an article appearing in the Black Panther Party newspaper in November of 1968. Including "older people" in the black community as part of his readership, Seale talked candidly about the BPP's moving aggressively into politics. He pledged that the BPP would replace local mayors and councilmen "by either voting power or by the gun." More important for local chapters was Seale's discussion of the four projects of service to the community that would become essential to the Panthers in 1969. The article contemplated a circulation in various cities of petitions to obtain a referendum on decentralization of city police forces.[46] Seale proposed what was to become the controversial free breakfast program for schoolchildren of welfare recipients. These meals were served in neighborhood churches. Free health clinics were to begin in black communities. The remaining project was for the creation of black liberation schools to promote black culture in the urban centers. According to Seale, the project would include classes in black history, taught to children after school in the same churches that provided them with free breakfasts.[47]

The purpose of the program was to unite the members of the community with the BPP. In an article in the radical publication *The Guardian*, Seale used the example of Cuban revolutionary Che Guevara, who had supposedly claimed that revolutionary struggles must also relate to the "momentary desires of the people." An editorial entitled "The Roots of the Party" that appeared in the May 25, 1969 issue of *The Black Panther* best summarized this objective: "The Black Panther is for the people, by the people and of the people. This is the crucial difference between our party and many other black organizations."[48]

Charles William Hopkins, in "The Deradicalization of the Black Panther Party, 1967–1973," argues that government harassment of the BPP was the main reason for its shift from radicalism to reformism. As a secondary cause, Hopkins identifies the Party's own ideological and organizational weaknesses. In its attempts to legitimize itself, the BPP grew even more attractive to poor blacks, white college students, and even some older black Americans. This made it a very real threat in the eyes of many officials. The Party in New Haven found itself attempting to identify with local issues while keeping abreast of national prosecutions of Panthers. The result was often halfhearted attempts to link local problems with problems faced by the BPP nationally.[49]

To the establishment the greatest threat from the Panthers came between 1969 and 1971, the period of their most successful community organizing efforts. Several polls taken in this period indicated growing support for the BPP as it changed its outlook. The assassination of Martin Luther King, Jr., created a leadership vacuum into which the BPP could move. A poll taken by the *Wall Street Journal* in January of 1970 found that sixty percent of the people polled expressed full support for both the philosophy and the tactics of the BPP. A survey published in *Time* magazine in the spring of 1970 also indicated significant support for the Panthers.[50]

The Party also took initial steps in what was to be a complete reorganization of its structure from the national to the local chapter level. This was to be completed in the summer of 1969. The disorderly manner in which local chapters were emerging was to be brought under control. Even as the Panthers recentered themselves in neighborhoods, their nationwide discipline tightened.

The BPP was adapting to changes taking place in 1968 and 1969. The decline in incidents of urban rioting in 1968 discouraged the notion of an imminent black uprising in America. Instead, during 1968 and 1969, rebellion took the form of mass campus demonstrations. Among the many groups protesting on hundreds of campuses in this period were radical groups such as Students for a Democratic Society and militant black student organizations with a nationalist orientation.

Rivals of the BPP continued the criticism of the Panthers for their various alliances with white radical groups. The Federal Bureau of Investigation, meanwhile, used the transformation to infiltrate the Party with informants and agent provocateurs. By late 1968, the BPP was forced to institute a nationwide purge of Panthers and rogue chapters that were not cooperating with the Party's national office. These purges served to reverse the growth of the Panthers. They also produced political infighting within the BPP that reduced membership even further.[51]

As Panthers in Los Angeles were attempting to help students institute a Black Studies program, in January of 1969 they were attacked by

members of Ron Karenga's US. The incident resulted in the death of two
Panthers, Jon Huggins and Alprentice Bunchy Carter. The Huggins murder would prove significant for New Haven. It was Ericka Huggins's
arrival in New Haven to bury her husband that resulted in a New Haven
chapter of the BPP.

Notes

1. U.S. Riot Commission, *Report of the National Advisory Commission on
Civil Disorder* (New York: Bantam, 1968), 391.
2. Jane Jacobs, *The Death and Life of Great American Cities* (New York: Vintage, 1961), 204.
3. Ibid., 206–207.
4. Ibid., 206–207.
5. Hill-Dwight Citizens Commission on Police Community Relations, *In
Search of Fair and Adequate Law Enforcement*, June 1967, 12–13; see also U.S.
Riot Commission, 308.
6. Bobby Seale, *Seize the Time* (Baltimore: Black Classic Press, 1991), 59–63;
Phillip Foner, *The Black Panthers Speak* (New York: Da Capo Press, 1995), xxv–
xxvi; Michael Newton, *Bitter Grain: The Story of Huey P. Newton and the Black
Panther Party* (Los Angeles: Holloway House, 1991), 13–15; Gene Marine, *The
Black Panthers* (New York: Signet, 1969), 24–34; Robert Brisbane, *Black Activism*
(Valley Forge, PA: Judson Press, 1974), 196–199; Henry Hampton and Steve
Fayer, eds., *Voices of Freedom* (New York: Bantam Books, 1990), 351–352; Louis
Heath, *Off the Pigs! The History and Literature of the Black Panther Party* (Metuchen, NJ: The Scarecrow Press, 1976).
7. Seale, *Seize the Time*, 59–63; Brisbane, 196; Marine, 24–34; Michael New-
ton, 12–14; Theodore Draper, *The Rediscovery of Black Nationalism* (New York:
The Viking Press, 1969), 97.
8. Seale, *Seize the Time*, 59–63; Brisbane, 196; Marine, 24–34; Draper, 97.
9. Seale, *Seize the Time*, 59–63; Brisbane, 197; Marine, 35–47; Foner, 1–6.
10. Whitney M. Young, "What Lies Ahead?" an address delivered before the
Sixth Annual Convention of the Southern Christian Leadership Conference, 27
September 1962, Birmingham, AL, and statistics quoted in State of Connecticut
Commission on Civil Rights, *Study of the Process of Urban Relocation in Con-
necticut* (1963), 12–13.
11. Seale, *Seize the Time*, 59–63; Huey Newton, *To Die for the People* (New
York: Random House, 1972; New York: Writers and Readers, 1995), 2–8; House
Committee on Internal Security, *Gun Barrel Politics: The BPP 1966–1971*, 92nd
Congress, 1st session (Washington, D.C.: US Government Printing Office, 1971),
1–5; House Committee on Internal Security, *The Black Panther Party: The Origins
and Development as Reflected in Its Official Weekly Newspaper, The Black Panther
Community News Service*, 92nd Congress, 1st session (Washington, D.C.: US
Government Printing Office, 1971); Kenneth B. Clark, *Dark Ghetto* (New York:
Harper and Row, 1965) as quoted in House Committee on Internal Security,
Gun Barrel Politics: The Black Panther Party, 1966–1971, 3.
12. Bobby Seale, *Seize the Time*, 16.
13. Bobby Seale's comments reported in House Committee on Internal
Security, *Gun Barrel Politics: The Black Panther Party, 1966–1971*, 5.

14. Seale, *Seize the Time*, 35–44; Michael Newton, 15–18; Brisbane, 197–201; Marine, 35–47; Foner, 8–14.

15. Huey Newton quoted in Hampton and Fayer, 351; for further discussion of Black Panthers origins and relations with police see Seale, *Seize the Time*, 44–56; Michael Newton, 15–18; Brisbane, 197–201; Marine, 35–47; Foner, 8–14; House Committee on Internal Security, *Gun Barrel Politics: The Black Panther Party, 1966–1971*, 1–8.

16. Marine writing in *Ramparts* magazine, 29 June 1968, as quoted in House Committee on Internal Security, *Gun Barrel Politics: The Black Panther Party, 1966–1971*, 4; Hugh Pearson published the controversial *Shadow of the Panther* in 1994. It advances the thesis that from its inception the BPP was little more than a criminal clique. Pearson identifies several chapters including New Haven which he says were serious about community organizing. On a whole, however, he argues that the Black Panther Party was largely a front for criminal activity. Hugh Pearson, *The Shadow of the Panther: Huey Newton and the Price of Power in America* (Reading, MA: Addison Wesley, 1994); "NAACP Claims Brutality by Police in L.A.," *Los Angeles Times*, 19 February 1962, (page unknown) contained in NAACP Papers Group III Folder A243, Manuscript Division, Library of Congress.

17. Seale, *Seize the Time*, 72–98; Brisbane, 200; Marine, 38–40; Michael Newton, 15–17.

18. Seale, *Seize the Time*, 79–84; Brisbane, 200–201; Marine, 40; Michael Newton, 16–17.

19. Hampton and Fayer, 351–357; Bobby Seale, *Seize the Time*, 72–79; Brisbane, 200–201; Gene Marine, 41; Michael Newton, 18.

20. Bobby Seale, *Seize the Time*, 134; Hampton and Fayer, 365–366; Marine, 53–56; Michael Newton, 22–26.

21. Ibid.

22. Kathleen Rout, *Eldridge Cleaver* (Boston: Twayne Publishers, 1991), 45; Robert Scheer, ed., *Eldridge Cleaver, Post Prison Writings* (New York: Random House, 1968), 35–36; Seale, *Seize the Time*, 127–134; Hampton and Fayer, 365–366; Marine, 53–56; Michael Newton, 22–26.

23. Seale, *Seize the Time*, 134; Hampton and Fayer, 365–366; Marine, 53–56; Michael Newton, 22–26.

24. Seale, *Seize the Time*, 153–166; Hampton and Fayer, 369–372; Marine, 62–66; Michael Newton, 30–31.

25. Newton could not attend because of parole restrictions stemming from previous arrests. On the steps of the capitol Seale read from a statement prepared by Newton. It read, "The Black Panther Party for self-defense calls upon the American people in general and Black people in particular to take careful note of the racist California legislature, which is now considering legislation aimed at keeping the Black people disarmed and powerless, at the very same time that racist police agencies throughout the country are intensifying the terror, brutality, murder and repression of Black people." Executive Mandate No. 1, 2 May 1967, reprinted in Huey Newton, *To Die for the People*, 8; Executive Mandate No. 1 is also reprinted in Phillip Foner, 40; for a description of the events leading up to the Mulford protest see Bobby Seale, *Seize the Time*, 153–166; Marine, 62–66; Michael Newton, 30–31.

26. Huey Newton, quoted in *The Black Panther*, 16 March 1968, 4; see also Phillip Foner, xxvii–xxxi; Huey P. Newton, *Revolutionary Suicide* (New York: Ballantine, 1973); Bobby Seale, *Seize the Time*, 153–166; Hampton and Fayer, 369–372; Marine, 62–66; Michael Newton, 30–31.

27. Bobby Seale, *Seize the Time*, 153–166; Hampton and Fayer, 369–372; Marine, 62–66; Michael Newton, 30–31.

28. Bobby Seale, 135–149; Phillip Foner, xxvii; Gilbert Moore, *A Special Rage* (New York: Harper and Row, 1971), 58.

29. Bobby Seale, *Seize the Time*, 134–149; Hampton and Fayer, 366–371; Foner, 8–14; Marine, 57–66; Michael Newton, 34–37; Sol Stern, "The Call of the Black Panthers," *The New York Times Magazine*, 6 August 1967, page unknown.

30. Deputy Attorney General Charles O'Brien from interview contained in Eyes on the Prize, Series II "Power," video, (The Eyes on the Prize Production group, PBS video series, 1989).

31. Sol Stern, "The Call of the Black Panthers," page unknown.

32. Ibid.

33. Ibid.

34. Executive Mandate No. 2, 29 June 1967, reprinted in Huey Newton, *To Die for the People*, 9–10; Bobby Seale, *Seize the Time*, 207–222; Michael Newton, 38–39; Marine, 121–123; Clayborne Carson, *In Struggle* (Cambridge: Harvard University Press), 277–279.

35. Foner, xxxii–xxxiii. It was from such a list that Officer John Frey would recognize the car driven by Huey Newton on the night of October 28, 1967. Bobby Seale, *Seize the Time*, 187–189; Hampton and Fayer, 372; Marine, 77–106; Michael Newton, 42–65.

36. Bobby Seale, *Seize the Time*, 187; Michael Newton, 38–39.

37. Convicted of voluntary manslaughter in September of 1968, Newton would serve an additional twenty-two months in prison before the Appellate Court of California reversed his conviction. After two more trails ended in hung juries, the state of California dismissed all charges against him. Meanwhile, state, local, and federal law enforcement agencies were actively pursuing BPP leaders and had succeeded for the most part in disrupting the internal cohesion of the Party, pitting Newton and Seale against Panther Minister of Information Eldridge Cleaver and fomenting general dissension within the Party, quite consistent with the 1966 Hoover Memorandum; Bobby Seale, *Seize the Time*, 187–189; Hampton and Fayer, 372; Foner, xxxii–xxxiii; Marine, 77–106; Michael Newton, 42–65.

38. Clayborne Carson, 279–281.

39. Ibid.

40. Ibid.

41. Ibid.

42. BPP membership statistics quoted in House Committee on Internal Security, *Gun Barrel Politics: The Black Panther Party, 1966–1971*, 69.

43. Marine, 77–106; Michael Newton, 155–161.

44. Bobby Seale, *Seize the Time*, 218; Marine, 77–106; Michael Newton, 155–161; Roy Wilkins and Ramsey Clark, *Search and Destroy: A Report by the Commission of Inquiry into the Black Panthers and the Police* (New York: Metropolitan Applied Research Center, Inc., 1973). One of the ways that the Black Panther Party sought to combat its membership growth after its suspension on recruiting was to ask prospective Panthers to form branches of the National Committee to Combat Fascism. Controversy continues to plague the discussion concerning the nature of Ronald Karenga's US organization. For the most part Karenga has been singled out as a police informant and agent provocateur. In a 1997 article in the *Journal of Black Studies*, Scott Nozi Brown offers a different perspective on the conflict. According to Brown US was as much a victim of the

FBI counterintelligence program as was the BPP. Brown points to the persistence of the organization being referred to as the "United Slaves," as an example of the widespread acceptance much of the negative propaganda initiated by the FBI has produced. While I tend to agree with Brown about the overall legacy of US, I am cautious about downplaying the use of informants. His thesis supports the idea that the FBI Counterintelligence program was far more sophisticated than many would suspect. But the FBI depended heavily on informants and agent provocateurs to carry out its work. While I agree that Karenga has been unfairly targeted, it is clear that many of the circumstances surrounding the US-Panther conflict defy logical explanation outside the realm of police provocation. This discrepancy certainly warrants a larger study of the problem. "The US Organization, Maulana Karenga, and Conflict with the Black Panther Party," Scott Nozi Brown, *Journal of Black Studies* Volume 28, Number 2/November 1997, 157–169.

45. Bobby Seale, *Seize the Time*, 187–189; Marine, 77–106; Michael Newton, 155–161.

46. Bobby Seale, *Seize the Time*, 187–189; Hampton and Fayer, 372; Foner, xxxii–xxxiii; Marine, 77–106; Michael Newton, 42–65.

47. House Committee on Internal Security, *Gun Barrel Politics: The Black Panther Party, 1966–1971*, 46–48; Charles W. Hopkins, "The Deradicalization of the Black Panther Party, 1967–1973" (Master's thesis, University of North Carolina at Chapel Hill, 1978), 1–10.

48. House Committee on Internal Security, *Gun Barrel Politics: The Black Panther Party, 1966–1971*, 46–48; "The Roots of the Party," *The Black Panther*, 25 May 1969.

49. Charles W. Hopkins, 1–10.

50. Polls cited in Charles W. Hopkins, 4–5.

51. Bobby Seale, *Seize the Time*, 370–371; for a good discussion of problems within the BPP see David Hilliard, *This Side of Glory* (Boston: Little and Brown, 1992), 234–246; Michael Newton, 198–201.

CHAPTER SEVEN
Servants of the People

J. Edgar Hoover called the BPP the greatest threat to the nation's internal security. Hugh Pearson, in *The Shadow of the Panther*, has concluded that the BPP never amounted to more than a group of organized criminals. Were the Panthers, asks Donald Freed, the same gang of thugs that Hoover, Vice President Spiro Agnew, and even the *New York Times* defined them as, or were they, as they called themselves, "servants of the people," the vanguard of the New American Revolution?[1] The answer is not so simple.

Agnew and other critics of the BPP were right in the sense that the Panthers, like the Black Muslims, recruited much of its members from individuals with criminal backgrounds. And not all of those prior arrests could be blamed on relations with the police. A congressional investigation of the Black Panther Party in 1970 found in the records of members a variety of criminal charges ranging from breach of peace and drunkenness to rape and murder. Until November of 1968 the BPP, unlike the Black Muslims, had no formal system to rehabilitate its recruits. According to both Bobby Seale and David Hilliard, it was not until 1968 that the Party adopted stricter rules for its members. In January of 1969 the BPP began purging itself of "jackanapes," people whom Seale defined as enemies of the people. The purges, which exposed the seedy underside of the Party, are also the best evidence of the BPP's sincere attempts to reform itself and make itself in the words of Huey Newton an "ox to be ridden by the people."[2]

The FBI and other critics of the BPP had fertile opportunity for criticism of an organization that exalted the "Brother off the block" whom many associated with the common criminal rather than what the Panthers defined as potentially disciplined revolutionists. In New Haven the HPA had been dealing with the same volatile groups. City administrators hoped that Harris could exercise some control over their frustration, but the riot destroyed Harris's credibility. The New Haven police used the criminal records of certain members of the organization as pretext to harass it. Harris's arrest in a predawn raid on a narcotics charge after city officials discovered that he had a drug problem is an instance.

Servants of the People **125**

The BPP, however, was far from a criminal clique. The years from 1968 to 1971, the high point of the federal, state, and local campaigns against it, was also the period of its most serious community activity. At the point at which the BPP seemed to be moving beyond adolescence, a hostile web of police agencies stunted its maturation, at the same time exposing and sharpening its growing pains.

The evolution of the New Haven chapter of the BPP was representative of the changes taking place in the Party as a whole after 1968. The emergence of the BPP in New Haven also demonstrates the nature of the shift from civil rights to Black Power to human rights protests that took place in the 1960s. The transition of national organizations and groups that operated in New Haven from 1954 to 1973 suggests Donald Freed's paradigm of the recent American human rights movement, which Freed defines as going through three phases.

In the first phase the movement was largely southern and agrarian. It was also Christian and nonviolent and sought to redeem the soul of America by exposing the degree to which the nation had not lived up to its promise of freedom and equality. Dr. King led the nonviolent civil rights movement, which began to lose ground to the militant nationalists movement after 1965.[3]

This accurately describes the New Haven of the late 1950s and early 1960s, when the NAACP and the Dixwell Ministerial Alliance battled each other for Mayor Lee's favor. In this period New Haven drew most of its leadership from former participants in the southern civil rights campaign like John Barber and Reverend Edmonds. They attempted to use the same tactics to define the parameters of the civil rights struggle in New Haven. Edmonds, in particular, believed that civil rights groups in New Haven should be receptive to Mayor Lee's willingness to take and adopt some of the changes encouraged by civil rights activists. The price was that Lee manipulated these organizations to work on his behalf.

Bernard Lafayette, a civil rights activist in Chicago, described a similar situation in that city. According to Lafayette, Chicago in the 1960s was of a kind with things that were happening in places like Newark, Detroit, Philadelphia, New York, and other large metropolitan areas.[4] Mayor Richard J. Daley, a Democrat, manipulated black organizations to support his political machine. John McDermont, another activist in Chicago, recalls that Daley used political favors to influence his critics. McDermont says of Daley, "He had a sense that we were Democrats. This was a liberal community. We had a human relations commission going back to the forties. His theory about Chicago was that the system was fair. All you had to do was cooperate with him and it worked for you, and that this was not a hotbed of racism." Dorothy Tillman, a long-time resident of Chicago and critic of Daley, has elaborated on Daley's control over the black community in Chicago:

You know down South you lived on the plantation, you worked it, and you had your food, clothing, and shelter. Up here they lived on a plantation with Boss Daley as slave master. Their jobs, their clothes, their shelter, food, all depended on Boss Daley. And everything was connected. Any little thing they did for you, you had to pay for it. You know: Okay, Mrs. Jones I'll move your garbage, now you go down and vote for so and so.[5]

"In the minds of many white people and the press," as McDermont observes, "it became hard to see Daley as some kind of enemy because he would always respond."[6]

Andrew Young, one of the leaders of SCLC, when it marched in Chicago in 1966, explains, "Mayor Daley was trying to keep together a political machine. We were trying to get more registered voters. He saw too many registered voters as a direct threat to his machine. We saw the machine as the basis of the slums, of the poverty, of the exploitation of Black folk." Daley's "machine had served the Black community well," Young remarks, "but its days were over, and we were there to announce that. The machine helped a certain segment of the Black community shift from race to class."[7]

Daley, like Lee, had blacks on staff who were loyal only to him. Dorothy Tillman remembers that the six black aldermen in Chicago bowed to Daley's pressure and would deliver the black community. According to Jesse Jackson, one-time head of Operation Breadbasket in Chicago, many black ministers and officials associated with the Daley machine had supported the efforts of Dr. King and SCLC in the South. But when the SCLC came to Daley's plantation in 1966, this same group "held press conferences and urged Dr. King to leave Chicago."[8]

This buying of black interests caused many activists to question what impact the nonviolent civil rights movement could have in the North. According to Andrew B. Haynes, between 1965 and 1967 a large percentage of blacks of moderate low income felt a vicarious identification with black militancy and militant figures. This was the high point of the HPA in New Haven. The fear of an urban riot provided the HPA with a great deal of leverage with the city government. Fred Harris wanted to frighten it into believing a black revolution was at hand. And when the HPA's black revolution did not materialize and the organization lost out in its confrontations with the New Haven police, many of its supporters left. By the time the BPP arrived, Fred Harris, Willie Counsel, and other New Haven militants had begun to take on the status of the "low grade entertainers" described by Haynes. Many people had come to expect rhetoric but not action from the once feared HPA.

For the remaining militants, the BPP represented a chance to renew protest efforts under the guise of a national organization. That the Panthers were independent of government funds, instead envisioning that the people would support their efforts to create a community health care center and freedom school, defined their ability to lead a popular rebellion. As Huey Newton explained in the pages of *The Black Panther Community News Service,* "We can no longer afford the dubious luxury of the terrible casualties wantonly inflicted upon us by the cops during these spontaneous rebellions. Black people must now move from the grassroots up through the perfumed circles of the Black bourgeois, to seize by any means necessary a proportionate share of the power vested and collected in the structure of America."[9] In the past, New Haven residents had waited for political leadership from the mayor, but the Panthers would seek out the help of ministers, grocery stores, and Yale students to build a program founded in community.[10] They began for New Haven what Donald Freed identifies as the second phase in the human rights movement: the time of Black Power.

The New Haven chapter emerged during the critical period when the BPP was in transition. New Haven enjoyed both the support of local militants and the presence of transplanted members from other chapters and the national offices of the BPP. The purges had hurt the national office and resulted in a population of floating Panthers looking for legitimate chapters to join.

Prior to the establishment of the New Haven chapter, the BPP maintained a small branch in Bridgeport, Connecticut. Early FBI reports show that most Panther activity in Bridgeport was limited to informational meetings and political education classes. In January of 1969, however, the *Bridgeport Post Telegram* reported that an Oakland Panther named Jose Gonzalez had surfaced in Connecticut claiming to be the head of BPP operations in the Constitution State. Gonzalez told a small audience that the BPP had actually been active in Connecticut for six months. He estimated the Party's strength statewide to be around one hundred members.[11] The FBI field agency in New Haven took the lead in identifying leaders and key members and determining the Party's actual strength in the state. Gonzalez, in the meanwhile, moved the Bridgeport chapter in the direction of protesting poor housing conditions and reaching out to the city's Puerto Rican population, a growing group in New Haven as well. At this time, the BPP divided its activities between Bridgeport and New Haven, with most of the work taking place in Bridgeport.[12] Things changed rapidly after Ericka Huggins arrived in New Haven in late January of 1969. Ericka Huggins's husband Jon had been a captain in the Los Angeles chapter of the BPP.

In the winter of 1968 he was attending UCLA as part of a special federally funded admissions program designed to draw students with college potential. The program proved attractive to other Los Angeles militants as well, including the BPP's chief nemesis in southern California,

Ronald Karenga's cultural nationalist group, the US. The BPP and US immediately battled for influence over the student body.[13]

Tensions increased after the university announced plans to create a Black Studies program. "It was not the Black students who had proposed the program," Elaine Brown, a student and Panther, observes, "but rather the university in an attempt to forestall the kind of black student agitation that was on the rise on most college campuses." The Panthers sensed an opportunity in the offer and began to organize the students toward creating a meaningful Black Studies program. US, however, had other plans.[14]

By January, the university was ready to select a chairperson for the new program and asked for the students' input. Karenga and US backed one candidate. Most students supported Jon Huggins and Alprentice Carter, both of whom insisted that the chairman of the new department should be chosen by the students themselves. Few knew at the time that the FBI and California state police were fueling the dispute between the BPP and US through a concentrated misinformation campaign. The debate over the Black Studies program coincided with a flurry of negative press on Karenga which intimated that he had met with some of the most influential politicians in the state of California, including the governor and the mayor of Los Angeles. These reports caused many to question Karenga's interest in choosing the director of the Black Studies program.[15]

UCLA's Black Student Union ultimately called for a meeting for January 17, to discuss both the directorship and the upcoming presidency of the BSU, for which Carter was running. On that evening the meeting, with about 150 people in attendance, broke up after a heated verbal confrontation between the students and representatives from US. After the meeting Carter and Huggins were ambushed by members of US while they were attempting to leave the building. Though two Panthers had been killed, the Los Angeles police subsequently raided the home of Ericka Huggins and arrested seventeen Panthers. They also took the couple's three-week-old infant to the jail. The seventeen were charged with various counts ranging from breach of peace to resisting arrest. The police would later claim that the arrests were to prevent retaliation for the murders.[16]

After being released, Ericka Huggins decided to take her husband's body home to New Haven for burial. At first she was unsure if she would stay. But when several people approached her about the possibility of starting a chapter of the BPP in New Haven, she decided to remain. Frances Carter, one of the earlier recruits to the Bridgeport BPP, recalls that after the memorial service, Huggins asked her and her sister Peggy whether they would be interested in joining, since "Elaine and some of the other sisters were leaving, and she was gonna stay on."[17] But the effort to start a New Haven chapter met with the rule informing a nation-wide suspension on recruiting and the organizers were ordered to link up with Gonzalez and the Bridgeport chapter. Early in February the San Francisco resident office of the FBI received confirmation that Ericka Huggins had attended a BPP meeting in Bridgeport, Connecticut.[18]

In Bridgeport, the BPP became involved in local issues such as the need for housing reform and a new antipoverty program. On April 4, for instance, the BPP led a protest at city hall after a tenement fire killed several children. But some members of the BPP wanted the chapter to relocate to New Haven. This was primarily because New Haven was much more cosmopolitan and because a number of the recruits lived there.[19] Huggins found a supportive base in New Haven consisting of local activists and Yale students. Among the first recruits were George Edwards, who had been a friend of Jon Huggins; Warren Kimbro, a local community activist; Peggy Hudgins and Frances Carter, the two sisters from Bridgeport; Jose Gonzalez, and Lonnie McLucas, formerly of the Newark chapter.[20]

Despite her warm reception, Ericka Huggins remained uneasy about New Haven. Originally from Washington, D.C., she was shocked by what she found in the Elm City. As she recalls:

Los Angeles and New Haven were light years apart in 1969. They were like different planets. New England was so conservative, as a matter of fact shockingly so. I had never seen anything that conservative in my life. There were times when I wished that I had been in the South. The South has a conservative quality but it's not polite. You can tell what's going on. In New England I could never tell what people truly felt. They were so polite it was as if they were lying. So I never quite knew what end was up. Just as we were figuring out how to work with people we were arrested.[21]

This appraisal goes closely with that of George Edwards, who had first come to New Haven in 1964:

I was not prepared for the lack of Black consciousness. I thought this was a place out of somebody's fantasy. I couldn't believe that Connecticut, the Constitution state, the home of so-called constitutional democracy, and integration and better race relations all the hype and propaganda . . . I really wasn't prepared for this place. I almost didn't stay here the first day I got in town. I thought where in the hell am I at. I thought this is the other side of the plantation that's all I thought. If I come from the southern side of the plantation this has got to be the other side of it and this was even worse. I didn't see any Black businesses. I didn't see any Black people smiling and friendly and hugging and speaking feeling a sense of joyfulness about their existence. Cold, distant, alienated they looked depressed. I saw the Black people but they looked like different kinds of people. They looked like they just really lost something in the human process.[22]

Once a presence had been established in New Haven, the local members helped to educate the Party on local issues, giving it a sense of connection with the community. The national officers gave the New Haven chapter a sense of legitimacy as transplanted staff provided for the political education of the new Panther recruits and coordinated the establishment of the new program in New Haven of service to the community. This was not the case in all chapters. Chapters with experienced members avoided the ramifications of the Party split between Newton and Cleaver that was more apparent after 1970 but definitely an issue before the Panther trial in New Haven. Ericka Huggins then in charge of political education, remained in constant contact with the national headquarters. All of this was not enough to avoid danger from another quarter. As Clayborne Carson has observed in his study of SNCC, by 1970 the BPP was heavily infiltrated by police informants.[23]

Yet, the New Haven chapter was able to accomplish some real changes early in its existence. Fred Harris and the HPA found it absolutely necessary to deal with the city government; the BPP not enticed by the dangling carrot of federal money, was free to pursue solutions to problems within the New Haven black community itself.[24] This made the BPP particularly appealing to young residents of the Hill who were attracted by the Party's image and its breakfast project and health clinic. From the very beginning the BPP in New Haven was a community organization. It did, however, retain some of the revolutionary language characteristic of the Panthers in their early formative period, of the kind typified in the words of Bobby Seale as represented in 1967 in *The Black Panther*: "if we want to exercise Black Power . . . the only thing what we can do now, brothers and sisters is to get our guns organized, forget the ins and shoot it out," or the pronouncement the same year by Huey Newton: "Only with the power of the gun can the Black masses halt the terror and brutality perpetrated against them by the armed racist power structure. . . . Black people were forced to build America and if forced to we will tear it down."[25]

The Panthers were quick to apply this to the local police, often creating fear and animosity. Eldridge Cleaver, for instance, rhetorically blasted Oakland Chief of Police Charles R. Gain and warned that the black community in Oakland was keeping a list of the names of policemen who "are going to be hunted down like the dogs they are and will receive the justice that Adolf Eiechman got."[26] Utilizing the same revolutionary language, the New Haven BPP moved into conflict with the New Haven police. While only a few months old, the chapter created a controversial flier charging the mayor and police chief with murder for using lead paint in what the BPP called "already inadequate housing." The flier read:

> Wanted for Murder by the people of New Haven for the use of lead paint in already inadequate Housing. We Charge these people: Murderer No #1 Mayor Richard C. Lee, Police Chief James Ahern . . . with these crimes: conspiracy with the intent to commit murder, premeditated murder. We charge all slum land lords with the same crimes.[27]

Mayor Lee soon found the presence of the BPP a political threat as well. On March 17, 1969, the *New Haven Journal Courier* reported the comments of the Republican mayoral candidate, John J. Moffitt, that the Panthers were "doing more harm to the Black community than to its white neighbors." Moffitt charged the BPP with intending the "complete destruction of our schools, our society, our city and the nation." Making reference to an incident in which a member of the BPP was arrested for organizing students outside Lee High School and another of BPP literature distributed at other schools, Moffitt reserved his greatest criticism for Lee: "we must rid the city of an administration which permits the distribution of this type of literature in our schools."[28]

George Edwards explains the basic strategy of the BPP in this period, "In order to affect any sort of meaningful change here you have to approach an extreme radical view and then moderate it going toward something else." The position of the BPP allowed the HPA and the Black Coalition to look centrist. John Daniels says of the Panthers' role in New Haven:

> African-American leaders at the time, we were talking about these things we were talking about poverty we were talking about jobs, that we needed to do more about it, but we were talking about that for years and we were talking but we were talking about it from the inside in a very non threatening non militant manner and now here comes the Black Panthers and they were talking the same thing we were talking but they were more militant in their concerns.[29]

The emergence of yet another radical group gave the consensus-seeking Black Coalition even more leverage. The BPP proved far more threatening to city officials because it was made up primarily of out-

siders. No one could control it. The HPA, despite some initial reservations, granted the Party a small office space within its community outreach offices in the Hill. When Mayor Lee and the CPI found out, both
the HPA and the Panthers were evicted. The Reverend Edwin Edmonds
and John Daniels agree that the BPP played an important part in bringing greater awareness to issues concerning blacks in New Haven. At the
same time, their confrontational style scared away a lot of potential supporters and made things very difficult for them in dealing with the local
authorities.[30]

The FBI first began investigating the BPP late in 1966 for its con-
forntations with police and calls for a black revolution. In a broad memorandum in 1968, FBI Director J. Edgar Hoover instructed FBI agents to
"expose, disrupt, misdirect, discredit, or otherwise neutralize the activities of Black nationalist, hate type organizations and groupings, their
leadership, spokesman, membership, and supporters, and to counter
their propensity for violence and civil disorder. The activities of all such
groups of intelligence interests to this Bureau must be followed on a
continuous basis so we will be in a position to promptly take advantage
of all opportunities for counterintelligence and to inspire action in in-
stances where circumstances warrant." The Hoover memorandum had
an immediate impact on state and local police agencies as well. Harold
Saffold, a black Chicago policeman in the 1960s, explains: "the police
community has a sort of built in reward and punishment system of its
own and you get a lot of rewards when you go after who the boss says is
the bad guy and you get him. . . . I think what J. Edgar Hoover was able
to do was to give police officers the impression that it was ok. It was
open season. You didn't have to worry about the law."[31]

Around the time that Ericka Huggins arrived in Connecticut, the
Bridgeport chapter was the subject of the intense investigation by the
FBI that the claims by Jose Gonzalez on the presence of the Panthers
there had prompted. On February 19, 1969, the Boston resident field
agency reported the comments of Gonzalez during a meeting of BPP
brass in which he reportedly threatened the life of an FBI special agent.
During the meeting Gonzalez complained that William Gunderson, the
assistant special agent in charge of the New Haven office, represented a
real problem for the Party in Connecticut. Gonzalez further suggested
that Gunderson be "eliminated." This prompted an urgent teletype from
the FBI resident agency in Boston to the special agent in charge of New
Haven and the director of the FBI.[32]

When the Boston field office suggested that the Bureau initiate an
investigation, Director Hoover wrote "press vigorously" in the margins
of the memo. In a subsequent memo dated February 27, Hoover told the
New Haven field office to "institute an intensive in-depth investigation"
of the Bridgeport/New Haven chapter of the BPP. Hoover noted again

that the investigation should "press vigorously with an eye toward establishing information indicating a possible violation of the assault on a federal officer statute."[33]

This was the beginning of serious problems for the Bridgeport/New Haven chapter with both federal and local law enforcement agencies. As a result of the nationwide raids against the Party by federal and local police agencies in January of 1969, the BPP adopted a new no-nonsense policy aimed at removing suspect influences from the Party. As Chief of Staff David Hilliard recalls, "Every time Bobby and I look around during the Spring of 1969 someone's opening up a chapter. The paper appears like clockwork and the new serve the people programs start everywhere: free clothes, food distribution centers, medical and legal clinics." Hilliard and Seale appreciated the new problems associated with the Party's rapid expansion. Seale surmised that the raids on the BPP were part of a campaign by federal agencies to deplete the Party's funds.[34]

Conscious of the rapid expansion of the Party and the growing amount of state and federal police harassment against it, the national BPP began making a serious attempt to weed out jackanapes and police agents. The BPP announced that no bail money would be available except in special cases approved by headquarters. The Party also suspended recruitment for the next three months—the suspension that the attempt to organize a separate New Haven chapter ran against. The Panther purge, once begun, was widely felt between March and August of 1969. The BPP played into the hands of the FBI by regularly publishing the names of expellees in the pages of *The Black Panther*.[35] In a letter to the special agent in charge of the Albany, New York, field office which was distributed to twenty-four other offices including that in New Haven, Hoover referred to the Panther purges as "an opportunity to further plant the seeds of suspicion concerning disloyalty among ranking officials in order to further disrupt and exploit BPP fears in this regard." Claiming that the "Central Committee of the BPP is attempting to assume total power over BPP affairs on a national scale, to the exclusion of BPP leaders in other parts of the country," Hoover concluded: "These and other vulnerabilities of the BPP should be the subject of hard hitting imaginative counterintelligence proposals which will render this Black extremist organization ineffectual."[36]

All this corresponded with a period in which the BPP was trying to move beyond its violent image. As California Chief Deputy Attorney General O'Brien was to recall, "The Panthers seemed to be in deliberate, open, provocative confrontation with police departments in their early periods. They used revolutionary language, provocative language, and seemed to be deliberately seeking to confront established authority particularly police authority. But then we observed they seemed to have a social side, a concept of doing something beyond these angry confrontations." Even Hoover was forced to admit that the BPP had embarked on what he described as a "series of steps designed to create a new and better image of itself."[37]

Hoover, however, remained bent on destroying the Black Panther Party. His obsession appeared irrational even to some of his own agents. The special agent in charge of the San Francisco office, for instance, sent Hoover an Airtel on May 14, 1969, criticizing the FBI's secret war on the Panthers. In a three-page document the SAC questioned the legality of the FBI's counterintelligence program. He also criticized it for attacking initiatives like the program of breakfast for children, which "many prominent humanitarians, whites as well as Blacks" were supporting. Hoover responded in an angry four-page memorandum chastising the SAC for his misplaced sympathies.[38] As Hoover explained:

> As it concerns the BPP, you point out that results achieved by utilizing counterintelligence ideas such as publicizing the evils of the violence, the lack of morals, the widespread use of narcotics and anonymous mailings, have not been outstanding. This is because the typical Black supporter of the BPP is not disturbed by allegations which would upset a white community.[39]

Hoover continued:

> You must recognize that one of our primary aims in counterintelligence as it concerns the BPP is to keep this group isolated from the moderate Black and white community which may surround it. This is most emphatically pointed out in their Breakfast for Children Program, where they are actively soliciting and receiving support from uninformed whites and moderate Blacks.[40]

Despite Hoover's insistence, FBI informants and resident field offices were continually frustrated in trying to come up with unfavorable information on the Party. In New Haven, the resident agency had an especially hard time complying with Hoover's request for biweekly reports. On March 5, the SAC of New Haven sent the Director a letter acknowledging that the division "is aware of the importance of an effective counterintelligence program and every effort will be made to penetrate and disrupt the Black Nationalist Movement in Connecticut." But the office was unable to propose little more than furnishing information to a local news personality to be used on his television show concerning the BPP: "The New Haven Office does not have any specific counterintelligence operation in effect other than that set forth above."[41]

On March 28, Director Hoover sent the resident agency in New Haven his reply castigating it for failing to come up with information on the BPP: "To date you have submitted no concrete recommendations under this program concerning the Black Panther Party, despite the fact this extremely dangerous organization is active in four cities in your Division." Hoover instructed the New Haven office "by 4/14/69, and every two weeks thereafter, submit to the Bureau your proposals to disrupt the BPP and fully comply with the instructions contained in Bureau letter 1/30/69."[42]

In the meanwhile, the New Haven police department had initiated its own investigation of the BPP early in February of 1969. Under Chief James Ahern, the department in hopes of linking the Party with some type of criminal activity initiated electronic and physical surveillance on members' homes and BPP headquarters. Though this electronic surveillance was a direct violation of the 1968 legislation, FBI agents regularly referred to it in conversations with Ahern's intelligence squad about the activities of the BPP and other militant groups in New Haven. The FBI also provided the special register tapes needed to produce the wiretaps. The FBI's role, however, was neither supervisory nor managerial. Stephen Ahern, head of intelligence for New Haven, called the shots and directed most of the surveillance against the BPP, willingly sharing information with the FBI on BPP activities.[43]

This federal and local investigation coincided with difficulties within the Bridgeport BPP and problems between the Connecticut Panthers and the national headquarters. Most of these internal problems concerned State Captain Jose Gonzalez, who got along with few of the local members. At this time the core of the Panther membership consisted of Gonzalez, Ericka Huggins, Kimbro, Edwards, McLucas, the Carter sisters, Rosemarie Smith, who was identified as the BPP Lieutenant of Culture, Maude L. Frances, described as the Second Lieutenant of Labor, and Jeannie Wilson, the First Lieutenant of Information. The total membership of the Bridgeport/New Haven chapter fluctuated between fifteen and twenty-five members. A tangled web of political infighting within the local BPP, strained relations with the national office, attempts by the national office to bring the New Haven chapter under greater control, and FBI and local surveillance and attempted disruption of the Party, created a general atmosphere of fear and distrust

The beginning of the end came in late April when Lonnie McLucas and Jose Gonzalez fell into a dispute over who was responsible for a minor theft at the home of another Panther. Both called the national office which, believing Gonzalez, threatened to expel McLucas from the Party. On April 14, the San Francisco FBI office reported the text of a telephone conversation with Lonnie McLucas, who was informed he was being expelled for stealing money. On the same day, Ericka Huggins contacted David Hilliard to complain that "untrue reports and gross exaggerations" were being made about the New Haven chapter. She identified Jose Gonzalez as the source of these reports and told Hilliard that the New Haven chapter would begin making regular reports to the national offices to avoid confusion.[44]

Soon Gonzalez began to behave strangely. Around the first of May he mysteriously disappeared. He left New Haven shortly after May 4 and on May 12, reappeared in North Carolina, where he told the assistant chief of staff for the national offices, Roosevelt Hilliard, that he was working to help organize a chapter of the BPP there. In a telephone conversation subject to FBI surveillance, Hilliard sharply reprimanded Gonzalez for violating the ban on recruiting and ordered him to return to New Haven. Hilliard subsequently placed a call to Landon Williams in New York. Williams was on an official inspection visit for the BPP national offices and was in New York reviewing chapters in the Northeast. An FBI report says that Hilliard told Williams to "go up to New Haven and impress on those MF's that they weren't organizing anything outside of their city." Williams, Hilliard informed him, had the option of deciding whether to impose some sort of disciplinary action on Gonzalez for attempting to organize a chapter in North Carolina. Gonzalez, however, never returned to New Haven.[45]

Following Gonzalez's departure, the New Haven FBI field office reported a decrease of activities in the Bridgeport area. Before he left Connecticut Gonzalez had told reporters on April 5, that the BPP in Bridgeport had obtained thirty-five applications for membership. The New Haven FBI office confirmed Gonzalez's estimate observing that "most of the hardcore workers" had moved to New Haven where a state headquarters had been established at 285 Putnam Avenue.[46]

With the move to New Haven the BPP became much more active. As the New Haven BPP struggled to get its programs off the ground, the police placed telephone taps on the Party headquarters, which, after the eviction from the HPA offices, were located in the home of Warren Kimbro at 365 Orchard Street. By mid-May, the New Haven chapter claimed thirty-five full-time members and the chapter began making preparations for Party Chairman Bobby Seale to speak at Yale University. Seale was on a nationwide speaking tour designed to generate money for the national office, drained of funds by the police raids. Ahern's men quickly expanded surveillance, pressing informants for details and turning the information over to the FBI for use in covert initiatives against the BPP.[47]

At this time the FBI was concentrating on Seale. The Bureau had first targeted Seale late in 1967. But, despite the best efforts of the FBI, together with the California state and local police, he managed to evade serious legal trouble until February of 1968. In that month police raided Seale's Berkeley apartment after receiving a call from a concerned neighbor who claimed to overhear Seale and others plotting a murder.

Bobby Seale on a talk show
shortly before he left the Black
Panther Party. Seale helped to
inaugurate the Serve-the-People
objectives of the Party in 1968.
He was arrested along with
eight other Panthers in connection with the murder of Alex
Rackley in New Haven in May
of 1969. *(Copyright* Washington
Post; *Reprinted by permission of
the D.C. Public Library)*

Charges were later dropped when an Oakland judge ruled that the officers didn't have probable cause to search Seale's apartment. Seale was
freed, but the foundation for a deadly game had been laid. In 1968 he
was one of several radical speakers charged with disrupting the Democratic National Convention in Chicago. Seale would twice more be accused of plotting the murder of renegade Party members: in New Haven,
Connecticut in May of 1969 and by FBI informant Thomas E. Mosher
before a Senate subcommittee in 1971.[48]

The New Haven police department's telephone taps let the FBI know
of Bobby Seale's visit well in adavnce and of the upcoming inspection
visit by officials from the national headquarters stemming from the
problems with Gonzalez. In return, the FBI kept the New Haven police
informed about Seale's legal troubles in connection with the 1968 Democratic National Convention in Chicago and his prior arrests in California. Agents also shared the fruits of the FBI San Francisco taps, which
revealed the escalating problems developing in New Haven and its problems with the national office over Gonzalez.[49] The FBI instructed its
New Haven office that the inspections were part of a national program
instituted by Seale to purge all infiltrators from the BPP, a provision that
the Bureau seized on for counterintelligence initiatives. In a memorandum to all resident agencies dated November 25, 1968, Hoover declared
that the new Panther policy "presents an opportunity to further plant the
seeds of suspicion concerning disloyalty among ranking officials in or-

der to further disrupt and exploit BPP fears in this regard." Hoover instructed agents to refrain from "endangering Bureau informants; moreover, counterintelligence in this regard should throw off suspicion."[50]

On May 15, 1969, the FBI branch in New Haven requested permission from the Bureau to disseminate an anonymous letter to a selected group of moderate black businessmen in the Bridgeport, New Haven, Hartford, and Middletown, Connecticut, areas with the intention of disrupting the BPP chapter's highly successful program of breakfast for children. The letter contained obscenities and warned that black businessmen who did not support the BPP would be branded enemies of the black people. Hoover denied New Haven's request, pointing out that a similar ruse had already been published in the BPP newspaper. He further advised New Haven that the office should pursue "a situation existing in New Haven whereby the local hoodlums and the BPP are criticizing each other. Hoover concluded: "We are calling for a suggested counterintelligence program concerning this."[51]

This communication underscores two things: the effectiveness of the FBI's intelligence web with regards to the BPP, and the damage that the very public infighting within the BPP was doing to the organization. From November 1968 through June 1969 similar patterns can be observed in several cities. The FBI, in connection with state and local law enforcement officials, directed operations against BPP chapters that were new, in bad standing, or feuding with the national headquarters. A Panther, usually of dubious reputation, would arrive with a message from national headquarters either ordering the target chapter underground or claiming that he had been sent to straighten the chapter out. With the help of agent provocateurs within the BPP, the FBI, along with state and local police agencies, created an atmosphere of fear and distrust that resulted in acts of violence often misdirected against BPP members. These attempts were often facilitated by the degree of political infighting within the Party itself and efforts by the national office to bring its chapters under some organizational structure.[52]

In the February 17, 1969 issue of *The Black Panther* newspaper, opposite the last statement of the late Jon Huggins, was an article by the Chicago BPP Head of Security William O' Neal entitled "All Panthers Beware," detailing a security breach in Chicago that was indicative of things to come in New Haven. O'Neal—himself later revealed to be an agent provocateur for the FBI—reported that a "brother" dressed like a Black Panther had entered the central office of the Illinois Black Panther Party, stated his name, Derek Phemster, and claimed to be Minister of Information for an underground organization of Black Panthers in Indianapolis, Indiana. Phemster told the Chicago Panthers that he had direct orders from Seale and Hilliard authorizing him to come to Chicago and order the Black Panther Party there underground. When Chicago's deputy minister of defense, Bobby Rush, checked Phemster's story with a phone call to the national offices, however, he was uncovered as a spy.[53] The article goes on to discuss Panther methods of handling suspected informers that included beatings and torture. After confronting Phemster, O'Neal wrote, "We went into a more intensive stage of questioning. We used methods which proved very effective . . . after about three and a half hours of interrogation, he then admitted all charges of dismissal from the Black Panther Party in Indiana because of informing."[54]

In the same period, several chapters reported similar attempts at disruption. Several persons of suspect background became involved in the New Haven chapter. Demonstrating the effectiveness of the FBI's program, one local Panther recalls, "As we found out . . . there are people who . . . we are not clear on who they worked for." After Gonzalez disappeared, rumors circulated that he had once been a cadet at the Brooklyn, New York, police academy.[55]

Around the same time Gonzalez arrived in North Carolina, George Sams, a clinically diagnosed moron with a reputation for violence, showed up in New York. Sams claimed to be a security enforcer from national headquarters sent to straighten out the New York chapter. He threatened to kill whoever was responsible for informing on twenty-one Panthers accused in a bombing plot against the New York City government. He also announced that he had the power to expel members who were not in line with BPP national directives.

At the time the New York chapter was divided over the changes in Panther policy and experiencing the same political infighting and atmosphere of mistrust that was developing in New Haven. As early as March of 1969, the New York 21 bombing plot exposed the deep divisions within the BPP. Many New York Panthers either left the Party or broke with the national offices, rejecting the new "serve the people" themes and accusing the party of becoming revisionist and not revolutionary. Eldridge Cleaver, in exile in Algeria, became the leader of this faction within the Party. In Seale's explanation, "they had a whole negative thing against organizing breakfast programs organizing free health clinics they had a whole negative thing. These dudes wanted anarchy. In other words they wanted to start shooting police in the back, fuck it. That's anarchy." And it would be destructive of revolutionary unity:

> In other words so you shooting some police; that does not make
> a revolution for the people. My point was that you must put the
> programs together, unite the people behind the programs. With
> the programs uniting the people and with meetings and rallies
> . . . you educate the people. You also network the community,
> step by step and with the networked community then you got the

majority of people on your side. But, when you're dealing with revolution you must be rational, specific and particular and deal with and find particulars of organizing and raising the consciousness of the people. So, this is where these guys split later on while I was in jail.[56]

Although he was not demonstrably a police agent, the circumstantial evidence against Sams is weighty. FBI memos reflected the growing sentiment in the Bureau that infiltrators too readily crossed the line into provocation. According to Seale, Sams had been expelled from the Party after he had "jumped on" a couple of Party members out in San Francisco. Sams was subsequently reinstated at the behest of Stokley Carmichael, then serving in the honorary position of the Panthers' prime minister, but his suspect behavior continued.[57] In New York, Sams terrorized Party members and raped and beat a female Party member after she refused his advances. He also openly violated Party rules, abusing drugs and alcohol in the presence of Party members and brazenly displaying his loaded .45. After being told that two other emissaries, Landon Williams and Roy Hithe, were scheduled to arrive from the West Coast, Sams unceremoniously announced that he would be leaving to go on an inspection visit to New Haven. Before leaving, however, he recruited to accompany him Alex Rackley, a twenty-four-year-old martial arts instructor and security officer in the Harlem chapter.[58]

Despite his erratic behavior no one thought to investigate Sams's Party credentials. This laxness was part of the organizational problems the BPP had experienced from its inception and a reason Hilliard and Seale were attempting to bring the Party under greater control. Of the success of their efforts in 1969, Huggins recalls, "everything that was done everywhere had its source at the national headquarters and you could almost . . . tell when something didn't have to do with national headquarters because it was so atypical." From his arrival in New York to his "unexpected" appearance in New Haven, everything about George Sams was atypical.

On May 17, Sams and Rackley arrived in New Haven. There, as in New York, Sams used fear and dissension to bolster his authority. According to Frances Carter, Sams was "the kiss of death," and with his arrival "the whole family cohesiveness-camaraderie we were experiencing stopped." Sams denounced Rackley as a police informant and ordered him bound and held for interrogation in the basement of the Panther headquarters.[59] For three days members of the New Haven chapter, under the direction of Sams, tortured and interrogated Rackley in the cellar of Warren Kimbro's home. While the New Haven police force listened in, members intermittently beat Rackley and doused his body with boiling water in an effort to extract a confession. Sams ordered Ericka Huggins to record the interrogation for national headquarters. That recording would eventually become a key piece of evidence against the New Haven Panthers.[60]

When Landon Williams arrived with Roy Hithe on his official inspection visit to New Haven on May 18, he found George Sams in control of the New Haven chapter with Alex Rackley held as a police informer bound and gagged in an upstairs bedroom. Both pairs of inspectors arrived just days before Seale's speaking engagement at Yale University on May 19. The New Haven prosecutor, Arnold Markle, would later argue that Seale gave the order for the murder of Rackley. Seale notes that after his speech at Battell chapel he only stopped by Panther headquarters for a few moments while Ericka Huggins and Warren Kimbro retrieved some things inside. While waiting in the car, Seale explains he was approached by Williams, who told him: "I have a problem with George Sams." Seale says that he shortly informed Williams that Sams had been expelled from the Party and ordered them to release Rackley. The following evening, May 20, Sams told Rackley that he would be released and arranged for Rackley, still bound with coat hangers, to be placed in a waiting car with Sams, Lonnie McLucas and Warren Kimbro.[61]

The four men took the interstate to Middlefield, Connecticut, roughly twenty minutes from New Haven. There in a marshy swamp adjacent to a river, Sams informed Rackley that there was a boat waiting to take him back to New York. As Rackley made his way in the crisp night air through the marsh into a small clearing, Sams handed Warren Kimbro a .45. Sams pointed in the direction of Rackley and told Kimbro, "These [orders] are from national—ice him." Kimbro followed Rackley into the brush and fired one shot, striking Rackley in the head. Sams then gave the gun to Lonnie McLucas and told him to fire a safety shot to make sure Rackley was dead.[62]

Ahern recorded the official sequence of events in his book *Police in Trouble*. In his own words, May 20 brought an "uneasy evening." The New Haven Police Department had received information that members of the New Haven Black Panther Party had kidnapped a New York Panther and were holding him for interrogation. "We did not have enough information to make arrests, but we had the apartment under surveillance."[63] Fearing the worst, Ahern, by his account, ordered several more units to Kimbro's home but the Panthers, knowing that they were being watched, split up into four cars and left in different directions. In the confusion, the car containing Rackley "slipped away" and despite an all-points bulletin for suspicion of kidnapping somehow managed to wind its way twenty miles up Interstate 91 to Middlefield and back, escaping the notice of state and local police. Rackley's lifeless body was discovered the next morning. He had been beaten, tortured, scalded, burned, and shot once in the head and once in the chest.[64]

The next memo from the New Haven FBI to San Francisco, Los

Angeles, Sacramento, San Diego, New York, and Chicago detailed the murder of Rackley. The New Haven resident agency reported, "Based on interviews conducted to date during [the] period Rackley was in captivity, Saturday, May 17, last Tuesday, May 20, last he was accused on numerous occasions of being a police informant and was tortured." The FBI observed that the kangaroo court conducted by the BPP had been directed by the national offices of the Party. The bureau report concluded, however, that there was no evidence indicating Bobby Seale had "any knowledge" or that he was "directly involved in [the] murder, although he was believed to have spent the night of May 19 last at BPP headquarters New Haven."[65]

The New Haven police quickly rounded up six women and two men and held them without bail on charges of murder, kidnapping, binding, and conspiracy. Police announced that they were also seeking the fugitive Panthers Landon Williams and Roy Hithe, both later arrested in Denver, and Lonnie McLucas, who was later captured in Salt Lake City, as well as George Sams. Despite a statewide manhunt, Sams managed to get to Chicago where he would later claim he had been ordered by the Party to kill Fred Hampton, the head of the Chicago BPP. In Chicago Sams was held under house arrest by Phemster interrogator William O'Neal, who was working as an informant and agent provocateur for the Chicago FBI. Sams was later to testify that moments before a police raid on a warrant for his arrest was executed, O'Neal allowed him to escape and he walked through a line of police surrounding Chicago BPP offices armed with a .38 without being noticed. He subsequently fled to Canada.[66]

The FBI used Sams's fugitive status to conduct raids on Panther offices throughout the nation. This further depleted Panther funds and influenced public opinion against the BPP. In Chicago the initial search for Sams also set off a series of violent confrontations between Panthers and police that ultimately resulted in the murders of Fred Hampton and Mark Clark by Chicago police during a predawn assault in December of 1969.

The Rackley murder had consequences for the New Haven chapter. On June 3 the New Haven FBI field office announced that "there were only five Panthers left because of all of the arrests in New Haven and the local chapter had not been able to get any help from New York." But the arrest of the New Haven Nine, as the incarcerated Panthers came to be known, marked the beginning of a rejuvenated Black Panther Party in New Haven. Although the FBI observed that after September the majority of BPP activity in New Haven was directed by transplanted national officers and that former supporters in New Haven had left the BPP to "go it alone," by December the BPP was able to turn much of its misfortune around and began attracting new supporters to its programs.[67]

In an effort to reconnect with the community at large the New Haven BPP moved to implement the four service programs of the previous winter. In the *Ministry of Information Bulletin* for December 24, 1969, the New Haven chapter boasted a community political education class and a program of free breakfast for schoolchildren and announced a free clothing program to begin sometime in January of 1970. The breakfast program, held Monday through Friday at the Newhallville Teen Lounge, continued to be the chapter's most successful endeavor, and the BPP estimated that it served between seventy and ninety children a day. The BPP also provided telephone numbers in its newsletter for parents to arrange for their children's transportation to the program.[68]

The BPP appealed directly to the community for help. An ad in the *Ministry of Information Bulletin* #5 announced: "In order for the Black Panther Party to serve the people better, we need typists and photographers to help with leaflets and with the People's news service; drivers

Table 7.1

Welfare Department Expenditures, New Haven, 1955–1969
(thousands of dollars)

Year	Total Expenditure ($)	Personnel	Non-Personnel	Personnel as Percent of Total
1955	959	154	805	16.1
1956	952	165	787	17.3
1957	1,243	216	1,028	17.4
1958	1,669	261	1,408	15.6
1959	1,776	290	1,478	16.3
1960	1,465	299	1,166	20.4
1961	1,456	323	1,133	22.4
1962	1,282	353	928	27.5
1963	1,348	380	968	28.5
1964	1,240	399	841	32.2
1965	1,412	450	962	31.9
1966	1,352	455	896	33.7
1967	1,473	516	958	35.0
1968	1,573*	567	1,006	36.0
1969	1,581*	303†	1,278	19.2

*Budget.
†This large personnel decrease was due to the close of a convalescent home operated by the city.

Source: Claudia Scott, City Budgets, 1955–1969, 27.

and help with the breakfast program; and volunteers with skills such as carpentry to donate a few hours per week." The ad concluded, "give your time and talent to the Black liberation movement." When local officials threatened to close down the breakfast program in 1970, the BPP also sought the support of the people. The matter was referred to a vote by the Newhallville Youth Centers Executive Board. The BPP circulated a flier urging that the public get out and prevent the board from the closing. "The Free Breakfast for Children Program is the community's program," a BPP flier proclaimed to the community. "If you [the community] do care about this program, your presence at the UNO Executive Board Hearing is needed."[69]

The New Haven BPP eagerly worked on behalf of welfare mothers in the same way that Fred Harris and the HPA had done back in 1965. In a sharply worded article appearing in the New Haven BPP newsletter, Elise Brown charged, "the New Haven welfare mothers are demanding that this racist power structure give them a sufficient amount of money to purchase back to school clothing for their children." Showing how well they had become acquainted with local issues, the Panthers pointed out that in Connecticut, welfare recipients were allowed $12.50 to pur-

Table 7.2

Average Monthly Welfare Department Caseload, New Haven, 1964–1968

Year	Average Monthly Caseload
1964	1,162
1965	1,533
1966	1,533
1967	1,588
1968	1,987

Note: Tables 7.1 and 7.2 show the pattern of welfare expenditures for the past fifteen years. According to Claudia Scott, nonpersonnel expenditures constituted a large part of the total since the major function of the welfare department was the disbursement of relief payments. The demand for increased welfare services, as with the integration of schools, accompanied the rise of New Haven's nonwhite population. The rise in the need for welfare services can be observed in the growth of the average monthly caseload, as shown in Table 7.2. New Haven experienced most radical expression in the years when black migration from the South peaked and the city's welfare caseload markedly increased. The HPA emerged the year after the caseload increased by almost four hundred people. The BPP came along at a period when the welfare caseload had also grown by three hundred.

Source: Claudia Scott, *Annual Reports*, Department of Welfare, New Haven, 1964–1968, 27.

chase winter coats for a growing boy of thirteen. The average monthly clothing allowance of $6.80 per child the BPP described as "totally inadequate." After a failed meeting with State Welfare Commissioner Edward Shapiro, the Panthers reported: "The demagogic (lying, deceiving) punk ran away hiding after he got word that the mothers were on their way to Hartford with their children. Rather than face the mothers, their children, and have to deal with their needs he had his flunkies report that he had just received a hay fever attack"[70] (see Tables 7.1–7.2).

New problems, however, developed for the New Haven BPP. After the arrest of the Panthers, the New Haven Nine became a national cause. Yale students and white radical groups flocked to support the BPP. This left New Haven blacks to ponder again what group would not desert their interest in search of white support. But the event also invited among Panthers an articulation of what Donald Freed was to define as the third and broadest stage in the human rights movement.[71]

Notes

1. Donald Freed, *Agony in New Haven: The Trial of Bobby Seale, Ericka Huggins and the Black Panther Party* (New York: Simon and Shuster, 1973), 17.

2. Ibid.

3. Ibid., 19.

4. Henry Hampton and Steve Fayer, *Voices of Freedom* (New York: Bantam, 1991), 299.

5. Ibid., 300–301.

6. Ibid., 303.

7. Ibid., 302.

8. Ibid., 300–301.

9. *The Black Panther*, 20 June 1967, 4, 15.

10. Andrew Haynes, "Police–Black Panther Conflict," 103–105.

11. Gonzalez's decision to reveal his organizing efforts in Bridgeport may partly be explained by the murders in LA. After being released from jail Ericka Huggins, escorted by Elaine Brown, returned to New Haven to bury her husband. David Hilliard records that after the killings, Brown and Huggins went to Bridgeport, Connecticut, which he misidentifies as Jon's home, to start a new branch. Huggins and several recruits from New Haven attached themselves to Gonzalez and the Bridgeport chapter in fact until March of 1969 when they applied to form a new chapter in New Haven. David Hilliard, 240; *Bridgeport Telegram*, 29 January 1969, cited in Confidential Report, FBI, New Haven, Re: Black Panther Party, 5 February 1969, John R. Williams Papers RG 1398 Box 1, Manuscripts and Archives, Yale University Library; SAC, New Haven, to Director of FBI, via Airtel, Subject: Black Panther Party, 12 February 1969, John R. Williams Papers RG 1398 Box 1 Folder 1, Manuscripts and Archives, Yale University Library; "Panthers Take Spotlight At Dunham-Led Forum," *Bridgeport Post Telegram*, 7 February 1969; SAC, San Francisco, to Director of FBI, Washington, D.C., Subject: BPP–New Haven Division, 4 May 1969; FBI Boston Teletype, 19 February 1969; George Edwards interview; Michael Newton, 163–172.

12. Ibid.

13. Bobby Seale, *Seize the Time*, 270–271; Marine, 208–209; Elaine Brown, *Taste of Power* (New York: Doubleday, 1994), 156–170; Hilliard, 236–240.

14. Brown, 161; Seale, *Seize the Time*, 270–271; Marine, 208–209.

15. Freed, 22–23. Please refer to footnote 44 in Chapter 6 for a discussion of suspicions regarding Ronald Karenga's involvement in the police-Panther conflict.

16. Brown, 161–170; Marine, 209; Seale, *Seize the Time*, 270–271.

17. Francis Carter quoted in Hilliard, 242.

18. SAC, New Haven, to Director of FBI, via Airtel, Subject: Black Panther Party, 24 February 1969, John R. Williams Papers RG 1398 Box 1, Manuscripts and Archives, Yale University Library; SAC, San Francisco, to Director of FBI, Subject: BPP–New Haven Division, 19 February 1969, John R. Williams Papers RG 1398 Box 1, Manuscripts and Archives, Yale University Library.

19. SAC, New Haven, to Director of FBI, 21 April 1969.

20. Ericka Huggins interview; George Edwards interview.

21. Ericka Huggins interview.

22. George Edwards interview.

23. SAC, San Francisco, to Director of FBI, Washington, D.C., Subject: BPP–New Haven Division, 4 May 1969, Manuscripts and Archives, Yale University Library; FBI Boston Teletype, 19 February 1969, John R. Williams Papers RG 1398 Box 1 Folder 2, Manuscripts and Archives, Yale University Library; George Edwards, interview by author, 5 August 1995; Ericka Huggins, interview by author, 10 July 1995; Bobby Seale, interview by author, 2 January 1996; Attorney Michael Koskoff, interview by author, 5 May 1995; Michael Newton, 163–172; Clayborne Carson in foreword to Phillip Foner's *The Black Panthers Speak*, xiv–xv; on the FBI's infiltration of the BPP see Huey P. Newton, *The War Against the Panthers: A Study in Repression in America* (Ph.D. diss., University of California at Santa Cruz, 1980); Kenneth O'Reilly, *"Racial Matters": The FBI's Secret File on Black America, 1960–1972* (New York: The Free Press, 1989); Ward Churchill and Jim Vander Wall, *Agents of Repression: The FBI's Secret War Against the Black Panther Party and the American Indian Movement* (Boston: South End Press, 1990).

24. FBI Boston Teletype, 19 February 1969; SAC, San Francisco, to Director of FBI, Washington, D.C., Subject: BPP–New Haven Division; George Edwards interview; Ericka Huggins interview; Bobby Seale interview; Michael Newton, 163–172.

25. *The Black Panther*, 20 June 1967, 4, 15.

26. *The Black Panther*, 10 June 1968, 6.

27. BPP flier contained in John R. Williams Papers 1398 Box 33 Sub A, Manuscripts and Archives, Yale University Library.

28. Moffitt's comments contained in *New Haven Journal Courier*, 17 March 1969; mayor's clippings file contained in Richard C. Lee Papers, Manuscripts and Archives, Yale University Library.

29. John Daniels interview.

30. "Welfare Moms," Elise Brown, *Ministry of Information Bulletin #5*, 24 December 1969, 3; FBI Boston Teletype, 19 February 1969; SAC, San Francisco, to Director of FBI, Washington, D.C., Subject: BPP–New Haven Division, 4 May 1969; Edwin Edmonds interview; John Daniels interview.

31. Harold Saffold's comments presented in The Eyes on the Prize Civil Rights Series II, "A Nation of Law," Blackside Productions, 1990.

32. FBI Boston Teletype to Director of FBI, 19 February 1969.

33. Director of FBI, to SAC, New Haven, 27 February 1969, John R. Williams Papers RG 1398 Box 1 Folder 1, Manuscripts and Archives, Yale University Library.

34. Hilliard, 246; Seale, *Seize the Time*, 370–371; Bobby Seale interview.

35. Michael Newton, 198–199.

36. Director of FBI, to SAC, Albany, New York, Re: Bulet to Baltimore dated 11/25/68, 1 January 1969, File number 100-448006, Subject (BPP), Freedom of Information Act Reading Room, FBI Headquarters, Washington, D.C.

37. O'Brien's comments contained in Eyes on the Prize, "Power"; Director of FBI to SAC, Albany, New York, 1 January 1969.

38. SAC, San Francisco, to Director of FBI, Re: Bureau Airtel dated 5/2/69, 14 May 1969, File number 100-448006, Subject (BPP), Freedom of Information Act Reading Room, FBI Headquarters, Washington D.C.

39. Director of FBI, Washington, D.C., to SAC, San Francisco, Re: SF Airtel 5/14/69, 27 May 1969, File number 100-448006, Subject (BPP), Freedom of Information Act Reading Room, FBI Headquarters, Washington, D.C.

40. Ibid.

41. SAC, New Haven, to Director of FBI, Washington, D.C., Re: New Haven letter to Bureau 1/6/69 and New Haven letter to Bureau 2/17/69, 5 March 1969, File number 100-448006, Subject (BPP), Freedom of Information Act Reading Room, FBI Headquarters, Washington, D.C.

42. Director of FBI, Washington, D.C., to SAC, New Haven, 28 March 1969, Freedom of Information Act Reading Room, FBI Headquarters, Washington, D.C., File number 100-448006, Subject (BPP), the Bureau letter from 1 January 1969 instructed all FBI BPP offices to submit biweekly letters to the Bureau containing "proposed counterintelligence maneuvers aimed against the BPP and accomplishments obtained during the previous two week period."

43. Andrew Houlding, "The Wiring of New Haven," *The Nation*, 7 June 1980, 668; Jamie Workman, "Suspicion and Paranoia: The Secrets of the May Day Security Machine," *The New Journal*, 2 February 1990, 39; Herman Schwartz, "The Intrusive Ears of the Law," *The Nation*, 16 July 1995, 722; Bruce Shapiro, "Are Your Local Police Listening?" *The Nation*, 5 February 1990, 157–160.

44. SAC, San Francisco, to Director of FBI, Washington, D.C., 4 April 1969, John L. Williams Papers RG 1398 Box 1 Folder 1, Manuscripts and Archives, Yale University Library.

45. Police harassment along with personal difficulties with the other members in the area are some possible reasons given for Gonzalez's leaving Bridgeport. SAC, New Haven, to Director of FBI, Washington, D.C., 14 May 1969, John R. Williams Papers RG 1398 Box 1 Folder 2, Manuscripts and Archives, Yale University Library; George Edwards interview; Bobby Seale interview; Ericka Huggins interview.

46. FBI, New Haven, Connecticut, Confidential Report Black Panther Party, 5 April 1969, John R. Williams Papers RG 1398 Box 1 Folder 1, Manuscripts and Archives, Yale University Library.

47. Bobby Seale interview.

48. Bobby Seale interview; Marine, 130–132.

49. Director of FBI, Washington, D.C., to SAC, New Haven, Re: SF Airtel 9 May 1969, entitled "Black Panther Party New Haven Division, RM-BPP," 15 May 1969, Manuscripts and Archives, Yale University Library; SAC, New Haven, to Director of FBI, Washington, D.C., 9 May 1969, Manuscripts and Archives, Yale University Library; George Edwards interview; Michael P. Koskoff interview; Bobby Seale interview; James Ahern, 33. On Seale and the Democratic National Convention see Deborah Cox et al., *The Conspiracy: The Chicago Eight Speak Out!* (New York: Dell, 1969).

50. SAC, New Haven, to Director of FBI, Re: New Haven letter to Bureau, 3 June 1969, 17 February 1969.

51. Director of FBI, Washington, D.C., to SAC, New Haven, Re: NHlet 4/28/69, 15 May 1969; SAC, New Haven, to Director of FBI, Washington, D.C., Re: New Haven letter to Bureau 4/10/69 and Bulet to San Francisco, 4/23/69, 28 April 1969, Manuscripts and Archives, Yale University Library.

52. Frank J. Donner, "Hoover's Legacy: A Nationwide System of Political Surveillance Based on the Spurious Authority of a Press Release," *Nation*, 218 (June 1, 1974), 34–51; "Electronic Surveillance: The National Security Game," *Civil Liberties Review* 2, (summer 1975), 15–17; Nelson Blackstock, *Cointelpro: The FBI's Secret War on Political Freedom* (New York: Vintage Books, 1975); Frank J. Donner, *The Age of Surveillance: The Aims and Methods of America's Political Intelligence System* (New York: Alfred A. Knopf, 1980); Ward Churchill and Jim Vander Wall, *Agents of Repression: The FBI's Secret War Against the Black Panther Party and the American Indian Movement* (Boston: South End Press, 1990).

53. William O'Neal, "All Panthers Beware," *Black Panther Community News Service*, 17 February 1969, Vol. 11, No 23, 9–10.

54. Ibid.

55. Bobby Seale interview; Ericka Huggins interview; George Edwards interview; Michael P. Koskoff interview; Freed, 246–267.

56. Bobby Seale interview.

57. Freed, 264–267 and 302–304; Donner, 226; Churchill and Vander Wall, *The Cointelpro Papers*, 360; Damien Formisano, "Court Denies New Mental Test For Sams," *New Haven Register*, 23 March 1971, 38; Donald Marchione, "2nd Psychiatric Exam Sought For Sams," *New Haven Register*, 23 March 1971, 32.

58. Ericka Huggins interview; on Sams see "Ice Him," *Newsweek*, 3 August 1970, 25; "The Enforcer," *Newsweek*, 17 August 1970; Frank J. Donner, *The Age of Surveillance: The Aims and Methods of America's Political Intelligence System*, 226; Ward Churchill and Jim Vander Wall, *The Cointelpro Papers*, 360; Damien Formisano, "Court Denies New Mental Test For Sams," *New Haven Register*, 23 March 1971, 38; Donald Marchione, "2nd Psychiatric Exam Sought For Sams," *New Haven Register*, 23 March 1971, 32; David Hilliard, 248–250.

59. Ericka Huggins interview; for Frances Carter's account of Sams's visit see David Hilliard, 248–250.

60. James Ahern, *Police in Trouble* (New York: Hawthorne, 1972), 33.

61. Ibid.

62. "Ice Him," *Newsweek*, 3 August 1970, 25; "The Enforcer," *Newsweek*, 17 August 1970; Frank Donner, *The Age of Surveillance: The Aims and Methods of America's Political Intelligence System*, 226; Churchill and Vander Wall, *The Cointelpro Papers*, 360; Damien Formisano, "Court Denies New Mental Test For Sams," 38; Donald Marchione, "2nd Psychiatric Exam Sought For Sams," 32; Michael Newton, 163–171; Donald Freed, 15–17.

63. Ahern, 33.

64. Freed, 27; Sheehy, *Panthermania* (New York: Harper and Row, 1971), 108; Donner, 226; Churchill and Vander Wall, *The Cointelpro Papers*, 360; Damien Formisano, "Court Denies New Mental Test For Sams," *New Haven Register*, 23 March 1971, 38; Donald Marchione, "2nd Psychiatric Exam Sought For Sams," *New Haven Register*, 23 March 1971, 32; "8 Panthers Held In Murder Plot," *The New Haven Register*, 22 May 1969; "Second Victim Sought In Panther Case," *The New Haven Register*, 23 May 1969, page unknown, clippings file, Black Panther Party, Local History Collection, New Haven Public Library.

65. FBI New Haven, 22 May 1969, John R. Williams Papers RG 1398 Box 1 Folder 2, Manuscripts and Archives, Yale University Library.

66. Sheehy, 109; Freed, 247–258; Churchill and Vander Wall, *Agents of Repression*, 53.

67. SAC, New Haven, to Director of FBI, Washington, D.C., Re: Bureau Airtel to Albany 3/4/68, 3 September 1969, Freedom of Information Act Reading Room, FBI Headquarters, Washington D.C., File number 100-448006, Subject (BPP).

68. *Ministry of Information Bulletin #5*, 24 December 1969, John R. Williams Papers RG 1398 Box 33 Sub H, Manuscripts and Archives, Yale University Library.

69. *Ministry of Information Bulletin #5*, 24 December 1969; BPP flier, "Support the Free Breakfast for Children Program," John R. Williams Papers RG 1398 Box 33 Sub J, Manuscripts and Archives, Yale University Library.

70. "Welfare Pigs Refuse to Give Mothers Money to Purchase Back to School Clothing for their Children," John R. Williams Papers RG 1398 Box 33 Sub D, John Williams Papers RG 1398 Box 33 Sub J, Manuscripts and Archives, Yale University Library.

71. SAC, New Haven, to Director of FBI, Washington, D.C., Re: NH letter 5/12/69, NH Airtel to Bureau 6/2/69, 3 June 1969, John R. Williams Papers RG 1398 Box 33 Sub J, Manuscripts and Archives, Yale University Library.

CHAPTER EIGHT
No Haven

The government persists in "generating public enemies" wherever it is convenient for it to find them. . . . The lone juror who is reported to have voted for conviction in the Seale case said she believed "she owed the prosecution something." But of course neither she nor the prosecution itself, so far as that goes, owes anything to anybody but a search for the truth.

—Editorial, *The Boston Globe*,
May 29, 1971

People who preach liberalization are the ones who are the least liberal. They are supposed to be against the rich, but they make laws . . . that legislate against the poor. . . . The rich are not hurting—only the backbone of America. The liberals are tearing the backbone of America apart. What they are doing is the opposite of Constitutionality. Freedom of choice is what all my mail says—even from the black community. This thing works in reverse. What they are doing is the opposite of what they are supposed to be doing. When you get far to the left, you begin to move toward totalitarianism.

—Martha Mitchell, wife of
Attorney General John
Mitchell, May 2, 1971

Immediately following the arrests of the New Haven Panthers, the prosecution attempted to strengthen its case by offering deals to the accused in exchange for their testimony. Six pleaded guilty to lesser charges while the cases of two others were disposed of in juvenile court and charges against one were dropped altogether. The Panther emissaries, Landon Williams and Roy Hithe, remained in Colorado, still fighting rendition to New Haven on charges stemming from the Rackley murder. George Sams, in the meantime, emerged as the prosecution's chief wit-

Yale students and other Panther supporters gathered for May Day protests on the campus of Yale University. This outpouring of popular support for the Panthers led some to question the Panthers' militancy. *(Copyright* Washington Post; *Reprinted by permission of the D.C. Public Library)*

ness along with Warren Kimbro: a crushing blow to the New Haven Panthers, who had been growing increasingly suspicious about Kimbro and his association with the New Haven police. Shortly after his arrest, New Haven detectives had arranged for Kimbro's brother, a Miami policeman, to fly to New Haven to meet with him. Kimbro subsequently turned states evidence. He was also to receive a series of deals that strongly suggest his collusion with the police.[1]

On July 3, 1969, the New Haven FBI reported that "as a direct result of the action taken by FBI, New Haven, and the New Haven Police Department in connection with the homicide investigation of Alex Rackley, the overall effective leadership of the BPP has been seriously disrupted."[2] The memo boasted that, in addition to the arrests in New Haven, "thirty-four arrests have directly or indirectly resulted from the investigation of the Rackley murder." Despite the success of the Bureau's operation in New Haven, Hoover instructed agents that, in disseminating further incriminating information on the Panthers to a television station friendly to the Bureau, they were to withhold any comment on Rackley's murder.[3] In response to a request from the SAC of Las Vegas to attempt a similar operation in Nevada, Hoover replied, "your suggestion . . . is being denied since such action could possibly result in a situation similar to that which occurred in Connecticut in May 1969, when

Alex Rackley was tortured and killed by BPP members, if the allegation was believed."[4]

In an effort to ensure a conviction against Bobby Seale and Ericka Huggins, the prosecution elected to try Lonnie McLucas first. The Panthers concentrated on providing him with a solid defense. He would be represented by Theodore Koskoff, a brilliant legal tactician who had a well-established reputation in the state, and by Michael Koskoff, Theodore's youthful but perspicacious son, who was himself earning a reputation for representing underdog clients and had been his father's link to the Panthers. The younger Koskoff had been approached by Frances Carter's sister about representing her, but the Panthers asked the Koskoffs to represent McLucas instead. The attorneys initially had some reservations about taking the case. Theodore Koskoff had once turned down a request to defend the Communist Party in Connecticut because the organization refused to relinquish complete control of the defense to him. He was wary that the Panthers might be inclined toward the same policy of sacrificing a client to make a political statement. Only after the Panthers assured them that saving McLucas was their priority did the Koskoffs agree to take the case. According to Michael Koskoff, he and his father were well aware of the political ramifications of the trial and wanted the case for acquittal to be based on the evidence. To this end, the Koskoffs planned a two-tiered defense to show that in participating in the torture of Rackley, McLucas had acted out of fear of George Sams and that the safety shot fired by their client was not the one that killed Rackley.[5]

As early as September of 1969, concerned citizens and seventeen community organizations united to form the Coalition to Defend the New Haven Panthers. Robert H. Abramovitz, M.D. was elected coalition chairman and immediately began work on raising the estimated $70,000 in legal fees. After uncovering tapes of an interview Judge Harold Mulvey had given with a University of Connecticut sociology professor, J. David Coffin, while serving as state attorney general in 1966, the coalition worked to remove him from the case. Describing black migrants as "those slobs who come here from the farm and undermine New Haven Blacks," Mulvey had declared that "racial integration had damaged New Haven schools and had driven whites to the suburbs." Commenting on the absence of black leadership in New Haven, Mulvey concluded, "Anyone who drives a Cadillac among Blacks has influence."[6]

The Panthers disclosed plans for three days of fund-raising activities on the New Haven green, beginning on May 1, 1970. As David Hilliard recalls, "all we've announced is a mass gathering, nothing more, but they act like they believe Yale will be destroyed." William Porter III, one of the participants in the demonstrations in support of the Panthers, remembers: "We were the center of the universe for a few moments. We

Demonstrators display signs that illustrate the humanistic element of the Black Panther Party program. While many detractors were quick to denounce the Party as a Black Power organization, the Panthers, in their middle and later periods (1968–1974), worked actively to project the image of a human rights organization concerned first with the struggle for black equality but giving equal concern to the struggles of other oppressed groups. *(Reprinted with the permission of Manuscripts and Archives, Yale University Library)*

made the national news." But the Panthers and the Yale protest turned the spotlight from the issues that had brought the BPP to New Haven in the first place. That was the problem. Yale students began organizing their own demonstrations in support of the Panthers. In the same way Mayor Lee had exploited the NAACP for his own agenda, the left manipulated the BPP during the New Haven trials. Radical groups from all over the nation gathered in New Haven for the protest. Many participants made the demonstrations a forum for other protests, notably against the Vietnam War.

While university officials debated what course to take regarding the demonstrations, Yale students proved remarkably receptive to the cause developing in their backyard. When a waitress at one of the university dining halls was fired for taking a day off to care for a sick child, a number of students, led by Mary Pearl and Kurt Schmoke, helped to establish a child care facility for Yale employees. Students engaged in teach-ins and, at a rally on April 15, more than four hundred of them met to consider several proposals for expressing their support of the Panthers.

They called on the Yale Corporation to donate $500,000 to the BPP's defense efforts. They also proposed a four-day teach-in and a moratorium on classes.

Yale's president, Kingman Brewster, touched off a national debate when, during a faculty meeting the following week, he expressed his doubts that a black revolutionary could receive a fair trial in the United States. Brewster was bitterly attacked in the national press. His harshest critic was Vice President Spiro Agnew, who suggested that alumni start a letter writing campaign to have him ousted. Brewster's comments galvanized the left. Yale's activist chaplain, William Sloane Coffin, Jr., argued that "the Panther program was really asking of whites no more than our forebears 200 years before had asked of the British Parliament."[7]

Meanwhile, Brewster worked quietly to quell the potential for violence associated with the demonstrations. In secret meetings with everyone from the New Haven police to officials from the federal Department of Justice, Brewster sought to make the university secure. In what appeared to be a genuine response to student demands, he promised to open up the campus to the demonstrators and pledged that Yale would provide shelter and food for BPP supporters coming to New Haven to participate.[8] According to Henry Chauncey, Jr., who served as a special assistant to Brewster during the May Day demonstrations, the president's actions were not based on "some high and lofty principle." ". . . This was a pragmatic decision. If we didn't open the college what would happen? The answer was it would probably cause a hell of a lot of trouble." By opening up the campus to the radicals, Brewster was inviting them into an intelligence web far more sophisticated than anyone could imagine.[9]

As the New Haven police apparatus went into overdrive, Governor John Dempsey instructed the department to cancel all leaves and asked that police agencies in the greater New Haven area remain on twenty-four hour alert. He also took steps to mobilize state units of the national guard to support the police. The federal government followed suit. United States Attorney General John Mitchell requested the Pentagon to station four thousand marines and paratroopers near New Haven to assist in case of an emergency. Police Chief Ahern, however, called for calm and persuaded the governor that the New Haven police would be well prepared to deal with the scheduled events. Only a few minor incidents were reported during the demonstrations, including, a minor explosion and several small fires.

Ahern would later credit a "constant flow of information in our intelligence division" with helping him control the demonstrations. Citing sources that ranged from "reliable informants, to phone calls from the public, to generally circulating rumors," Ahern contended that "although gaining information from informants may seem a questionable tactic

Students hold up a Free Bobby
Seale poster in front of a Yale
University administration building. Panther supporters remained
nonviolent while police used dirty
tricks and disinformation to stifle
the protest. *(Copyright* Washington Post; *Reprinted by permission
of the D.C. Public Library)*

and obviously subject to abuses, in many situations police must have
information on organizations that may be a threat to life or to law."
Ahern also mentioned pejoratively "such gimmicks as wiretapping,"
which he dismissed as the excesses of the Nixon Administrations' policy
to take the handcuffs off the police. In fact, "reliable informant" was a
code word for New Haven's extensive wiretap machinery. Again, Ahern's
successes were largely based on the work of his brother, who provided
the chief with constant reports on the plans of the May Day organizers.
Ahern's men learned from the wiretaps that the protesters had called for
nonviolence, a fact the media ignored in heralding Ahern for keeping the
peace. Nevertheless, Ahern authorized additional covert activities aimed
at incapacitating the Panthers' supporters, among them slashing tires,
vandalizing homes and vehicles, and making lewd and threatening
phone calls.[10] Years later in an interview with Yale student David Greenberg, Henry Chauncey was to recall one of Ahern's more devious tricks.
After learning from a Harvard administrator that the Weathermen, a violent faction of the SDS, had chartered a pair of buses to come to New
Haven for May Day, Ahern and Chauncey paid for insurance on the
buses and then took the radical students for a proverbial ride. They
replaced the bus drivers with two state police officers, who allowed the
students to board and proceeded on to the Massachusetts turnpike.

The lead bus pulled over as though something was wrong, and
the second bus pulled behind it. And the two drivers huddled

underneath the hood. All of a sudden a police car came along and picked the two up and just left the Weathermen right there on the Mass Turnpike. They picked a place where you could walk five miles in any direction and still not get any where. They all got out and went left and right and were never seen again, as far as New Haven was concerned.[11]

The McLucas trial began without incident in June. According to *Newsweek*, "from the start of the eleven week trial, the government credited the Panthers with a far tighter chain of control than the revolutionaries were willing to admit." During the trial the state contended that Rackley had been tortured and killed not because of the pressure from Sams, but because he was suspected of being a police informer within the Black Panther Party. To support the argument, the state introduced evidence of the BPP's violent rhetoric and sweeping Panther purges. McLucas testified that he was fearful of Sams and Warren Kimbro. He had believed that if he did not fire he would be killed as well. For the prosecution, Kimbro admitted to having fired the first shot, but claimed that Sams had then ordered McLucas to shoot a second time to make sure Rackley was dead.[12]

The jury deliberated for six days. The arguments were tense, with the majority in favor of dismissal on the three most serious charges facing McLucas. The holdouts wanted to find McLucas guilty of more than the charge of conspiracy to commit murder, but capitulated after the judge delivered a Chip Smith charge, a legal device in which the judge admonishes the minority to reconsider the opinion of the majority. The verdict, rendered on August 31, found McLucas guilty of conspiracy to commit murder, but acquitted him of the three more serious counts, all of which carried the death penalty. "It's McLucas' testimony that freed him, not his defense," one juror commented. "He was as honest as the FBI and the New Haven Police."[13]

In between the McLucas trial and that of Seale and Huggins, the New Haven Panthers continued to be the subject of harassment at the hands of police, prison officials, and the FBI. Before their various plea bargains, Ericka Huggins and Frances Carter, along with the other female Panthers, were imprisoned at the women's facility at Niantic. Bobby Seale and George Edwards were incarcerated at Montville. The Panthers, much to the irritation of prison officials, tried to organize among the other inmates. Bobby Seale went on a ten-day hunger strike to protest a rule against the wearing of long hair and beards at the prison. The women, led by Ericka Huggins, demanded that female prisoners be granted better health care. They used the experience of Frances Carter as their model. Carter, pregnant when she was arrested, was forced to give birth with FBI agents present in the delivery room. She suffered greater abuse after the FBI attempted to use her newborn child to force her to testify against the others. She was released on a writ of habeas corpus only after she contracted gangrene and a host of other ailments while in solitary confinement, where she had been placed for asking her sister Peggy, who was also imprisoned, to call her lawyer while she was being treated in the prison's medical wing. The Bureau also continued to try to link Seale to the murder of Rackley, picturing the BPP chairman as a murderous kingpin. In 1971, Thomas E. Mosher, an FBI informant, testified before a Senate subcommittee that, while he was undercover for the Bureau in Santa Cruz, California, he was told by other Panthers that Bobby Seale had ordered the murder of another Panther, Fred Bennett. Allegedly Seale, from his prison cell in New Haven, had condemned Bennett after hearing of an affair between Bennett and his wife.[14]

Despite the verdict in the McLucas case, many shared Brewster's reservations that a black revolutionary could not receive a fair trial in the United States. On the eve of the Seale and Huggins trial, newspaper editors from around the country largely asserted the federal court's ability to provide the remaining Panthers with a fair trial. An editorial in the *Richmond Times Dispatch* commented:

> Of course, the system can't win, it can't prove itself worthy, as far as the radicals are concerned. If a radical is convicted, that shows (it is alleged) that America oppresses dissenters. If he is acquitted that fact is cited merely as a freak and rare occurrence, or else the cry goes up that it proves the government had no case in the first place and was simply persecuting the poor defendants.[15]

But Seale, and his codefendant Huggins would be represented by a cadre of able attorneys including Catherine Roarbach, a well respected attorney known for taking on civil liberties cases; David Rosen, a twenty-seven year old graduate from Yale Law School; and the irrepressible legal activist Charles Garry, who had represented Huey Newton in his legal troubles in California and was now serving as Seale's counsel. Jury selection in the case lasted a staggering four months, as the defense and prosecution wrangled to find a sympathetic jury, while battling the incredible pretrial publicity.

At the opening of the trial, the prosecution attempted to establish that Bobby Seale had given the order for Rackley's execution. The prosecution's star witness, however, again proved a bitter disappointment. On the witness stand "Crazy George," as the Panthers had dubbed Sams, offered testimony that was allusive and erratic. Sams claimed that, after Seale delivered his speech, he had been briefed on the informant situation by Landon Williams and had even visited Panther headquarters, where Rackley was held. But the remaining Panthers, including the prosecution's other key witness, Warren Kimbro, testified that Seale had never been told of the kidnapping and never entered Kimbro's home. On May 29, 1971, after the jury reported that it was hopelessly deadlocked, the judge declared a mistrial. The following day, he dismissed the charges against the two defendants because of the publicity surrounding the case. Ericka Huggins was released while Seale was bound over to authorities in Illinois on charges stemming from the protest at the 1968 Democratic convention. Sams and Kimbro both received life sentences for their part in the murder.

A few days after the trial of Ericka Huggins and Bobby Seale, it was revealed that the jury had been deadlocked ten to two in favor of acquittal. Judge Mulvey's decision nonetheless stirred controversy.[16] An editorial in *The New York Times* observed:

> Justice can be perverted by juries determined to convict on the basis of their bias. But justice can also be paralyzed by pressures in the form of disruption or subtle exploitation of doubts and fears. . . . To read the events in New Haven as a victory of justice or mercy is to belittle the capacity of the courts to deal effectively with crimes that arouse political passions. The credibility of the judicial process suffers as much when justice bends with the winds of public opinion as when it surrenders to demands for vengeance.[17]

Similar was the declaration in *The Ann Arbor News*:

> The Bobby Seale–Ericka Huggins case is nothing to take pride in. . . . Dismissing cases for "publicity" and "biased juries" is active non justice, all that means is that attorneys who want to get controversial clients off need only to stir up attention. It's also called making a case into a cause.[18]

In the short term, the trial was peripheral to the problems of New Haven, bringing less discussion than the riot of 1967 on the failures of Mayor Lee or the city and more on the militants together with the national issues that could be associated with them. As one participant has recalled, May Day was the "last hurrah" for radical student groups. They made the most of the opportunity. In the long term, both trials had a favorable effect on the New Haven BPP. When Bobby Seale was implicated in the murder, the national offices had committed full resources to New Haven. Chief of Staff David Hilliard dispatched to New Haven people like Elbert "Big Man" Howard and Lu Lu Hudson. Both were knowledgeable and committed Panthers who greatly aided the local chapter. In the meanwhile, Douglass Miranda, a transplanted Oakland Panther captain, presided over the Panthers' remaining programs with orders to make New Haven a model chapter. As a result, the Panthers were able to devote more time to activities in the city. While a significant part of this activity was geared toward vindicating the Panthers in the eyes of the community, the Panthers also modified their existing programs in the Elm City.

In the summer of 1970, for example, the BPP expanded the program of breakfast for children after it obtained a larger meeting space on Legion Avenue. In creating the new facility, Miranda was aided by a Boston Panther, Andrea Jones. In June of 1970, an article appearing in *Modern Times*, the newsletter of the American Independent Movement, praised the BPP for meeting the needs of even more school children. The article noted that the breakfast servings were not the political indoctrination sessions that critics denounced them as being; though children were encouraged to return in the afternoon for the center's Party Liberation School, no real political agenda was discussed.[19]

At the same time, the divisions within the national Party that Bobby Seale first identified late in 1968 were growing. New York was to be the primary battleground of Panther conflict. Many New York Panther leaders, among them Richard Moore and Michael and Connie Tabor, refused to accept the redefinition of the Party that had taken place. Their discomfort was augmented after Huey Newton was released from prison on August 5, 1970. He immediately went to work further revising the Party, which had nearly tripled in size since his incarceration. His concept of "intercommunalism" squarely placed the BPP in the context of a worldwide freedom struggle. Black freedom fighters should therefore concentrate on building the revolutionary spirit of the people. The BPP would ally itself with any organization that expressed a similar commitment. Newton, in the interim, proclaimed himself Supreme Commander and then Supreme Servant of the People. This was a conscious change from the call to violence implicit in his former title, Minister of Defense.[20]

In 1973, historian Donald Freed would claim that the final stage of the human rights revolution was arriving. Changes in the BPP he found to be indicative of that final stage. Using revolutionary historical theory, Freed maintained that the conflict among black revolutionaries was inevitable. As Freed conceived the problem, when cultural nationalism "comes to a dead end it must freeze into a kind of reactionary racial separation or rise to the higher level of mature revolutionary nationalism, where class began to supersede caste or race" and develop into internationalism. For Freed, Newton's concept of intercommunalism indicated a similar path for the BPP. Like many others, Freed placed the Panthers at the vanguard of an international struggle against oppression.

The "psychological adolescent cultural nationalist movement" was giving way to the "mature, political revolutionary internationalist." However, Newton discovered that the "psychological adolescent" nationalists would not go without a fight.[21]

In February of 1971, Newton came to New Haven to attend the trial of the Panthers. Remaining in a secluded upscale guest suite located on the campus of Trumbull college at Yale, Newton touched off great controversy, and perhaps more confusion and frustration.

Much of the bewilderment came of a speaking engagement at Yale that Kai Erikson, the master of Trumbull college, who had facilitated Newton's lodging, arranged for him. A series of dialogues were to take place between Newton and Erik Erikson, professor emeritus of human development and lecturer in psychiatry at Harvard University. Kai Erikson's text coming out of the dialogues declares that Newton's visit to the city was a series of disappointments. During Newton's preliminary talk to the students, virtually everyone was disillusioned:

> Radicals because they wanted tougher words to stiffen their periodically limping spirits, moderates because they were anticipating another kind of entertainment, and conservatives because the sheer temperateness of Newton's tone deflated the indignation they were ready to feel. The circus had become a lecture.[22]

Newton began his presentation with an hour-long talk on Panther ideology. In the two hours remaining, according to Erikson, "The students were trying to lure Newton down from the high cerebral plane he had chosen so he could be the political activist they thought him to be, while Newton had come to discuss ideology and would not be discouraged from doing so." Newton was "clearly disappointed by the apparent indifference of the students to the Seale-Huggins trial." The students meanwhile were looking for a "call to action from these men of words."[23]

Between his talks and a series of parties held in his honor by prominent leftists and faculty at Yale, Newton found little time for meeting with the people he claimed to serve. For the critics of the BPP, this was evidence that Newton was out of touch. But Newton's relative isolation was also due to divisions within the Party. When free from his social obligations, he was engaged in secret meetings with renegade members from the New York BPP. Richard Moore and Michael and Connie Tabor represented the New York Panthers. On the evening of February 6, 1971, tensions snapped. The New York Panthers accused Newton of abandoning the revolutionary aims of the Party. When the meeting ended without resolution, the Tabors pilfered funds and personal papers belonging to Newton and escaped to Algeria, where they joined Eldridge Cleaver in denouncing Newton's faction of the Party as revisionist. In New York, the argument was soon to erupt into bloody conflict between Panthers.[24]

Despite the national problems, the New Haven BPP continued to flourish. In February of 1971, the chapter opened up the People's Free Health Clinic at 27 Dixwell Avenue. The clinic had been the brainchild of Frances Carter, Carolyn Jones, and Rosemary Mealy, who served as its medical coordinator. It was financed through donations, including a contribution of $1,000 from the student government at the University of New Haven, for which a group of conservative students threatened to take legal action.[25] The clinic was staffed by ten black physicians from New Haven. It also made use of student volunteers from Yale Medical School, who were associated with the university's Medical Committee on Human Rights. The staff offered medical advice on a rotating basis. Services were free of charge to anyone in the community. In addition, a network of doctors and pharmacists in New Haven took referrals from the clinic and provided free medical testing and prescriptions when necessary. The clinic proved so successful that representatives from the Nixon Administration visited in 1972 and expressed interest in taking the clinic over. The BPP refused. According to George Edwards, the clinic was a valuable asset to the Party in helping to bring together the BPP, the community, and Yale. Over time the Panthers became less involved and the clinic prospered on its own. Edwards argues that this was what the Panthers had always intended, a program for the people, run by the community. In reality, a decline in Party membership and problems within the national headquarters accounted for the decrease in Panther involvement as well.

While the violence between New York and the national headquarters was short-lived, it placed a strain on the Panthers' organizing efforts and membership. In 1972, Cleaver left the Party. The following year, Newton called all Panther chapters to Oakland to support Bobby Seale in a campaign to become mayor of that city. At this time, a number of BPP members, such as Panther Captain Doug Miranda, left New Haven. Although Seale came close to winning the election, the BPP continued to decline. In 1974, Seale left the BPP after confronting Newton about problems in the Party. Newton frequently abused drugs and alcohol and was thought to treat members contemptuously. In 1974, Newton fled to Cuba after he was implicated in the shooting death of Kathleen Smith, a sixteen-year-old prostitute. He was also accused of assault in another case. By that time the Party membership had dwindled to 150 members.[26]

The decline was felt in New Haven. Miranda's departure left Edwards in charge of the local branch. Between 1972 and 1973, Edwards and Elise Brown were able to keep many of the Panther programs functioning. At the time, the Panthers had expanded the free breakfast program to include a free clothing drive. The Panthers also launched a legal aid program. Political education classes were still held at the Panther headquarters and community members were encouraged to take advatage of the BPP's free library. By 1975, however, the Party was dwindling rapidly. Edwards remembers that fewer Panthers were circulating around the offices. Membership fluctuated between eight and ten core people. By 1973 only Elise Brown and Edwards remained.[27]

In 1974, after Newton's departure, Elaine Brown took control of the national organization and presided over its further decline. In Oakland, which had the largest concentration of Panthers, she engineered a modest revival of the Party, achieving some success in implementing the community survival plans the BPP had first announced in 1968. The Party was even somewhat successful in local politics. But while the BPP remained active in Oakland, the national organization was dead.[28]

In New Haven, the exodus of the BPP was at a period of intense controversy. The moderate Black Coalition was challenged when its director, Vernon Moore, resigned in the summer of 1970. As Moore told *Modern Times*, the Coalition was being exploited by the New Haven power structure. He accused Yale University of attempting to bribe the organization into passivity. As he explained, "They thought because they gave me $15,000 and a station wagon to drive they could buy me off. Everybody's got to realize money isn't everything." Moore praised the BPP for its innovative programs. For their failure to do the same, he censured the Black Coalition and Earnest Osbourne, director of Yale's Community Affairs Program, and the brother-in-law of one of the accused Panthers. Moore also expressed discontent that the Coalition was not involved in exposing the New Haven police department and "what's going down in the trial of the Panthers or in the whole court system."[29]

The New Haven police basked for a time in the limelight of their successful campaign against the Panthers and containment of student radicals. During his two-year tenure as chief, Ahern had earned the reputation as the region's top cop. Following the May Day demonstrations, he attained national recognition for being an expert on student unrest and police and community relations. After writing a book about his experiences, Ahern was selected to serve on the President's Commission on Campus Disorders, where he distinguished himself as a champion of student rights in the Kent State affair. In the early 1970s, Ahern left the police for a career in security. Meanwhile, the new chief, Biaggio "Ben" DiLieto, went about dismantling New Haven's wiretap apparatus attempting to dispose of all evidence of the operation. He entrusted this job to Sergeant Frank DeGrand, who smashed the wiretap machines but kept their broken remains stored in his basement.[30]

In 1977 a reporter, Andrew Houlding, exposed the New Haven police wiretapping operation in a series of articles appearing in the *Hartford Courant*. On the basis of Houlding's articles, 1,238 victims of New Haven's wiretap machinery were invited by a local New Haven attorney, John L. Williams, to make a claim against the city and the federal government. Also named in the suit were agents of the FBI. Documents secured by Williams revealed that with a memo from the director to the special agent in charge, outlining one final Cointelpro aimed at disrupting the Panthers breakfast for children program on the second anniversary of the Rackley murder, May 19, 1971, the FBI officially terminated its campaign against the New Haven Panthers.[31] James Ahern and his brother were also named in the suit and ordered to pay damages to the defendants. Ultimately the case resulted in a settlement of close to $2 million. The city of New Haven was saddled with the greater share of $1.85 million. The court also directed the Southern New England Telephone Company to pay $150,000. The court finally ordered the Ahern brothers to yield the remaining $35,000.[32]

During the civil case brought against the city, the men who monitored the machines testified that they had known the work they were doing was illegal. They also testified that chief Ahern had once entered the wiretap operations room and warned them, "If anyone comes in here throw those f———g machines out the window."[33] When the police board questioned Nicholas Pastore, an officer on Stephen Ahern's intelligence squad who had offered false testimony at the trial of the Panthers, about why he and others had not reported the wiretapping he replied, "Keep in mind I was working for a person who had a super cop image probably commended 100 times or more. His brother was a nationally acclaimed police chief—who was I?"[34]

Among the Panthers at the trial, many observers continue to be convinced that the real double agent was Warren Kimbro and that the Rackley murder may have been the result of a mixup between Kimbro and Sams, who was later revealed to have been an agent provocateur for the FBI. Described in the March 7, 1970 issue of the Black Panther Party newspaper as a provisional member of the Party, the New Haven native had gone to high school with New Haven prosecutor Arnold Markle and, until the Panthers arrived, remained on the fringes of all protest efforts in New Haven. At the close of the trial of Seale and Huggins, Markle appeared before the board of pardons to request that Kimbro's life sentence be reduced to four years: normally a life sentence carries a mandatory minimum of twenty years. Judge Mulvey stated: "For the record, I feel Mr. Kimbro has purged, has rehabilitated himself."[35] Kimbro received similar praises from prison authorities. While in prison, he was allowed to take part in a community counseling program that granted him liberal, unsupervised leave in the town of Willimantic, Connecticut. *The Willimantic Chronicle* found the convicted murderer and menacing Black Panther "no danger to the community." Kimbro, who was thirty-seven at the time of his arrest in connection with the Rackley slaying, told reporters, "I have rehabilitated myself and I'm back where I was before. . . . I was just a kid out there, who didn't know how to handle himself, and it was a slap in the face with cold, hard reality that turned

me around back to . . . what I was before 1969." Warden Richard Hills
of the Brooklyn Center called him "more than a model prisoner," while
Warden Harvey Karney observed, "He got the militant young blacks he
knew were going in the wrong direction and got them re-directed. He did
all this voluntarily; we didn't brainwash him." And the rewards kept
pouring in. The high school drop-out Kimbro was allowed, while in
prison, to take special classes at Eastern Connecticut State University.
Within months, he was accepted at Harvard University in the graduate
school of education.[36]

By the time Lonnie McLucas had his own sentence commuted in
1978 to time served, Kimbro had already completed his program and
was working in the field of education. George Sams, also released after
serving only four years, was placed in the federal witness protection program. He was subsequently groomed by the FBI as a witness in the
Chicago Hampton murder trial.[37] In spite of his supporting role in the
murder, McLucas became the fall guy for the entire operation, serving
more time and suffering from the adverse publicity of the trial. Released
on an appeal bond in October of 1973, McLucas found unforgiving the
same community that had embraced Kimbro. While serving out his sentence, McLucas had been promised a full-time job by J. Robert Smith,
director of the Youth Service Bureau of New London, Connecticut. But
upon his release, McLucas faced intense opposition from anxious city officials, including the city manager, C. Francis Driscoll. Driscoll branded
McLucas an "undesirable" and insisted that the seriousness of his conviction warranted his dismissal. Driscoll also barred McLucas from vol-
unteering until his appeal should be settled. After five years of scroung-
ing for work as a taxi driver and menial laborer in New London, McLucas received from the state parole board the judgment that he had
served, "a considerably greater sentence than any of his co-defendants,
some of whom were at least as culpable if not more culpable." Markle
opposed the reduction at first but later consented, after McLucas's attorney brought a federal suit on allegations of wiretapping and prosecutor-
ial misconduct. McLucas said he was happy to close a painful chapter in
his life. He subsequently returned to his family's home in North Carolina.[38]

As testament to the mixed legacy of the Black Panther Party, in
1992 third party presidential candidate Ross Perot claimed that in 1969
the Vietnamese government had sent a team of Black Panthers to as-
sassinate him. Perot's comments drew a curious response from Paul
McCaghren, head of Dallas police intelligence in 1969. "Well, there were
only about eight people here that belonged to the Black Panther Party,"
he explained, "Two of those people worked for us and they told us every
day what was happening."[39] Despite the vast amount of information on
police provocation and the cavalier attitude of many officials about the

abuses that accompanied surveillance of the Party, the violent image of the BPP remains the dominant view. Perot's suggestion that it was the North Vietnamese that sent the BPP demonstrates at least a basic awareness on the part of some about the potential the BPP represented. While Perot's charges were ultimately determined to be unfounded, it is clear that the Panthers deliberately attempted to abandon black power and black politics in search of a more humanistic and internationalist program. There is also ample evidence that in so doing the Panthers inspired a host of other race-based organizations with similar internationalist goals. The Panthers helped to politicize youth gangs like the Chicago Blackstone Rangers and the Puerto Rican dominated Young Lords. There is perhaps no better example of this than Panther negotiations with the inmates of Attica Prison, at Attica, New York, in 1971. The Panthers were called upon to represent the multiracial, multiethnic demands of the prisoners and shocked officials when, as part of a deal to end the disturbance, they offered political asylum to rioters in four different countries. Officials undoubtedly recognized that they were dealing with an organization that could claim, as the Panthers did, rightful leadership to a worldwide freedom struggle. In this sense the Panthers were in ideological agreement with Dr. Martin Luther King who wrote, "however deeply American Negroes are caught in the struggle to be at last home in our homeland of the United States, we cannot ignore the larger world house in which we are dwellers." "Equality with whites," Dr. King continued, "will not solve the problems of either whites or Negroes if it means equality in a world stricken by poverty and in a universe doomed to extinction by war." In 1968 the BPP recognized that this struggle could most effectively be won at the community level in organizing the "people" around common areas of oppression. It was essentially the same strategy Dr. Martin Luther King proposed with the Poor People's Campaign before he was brutally assassinated in Memphis, Tennessee, in April of 1968. The critical difference is that the Panthers endeavored to do it on a daily basis through community-based programs and not in the form of a singular event like the march promoted by Dr. King and the SCLC.[40]

This is not to say that the Panthers were not without flaws, but to suggest that greater scrutiny be applied to what the Panthers were able to accomplish on the local level as an extension of their internationalist and "Serve the People" themes. The institutions that the Panthers established were never race specific. For example their Breakfast for Children program was open to all school-age children, although few whites allowed their children to attend. In addition the Panther free health clinics were set up in economically depressed neighborhoods to serve the needs of all the people in those areas. This is the other shadow of the Panther which continues to be overlooked.

In New Haven, it is fair to say that while individuals like Fred and Rose Harris, George Edwards and others were receptive to the call of the Black Panthers and in fact had begun moving in the same political direction of the Party even before it materialized in Connecticut, others like those who ran the Black Coalition continued to pursue a solution through black politics. The Black Coalition and the NAACP remained active in local politics and, with their help, in 1989 New Haven elected its first black mayor, John Daniels of the NAACP. According to Daniels, many black organizations participated in his campaign. Through their united effort, they shattered the myth that black people did not vote. In the Democratic primary, Daniels marshaled more than seventy percent of the African-American vote, which guaranteed him victory.[41] Things, however, did not proceed well. In putting together his administration, Daniels sought consensus. To this end, he appointed as his chief of police Nicholas Pastore. At first, Pastore appeared to be a wise choice. For promoting his vision of community policing, in 1990 *Newsweek* hailed him as a "People's Cop." "He wants officers to leave the air-conditioned comforts of their patrol cars and the safety of their desks." The crime rate in the Elm City fell during the tenure of Pastore, but his tactics would soon come under fire. Like the Aherns, Pastore was accused of questionable investigative practices that included the use of informants.[42] The irony was not lost on everyone. George Edwards, who returned to New Haven after a brief stint with the Oakland Panthers, complains that after the years of struggle little has changed. Disappointed in the accomplishments of the Daniels Administration, the Reverend Edwin Edmonds feels much the same.[43]

The legacy of black indigenous protest in New Haven must be sought among the many obstacles national and local groups faced in attempting to do something meaningful for the community. Political infighting, poor leadership, class divisions, police harassment and the influence of civil administrators were all important in disrupting the efforts of black protest groups in New Haven. Nevertheless, the accomplishments of these groups were notable.

The NAACP, as an early instance, created a dialogue with Mayor Lee that gave the black community at least a voice in his administration. While Lee clearly benefitted from this relationship, there is no denying that many blacks were able to take advantage of his benevolence. The mayor appointed numerous black officials and helped to stimulate the growth of a black middle class in New Haven. At the same time, his unwillingness to countenance any form of dissent kept him from appreciating the needs of New Haven's rapidly expanding black population in the late 1950s and early 1960s.

In 1965, the frustration with the mayor's band-aid approach to civil rights resulted in the Hill Parents Association, which in many ways was a precursor to the Black Panther Party. Like many such organizations nationwide, the HPA was an example of what could be accomplished by indigenous black protest. It also revealed the limits of such protest. As the HPA came face to face with the reality of maintaining a community program without funding, it gravitated toward the mayor and CPI for support. Lacking the membership and national backing of groups like the NAACP and CORE, the HPA used the most potent weapon in its arsenal, the growing fear in American cities of urban unrest. The prospects of a sit-out greatly disturbed Lee in the 1960s. The promise of a riot terrified him. The HPA received funding, but the riot of 1967 destroyed its credibility with Lee, who had agreed to its program only to prevent such an occurrence. By late 1967 and 1968, the HPA found itself under assault by the New Haven police. Its usefulness to the mayor exhausted, the organization allied itself with the more moderate Black Coalition that still maintained Lee's ear.

By 1969, Mayor Lee was finishing up his last term. New Haven blacks had made some gains, but prospects seemed dim. After the riot, whites and middle-class blacks began leaving the city en masse and the poorest segments of the community were left to fend for themselves. Rising poverty and crime plagued the city. The Panthers arrived with a program remarkably similar to that of the HPA. They were able to make some real and enduring changes in New Haven, many of which are still evident. In this way, the BPP represented a true community organization at the local level. But the national offices of the BPP, like the national office of the NAACP, ultimately undermined the effectiveness of the Panthers' programs in New Haven. The national reputation of the BPP was at least partially responsible. The local branch lacked the organization and leadership that could have partly redeemed the situation.

In the small city of New Haven, the evolution from civil rights to Black Power also reveals the limits of liberalism in the 1960s. Circumstances in Connecticut at the arrival of the BPP were quite similar to what existed in other cities in 1969. By 1969, the political situation in New Haven was beginning to resemble what historian Gabriel Kolko, in discussing the Progressive movement of the 1910s, has described as "the triumph of conservatism" and what Robert Wiebe, discussing the same movement, has identified as the "search for order." Liberal progressive ideology in New Haven did not devolve into the conservative reactionary politics of the Nixon years, when the whole nation was obsessed with security and law and order. It had always been conservative, seeking to force conformity and maintain order in the guise of extending a charitable hand. This phenomenon was clearly evident in large cities like San Francisco and Chicago, where demonstrators were met with violence by some of the nation's best known liberal Democrats.[44]

The low point came with the 1968 Democratic National Convention held in Chicago. The facade of liberalism was exposed by Abraham Ribicoff of Connecticut, who verbally attacked Chicago Mayor Richard J. Daley for using "gestapo tactics" to suppress demonstrators in the streets. As Daley hurled insults at the podium, Ribicoff asked the convention, "How hard is it to accept the truth? How hard is it?"—this from a legislator from a state soon to perfect the technologies of repression of civil liberties. Just two years later, New Haven's police chief James Ahern would earn national praise for not utilizing similar tactics in dealing with Yale students demonstrating in support of the New Haven Panthers. Few were aware then that he was helping to create an electronic police state.[45]

In 1973, Richardson Preyer, chairman of the House of Representatives Committee on Internal Security, wrote of the community organizing of the BPP:

> Its hard to believe that only a little over a year ago the Panthers, despite their small number, ranked as the most celebrated ghetto militants. They fascinated the left, inflamed the police, terrified much of America, and had an extraordinary effect on the Black community. Even moderate Blacks, who disagreed with their violent tactics, felt that the Panthers served a purpose in focusing attention on ghetto problems and argued that they gave a sense of pride to the Black community.[46]

This was certainly true in New Haven, where the Panther program of breakfast for children, its free health clinic, and its legal aid program addressed the growing needs of the city's expanding black community. At the local level, the BPP was a viable community organization and, despite its size, helped to raise awareness about problems affecting blacks throughout the nation. Even in decline, the BPP achieved its stated objective of delivering power to the people, for many of its programs were taken over by the community. This is the enduring legacy of the BPP in New Haven, where illegal wiretapping and massive student protests once obscured the true accomplishments of the Panthers. Like the other organizations before them, however, they found no haven in New Haven.

Notes

1. In his doctoral dissertation, Huey P. Newton strongly suggests that Warren Kimbro was the informant within the New Haven BPP, basing this allegation on excerpts from FBI documents. While Newton never mentions Kimbro by name it is obvious to whom he is referring. Huey P. Newton, *A War Against the Panthers: A Study of Repression in America* (Ph.D. diss., University of California, Santa Cruz, 1980), 69; Michael P. Koskoff interview; George Edwards interview; Edwin Edmonds interview.

2. Memo to Director of FBI from SAC, New Haven, 3 July 1969.

3. Airtel to SAC, New Haven, from Director of FBI, 6 June 1969.

4. FBI Memo to SAC, Las Vegas, from Director of FBI, Re: LV Airtel, 13 April 1971.

5. Michael Koskoff interview; Diane Brozeck, "Koskoff Discusses Trial," *Connecticut Daily Campus*, Thursday, 12 November 1970, 1–2; "Legal Systems Flaws Cited By Lawyer," *The Bridgeport Post*, 12 November 1970, page unknown, clippings file, Office of Koskoff, Koskoff and Beider, Bridgeport, CT.

6. Ibid.

7. David Hilliard, 294; Comments of William Sloane Coffin, Jr. and William Porter III reported in Ellen Katz, "May Day—What Happened?" *The New Journal*, 2 February 1990, 7; on Kingman Brewster see David Greenberg, 16–19.

8. Ibid.

9. David Greenberg, "The King's Conundrum," *The New Journal*, 2 February 1990, 17.

10. James Ahern, 230; Andrew Houlding, "The Wiring of New Haven," *The Nation*, 7 June 1980, 686–687; Donald Freed, 197–198.

11. Among other things, Chauncey notes that the Harvard administrator that tipped him and Brewster off to the plans of the Weathermen was none other than Archibald Cox, who would later gain fame as a special prosecutor during Watergate. Chauncey explains that he and Brewster made contact with Cox in an isolated field in western Massachusetts, where the administrator handed them detailed files and photographs of the suspected student radicals. Cox's interest in the Weathermen was simple: a few months earlier they had staged a violent protest in Boston that had damaged Harvard. Chauncey's recollections support the notion of a well organized intelligence web that extended from state and local police to the FBI and the Department of Justice. Even campus police forces were not immune. Louis Cappiello, who was Yale's chief of police during the May Day protest, has noted that the police apparatus in New Haven was a "well planned wheel, run very smoothly, and I was just one of the spokes." Excerpts of Chauncey's interview with David Greenberg can be found in an inset in Jamie Workman, "Suspicion and Paranoia, The Secrets of May Day," *The New Journal*, 2 February 1990, 39–40.

12. "Ice Him," *Newsweek*, 3 August 1970, 25; "The Enforcer," *Newsweek*, 17 August 1970, page unknown; David Hilliard, 323; Donald Freed, 247–259; Joseph Lelyveld, "New Haven Panther Trial Told About Murder Night," *The New York Times*, 16 July 1970, page unknown, clippings file, Moorland Spingarn Research Center, Howard University, Washington, D.C.; Joseph Lelyveld, "Panthers Feared Sams, Court Told," *The New York Times*, 17 July 1970, page unknown, clippings file, Moorland Spingarn Research Center, Howard University, Washington, D.C.; Joseph Lelyveld, "Torture Is Described At Panther Trial In New Haven," *The New York Times*, 18 July 1970, 23; Joseph Lelyveld, "Role In Murder Laid To Panther," *The New York Times*, 1 August 1970, page unknown, clippings file, Moorland Spingarn Research Center, Howard University, Washington, D.C.; Joseph Lelyveld, "Panthers Lose Bid To Block Witness," *The New York Times*, 5 August 1970, page unknown, clippings file, Moorland Spingarn Research Center, Howard University, Washington, D.C.; Joseph Lelyveld, "Sams Takes Stand In Panther Trial," *The New York Times*, 6 August 1970, page unknown, clippings file, Moorland Spingarn Research Center, Howard University, Washington, D.C.; Joseph Lelyveld, "Former Panther Tells Of Dispute," *The New York Times*, 8 August 1970, 19; Joseph Lelyveld, "Prosecution Rests In Panther Trial In New Haven," *The New York Times*, 12 August 1970, page unknown, clippings file, Moorland Spingarn Research Center, Howard University, Washing-

ton, D.C.; Joseph Lelyveld, "Defense Begins Case In Panther Trial," *The New York Times*, 12 August 1970, page unknown, clippings file, Moorland Spingarn Research Center, Howard University, Washington, D.C.; Joseph Lelyveld, "Kunstler Is On The Stand In New Haven Panther Trial," *The New York Times*, 13 August 1970, 22.

13. "Black Panthers: Trial in New Haven," *Newsweek*, 27 July 1970, page unknown; "Verdict in New Haven," *Newsweek*, 14 September 1970, page unknown; "McLucas Convicted Of 1 Count," *Washington Star*, 31 August 1970, page unknown, clippings file, Washingtoniana Collection, Martin Luther King Public Library, Washington, D.C.; "Panther McLucas Gets 12–15 Years in Killing," *Washington Star*, 18 September 1970, page unknown, clippings file, Washingtoniana Collection, Martin Luther King Public Library, Washington, D.C.; "Sams, Kimbro Get Life Terms," *Washington Star*, 24 June 1970, page unknown, clippings file, Washingtoniana Collection, Martin Luther King Public Library, Washington, D.C.; "Panther Jury Is Still Out," *Washington Star*, 27 August 1970, page unknown; "Shot Rackley In Fear, Panther Testifies," *Washington Star*, 20 August 1970, page unknown, clippings file, Washingtoniana Collection, Martin Luther King Public Library, Washington, D.C.; Michael Koskoff interview.

14. "Testimony of Thomas E. Mosher, Hearings Before the Subcommittee to Investigate the Administration of the Internal Security Act of the Committee on the Judiciary United States Senate," 92nd Congress, 1st session, Part 2 (15 March 1971), 148; House Committee on Internal Security, *Gun Barrel Politics: The Black Panther Party, 1966–1971*, 92nd Congress, 1st session (Washington, D.C.: US Government Printing Office, 1971), 117–118.

15. Editorial, *Richmond Times Dispatch*, Richmond, Virginia, 30 May 1971.

16. Exerts from testimony contained in Donald Freed, *Agony in New Haven;* trail transcripts also part of the *John L. Williams Papers 1966–1977*, Yale University, Manuscripts and Archives; Bobby Seale interview; George Edwards interview; the FBI file of George Edwards, authors copy, August 1995.

17. Editorial, *The New York Times*, 31 May 1971.

18. Editorial, *The Ann Arbor News*, Ann Arbor, Michigan, 29 May 1971.

19. "Bacon and Pancakes: Panthers Combine Service and Politics," *Modern Times*, 15 June 1971, 8–9, contained in *Modern Times*, newsletter of AIM, the American Independent Movement, 1 May 1970–15 February 1972, on microfilm in the Yale University Library.

20. Donald Freed, 18–20.

21. Ibid.

22. Kai Erikson, ed., *In Search of Common Ground* (New York: Norton, 1973), 16.

23. Ibid., 18.

24. Ibid.

25. Linda Garson, "Free Health Clinic Opens," *Modern Times*, 15 February 1971, 12, contained in *Modern Times*, newsletter of AIM, the American Independent Movement, 1 May 1970–15 February 1972, on microfilm in the Yale University Library.

26. On the decline of the BPP nationally, see David Hilliard, *This Side of Glory* (Boston: Little and Brown, 1992); Bobby Seale, *A Lonely Rage* (New York: Time Books, 1978); Elaine Brown, *A Taste of Power* (New York: Pantheon, 1991); Michael Newton, *Bitter Grain* (Los Angeles: Holloway House, 1991).

27. George Edwards interview; Bobby Seale interview; Ericka Huggins interview; Linda Garson, 12.

28. David Hilliard, *This Side of Glory* (Boston: Little and Brown, 1992); Bobby Seale, *A Lonely Rage* (New York: Time Books, 1978); Elaine Brown, *A*

Taste of Power (New York: Pantheon, 1991); Michael Newton, *Bitter Grain* (Los Angeles: Holloway House, 1991).

29. Moore's comments reported in *Modern Times*, 15 July 1970, 2, contained in *Modern Times*, newsletter of AIM, the American Independent Movement, 1 May 1970–15 February 1972, on microfilm in the Yale University Library.

30. Andrew Houlding, 668–669; Herman Schwartz, 722; Carole and Paul Bass, "A City Bugged," *Connecticut*, September 1984, 75–83; Jamie Workman, 39.

31. Memo to Director of FBI from SAC, New Haven, Re: New Haven letter to Bureau, 25 March 1971 and Bureau airtel to Albany, 28 April 1971, May 1971; Andrew Houlding, 668–669; Herman Schwartz, 722; Carole and Paul Bass, 75–83; Jamie Workman, 39.

32. According to John L. Williams: "When the story broke I was contacted by a number of former activists, Panthers and bookmakers. They contacted me because I was the only one in town that was suing cops. Our suit became a massive class action suit on behalf of 1,200 people from literally all walks of life against the city of New Haven, the Mayor, the former Mayor, the former Chief of Police, the phone company, a number of other cops, the FBI and the former State's Attorney." Williams recalls: "To me it was wonderful because it united them. People of all political persuasions, from all walks of life, were united by the fact that they had all been victimized by a big brother police state." *The New York Times*, Late Edition, 7 November 1993, Connecticut Weekly, 3

33. Andrew Houlding, 688; Jamie Workman, 39–40.

34. Pastore testified under oath that he had seen Bobby Seale enter the home of Warren Kimbro the evening before the Rackley murder. The defense proved that Pastore could not have seen what he claimed from where he was parked because his view of the Panther headquarters was almost completely obscured. For Nicholas Pastore's testimony, see trial transcripts, John R. Williams Papers, Yale University; see also Jamie Workman, 39; Pastore testified that his actions were guided by the Aherns's; however, many doubt his sincerity and his practice of continuing to meet with informants recently came under fire as suspect; see Bob Cohn, "A People's Cop Ruffles His Macho Men," *Newsweek*, 27 August 1990, 38.

35. Michael Knight, "Murderer In 1969, Counselor Today," *The New York Times*, 14 September 1973, 41.

36. Lawrence Fellows, "Harvard Accepts Imprisoned Slayer," *The New York Times*, 9 June 1972; Michael Knight, "Murderer In 1969, Counselor Today," *The New York Times*, 14 September 1972; see also C. Newman, "Trails of the Black Panthers," *Harpers*, November 1973; "Black Panthers: Who Killed Alex Rackley?" *Newsweek*, 30 March 1970; "Shot Rackley In Fear, Panther Testifies," *Washington Star*, 20 August 1970; "Panther McLucas Gets 12–15 Years In Killing," *Washington Star*, 18 September 1970; "Panther Held Unfit As New London Aide," *New York Times*, 16 October 1973; Harry T. Clew, "Middlesex Nolles McLucas Indictment," *Hartford Courant*, 3 December 1970, 11; see also Stan Simon, "Panther Case Lawyer Hits System's Flaws," *Hartford Courant*, 12 November 1970, 18; George Gombossy, "McLucas Freed Of Prison Term," *Hartford Courant*, 29 March 1978, 1; Bill Bingham interview.

37. Michael Koskoff interview; Ward Churchill and Jim Vander Wall, *The Cointelpro Papers* (Boston: South End Press, 1990), 360; Ward Churchill and Jim Vander Wall, *Agents of Repression* (Boston: South End Press, 1990), 399; Gail Sheehy, 109; Frank J. Donner, *The Age of Surveillance* (New York: Alfred A. Knopf, 1980), 226.

38. Ibid.

39. "The 1992 Campaign: Candidate's Record; Perot Shows Penchant for

Seeking Conspiracy," Michael Kelley, *The New York Times*, Monday October 26, 1992, Section A p 12.

40. Martin Luther King, Jr., *Where Do We Go from Here—Chaos or Community?* (Boston: Beacon Press, 1967), 167; On the Panthers at Attica see Herman Badillo, et al., *A Bill of Rights: Attica and the America Prison System* (New York: Outerbridge and Lazard, 1972), 87; New York State Commission on Attica, *Attica: The Official Report of the New York State Special Commission* (New York: Bantam, 1972), 106–107.

41. George Edwards interview; John Daniels interview; Linda Garson, 12.

42. Stephen Ahern now owns a lucrative real estate and securities company. James Ahern passed away in 1986, shamed by the wiretap settlement but still widely regarded for keeping New Haven cool during May Day. Robert O. Boorstin, "James Ahern Dies; Expert On Police," *New York Times*, 3 March 1986; Bob Cohn, 38.

43. John Daniels interview; Edwin Edmonds interview; George Edwards interview; Bob Cohn, 38; George Edwards statement reported in Steve Hamm, "Ex Panther Retains Social Philosophy," *New Haven Register*, 13 May 1984, b5.

44. Gabriel Kolko, *The Triumph of Conservatism: A Reinterpretation of American History, 1900–1963* (New York: Harper and Row, 1963); Robert Wiebe, *The Search for Order* (New York, 1967) abstracted in Arthur Link and Richard McCormick, *Progressivism* (Arlington Heights, IL: Harlan Davidson, 1983).

45. The relevant portions of Abraham Ribicoff's speech in support of the candidacy of George McGovern are excerpted in Robert Daniels, *The Year of the Heroic Guerilla* (New York: Basic Books, 1989), 218.

46. Richardson Preyer comments recorded in House Committee on Internal Security, *Gun Barrel Politics: The Black Panther Party, 1966–1971*, 92nd Congress, 1st session (Washington, D.C.: US Government Printing Office, 1971), 143.

SELECTED BIBLIOGRAPHY

Primary Sources

Manuscript Collections

Counterintelligence Program Black Nationalist Hate Group Racial Intelligence (Black Panther Party) Federal Bureau of Investigations Reading Room, FBI Headquarters, Washington, DC.

The John L. Williams Papers, 1966–1977, Manuscripts and Archives, Yale University, New Haven, CT.

The NAACP Papers, 1950–1965, Manuscript Division, Library of Congress, Washington, DC.

The Richard C. Lee Papers, 1954–1968, Manuscripts and Archives, Yale University, New Haven, CT.

The LuLu Hudson Papers, Moorland-Spingarn Research Center, Howard University, Washington, DC.

The Congress of Racial Equality Papers, 1941–1967, Microfilm, Moorland-Spingarn Research Center, Howard University, Washington, DC.

The NAACP Papers, 1950–1966, Microfilm, Moorland-Spingarn Research Center, Howard University, Washington, DC.

The New Haven Free Public Library, Local History Collection, 133 Elm St, New Haven, CT.

Unpublished Interviews

Bingham, William. Interview by author, 19 September 1995, tape recording, New London, CT.

Daniels, John. Interview by author, 25 July 1997, tape recording, New Haven, CT.

Dowdy, Richard. Interview by author, 22 March 1999, telephone tape recording, Dover, DE.

Edmonds, Edwin. Interview by author, 23 July 1997, tape recording, New Haven, CT.

Edwards, George. Interview by author, 5 August 1995, tape recording, New Haven, CT.

Harris, Fred. Interview by author, 9, 11 April 1999, telephone tape recording, Dover, DE.

Huggins, Ericka. Interview by author, 10 July 1995, tape recording, Oakland, CA.

Koskoff, Michael P. Interview by author, 5 May 1995, tape recording, Bridgeport, CT.

Louis, Charles. Interview by author, 22 March 1999, tape recording, Washington, DC.

Louis, Joe. Interview by author, 22 May 1999, tape recording, Washington, DC.

Seale, Bobby. Interview by author, 2 January 1996, telephone tape recording, Philadelphia, PA.

———. Oral History Interview, Moorland-Spingarn Research Center, Howard University, Washington, DC.

Williams, Earl. Interview by author, 3 April 1999, telephone tape recording, Dover, DE.

Government Documents

Committee on Internal Security House of Representatives. *The Black Panther Party: The Origins and Development as Reflected in its Official Weekly Newspaper, The Black Panther Community News Service*. 92nd Congress, 1st Session, Washington, DC: US Government Printing Office, 1971.

National Advisory Commission on Civil Disorder. *Report of The National Advisory Commission on Civil Disorders*. Washington, DC: US Government Printing Office, 1968.

US Comptroller General. *FBI Domestic Intelligence Operations: An Uncertain Future. Report to the House Committee on the Judiciary*. Washington, DC: General Accounting Office, 1976.

US Comptroller General. *FBI Domestic Intelligence Operations Their Purpose and Scope: Issues that Need to be Resolved. Report to the House Committee on the Judiciary*. Washington, DC: General Accounting Office, 1976.

US House of Representatives Committee on Internal Security. *Gun Barrel Politics: The BPP 1966–1971*. 92nd Congress, 1st Session, Washington, DC: US Government Printing Office, 1971.

US House of Representatives Committee on the Judiciary. *FBI Counterintelligence Programs*. 93rd Congress, 2nd Session, Washington, DC: US Government Printing Office, 1974.

_____. *FBI Undercover Operations: Report of the Subcommittee on Civil and Constitutional Rights*. 98th Congress, 2nd Session, Washington, DC: US Government Printing Office, 1984.

US Senate Select Committee to Study Government Operations. *The FBI's Covert Program to Destroy the Black Panther Party*. Washington, DC: US Government Printing Office, 1976.

US Senate Select Committee to Study Government Operations. *Intelligence Activities and the Rights of Americans Book II*. 94th Congress, 2nd Session, Washington, DC: US Government Printing Office, 1976.

Newspapers and Periodicals

The Black Panther Party Community News Service, 25 April 1967; 20 June 1967; 10 June 1968; 17 February 1969; 25 May 1969; 25 October 1969; 13 December 1969.

Bridgeport Telegram, 29 January 1969, 7 February 1969.

Connecticut Sunday Herald, 27 August 1967.

Modern Times, 1 May 1970–15 February 1972.

NAACP Newsletter (New Haven, CT), 18 September 1959; 15 February 1959.

New Haven Journal Courier, 18 October 1961; 3, 4 April 1962; 3 October 1967; 2 November 1967.

New Haven Register, 19, 29 September 1961; 10 October 1961; 7 February 1962; 4 March 1962; 3, 24 April 1962; 25 May 1962; 16, 17, 23 October 1962; 10 November 1962; 27, 31 August 1964; 9 December 1964; 22, 23 May 1969; 23 March 1971.

New York Times, 23, 24, 25, 26, 27, 28 April 1969; 1, 2, 3, 4, 5 May 1970; 3 March 1986; 7 November 1986.

Open Gate News, 4 May 1962; 21 June–5 July 1963.

Washington Evening Star, 14 February 1958; 13, 17 November 1964; 9 January 1959; 8 April 1966; 4 September 1967; 25 December 1967; 1 August 1970; 18 September 1970; 16 October 1971.

Primary Books

Ahern, James. *Police in Trouble*. New York: Hawthorn, 1972.

Babcox, Michael and Deborah and Bob Abel, eds. *The Conspiracy: The Chicago 8 Speak Out!* New York: Dell, 1969.

Balzar, Richard. *Street Time: Text Based on Conversations with Fred Harris*. New York: Grossman Publishers, 1972.

Brent, William. *Long Time Gone*. New York: Times Books, 1996.

Brown, Elaine. *A Taste of Power: A Black Woman's Story*. New York: Pantheon Books, 1991.

Citizens Research and Investigation Committee. *The Glass House Tapes*. New York: Avon Books, 1973.

Erickson, Kai. *In Search of Common Ground*. New York: Norton, 1973.

Foner, Philip, ed. *The Black Panthers Speak*. Philadelphia: J.B. Lippincott Company, 1970; reprint New York: Da Capo, 1995.

Freed, Donald. *Agony in New Haven: The Trial of Bobby Seale, Ericka Huggins and the Black Panther Party.* New York: Simon and Shuster, 1973.

Hilliard, David. *This Side of Glory: The Autobiography of David Hilliard and the Story of the Black Panther Party.* Boston: Little and Brown, 1993.

Major, Reginald. *A Panther Is a Black Cat.* New York: William Morrow, 1971.

Miller, William. *The Fifteenth Ward and the Great Society: An Encounter with a Modern City.* Cambridge: The Riverside Press, 1966.

Motley, Constance Baker. *Equal Justice Under Law.* New York: Farrar, Starus Giroux, 1998.

Newton, Huey. *To Die for the People.* New York: Random House, 1972; New York: Writers and Readers, 1995.

_____. *Revolutionary Suicide.* New York: Ballantine Books, 1973.

Oudes, Bruce, ed. *From: The President, Richard Nixon's Secret Files.* New York: Harper and Row, 1989.

Seale, Bobby. *A Lonely Rage: The Autobiography of Bobby Seale.* New York: Times Books, 1978.

_____. *Seize the Time: The Story of the Black Panther Party and Huey P. Newton.* New York: Random House, 1970; Baltimore: Black Classic Press, 1991.

Sheehy, Gail. *Panthermania.* New York: Harper and Row, 1971.

Talbot, Allan R. *The Mayor's Game.* New York: Harper and Row, 1967.

Secondary Sources

Abron, JoNina. "Raising the Consciousness of the People: The Black Panther Party Intercommunal News Service, 1967–1980." In *Voices from the Underground: Insider Histories of the Vietnam Era Underground Press.* Ken Wachsberger, ed. Tempe, AZ: Mica Press, 1993.

Anthony, Earl. *Picking Up the Gun: A Report on the Black Panthers.* New York: Dial, 1970.

_____. *Spitting In the Wind: The True Story Behind the Violent Legacy of the Black Panther Party.* Santa Monica, CA: Roundtable, 1990.

Baldwin, James. *Nobody Knows My Name.* New York: Dell, 1962.

Banks, Louis, ed. *The Negro and the City.* New York: Time Life Books, 1968.

Blackstock, Nelson. *COINTELPRO: The FBI's Secret War on Political Freedom.* New York: Vintage Books, 1975.

Blumberg, Rhoda. *Civil Rights: The 1960s Freedom Struggle.* Boston: Twayne, 1984.

Boesel, David and Peter H. Rossi, eds. *Cities Under Siege: An Anatomy of the Ghetto Riots, 1964–1968.* New York: Basic Books, 1971.

Brisbane, Robert H. *Black Activism: Racial Revolution in the United States 1954–1970.* Valley Forge, PA: Judson Press, 1974.

Brooks, Thomas R. *Walls Come Tumbling Down: A History of the Civil Rights Movement, 1940–1970.* Englewood Cliffs, NJ: Prentice-Hall, 1974.

Carson, Clayborne, ed. *The Eyes on the Prize Civil Rights Reader.* New York: Viking Press, 1991.

Chevingny, Paul. *Cops and Rebels: A Study of Provocation.* New York: Curtis Books, 1972.

Churchill, Ward and Jim Vander Wall, eds. *Agents of Repression: The FBI's Secret War Against the BPP and the American Indian Movement.* Boston: South End Press, 1988.

_____. *The Cointelpro Papers.* Boston: South End Press, 1990.

Cleaver, Eldridge. *Eldridge Cleaver, Post Prison Writings.* Robert Scheer, ed. New York: Random House, 1968.

Collier, Peter and David Horowitz. *Destructive Generation, Second Thoughts about the Sixties.* New York: Summit, 1989.

Crowan, Paul, Nick Egelson, and Nat Hentoff. *State Secrets: Police Surveillance in America.* New York: Holt, Rhinehart and Winston, 1974.

Cruse, Harold. *The Crisis of the Negro Intellectual.* New York: Quill, 1984.

Dahl, Robert A. *Who Governs? Democracy and Power in an American City.* New Haven: Yale University Press, 1961.

Daniels, Robert. *The Year of the Heroic Guerilla.* New York: Basic Books, 1989.

Davis, James. *Spying on America: The FBI's Domestic Counterintelligence Program.* New York: Praeger, 1992.

Domhoff, William G. *Who Really Rules? New Haven and Community Power Re-examined*. New Brunswick, NJ: Transaction, 1978.

Draper, Theodore. *The Rediscovery of Black Nationalism*. New York: Viking Press, 1970.

Dubois, Ellen Carol. *Feminism and Suffrage*. Ithaca, NY: Cornell University Press, 1980.

Dumond, Dwight. *Anti-slavery: The Crusade for Freedom in America*. Ann Arbor: University of Michigan Press, 1961.

Eliff, John T. *Crime, Dissent and the Attorney General*. Beverly Hills, CA: Sage Publications, 1971.

_____. *The Reform of FBI Intelligence Operations*. Princeton, NJ: Princeton University Press, 1979.

Eyes on the Prize Production Group. Eyes On The Prize II. PBS video series. "Power" and "A Nation of Law?" Boston: Blackside Productions, 1989.

Fairclough, Adam. *Race and Democracy: The Civil Rights Struggle in Louisiana, 1915–1972*. Athens: University of Georgia Press, 1995.

Feagin, Joe and Harlan Hahn. *Ghetto Revolts*. New York: Macmillan, 1973.

Foner, Phillip and Josephine Pacheco. *Three Who Dared: Prudence Crandall, Margaret Douglass, Myrtilla Miner—Champions of Antebellum Black Education*. Westport, CT: Greenwood, 1984.

Fuller, Edmund. *Prudence Crandall: An Incident of Racism in Nineteenth Century Connecticut*. Middletown, CT: Weslyan University Press, 1971.

Garrow, David. *The FBI and Martin Luther King, Jr.: From "Solo" to Memphis*. New York: W.W. Norton and Company, 1981.

Gitlin, Todd. *The Sixties: Years of Hope, Days of Rage*. New York: Pantheon, 1988.

_____. *The Whole World Is Watching: Mass Media in the Making and Unmaking of the New Left*. Berkeley: University of California Press, 1980.

Goldstein, Robert. *Political Repression in Modern America: From 1870 to the Present*. Cambridge, MA: Schenkman Publishing Company, 1978.

Hall, Raymond. *Black Separatism in the United States*. Hanover, NH: University Press of New England, 1978.

Hampton, Henry and Steve Fayer, eds. *Voices of Freedom*. New York: Bantum Books, 1990.

Haring, Sidney L. *Policing a Class Society: The Experience of American Cities, 1865–1915*. Newark, NJ: Rutgers University Press, 1983.

Harrington, Michael. *The Other America: Poverty in the United States*. Baltimore: Penguin, 1971.

Harvey, James C. *Black Civil Rights During the Johnson Administration*. Jackson: University and College Press of Mississippi, 1973.

Heath, Louis G., ed. *Off the Pigs!: The History and Literature of the Black Panther Party*. Metuchen, NJ: The Scarecrow Press, 1976.

_____. *The Black Panther Leaders Speak*. Metuchen, NJ: The Scarecrow Press, 1976.

Hill, Norman, ed. *The Black Panther Menace: America's Neo Nazis*. New York: Popular Library, 1971.

Homel, Michael. *Down from Equality, Black Chicagoans and the Public Schools, 1920–1941*. Chicago: University of Chicago Press, 1984.

Honey, Michael. *Southern Labor and Black Civil Rights: Organizing Memphis Workers*. Urbana and Chicago: University of Illinois Press, 1993.

Jacobs, Jane. *The Death and Life of Great American Cities*. New York: Vintage Books, 1961.

Jennings, James. *The Politics of Black Empowerment: The Transformation of Black Activism in Urban America*. Detroit: Wayne State University Press, 1992.

Johnson, David R. *Law Enforcement: A History*. Saint Louis, MO: Forum Press, 1981.

Jones, Charles, ed. *The Black Panther Party Reconsidered*. Baltimore: Black Classic Press, 1998.

Jones, Howard. *Mutiny on the Amistad*. New York: Oxford University Press, 1987.

Karenga, Maulana Ron. *The Roots of the US-Panther Conflict: The Perverse and Deadly Games Police Play*. San Diego: Kawaida Publications, 1976.

Kelley, Robin. *Hammer and Hoe: Alabama Communists during the Great Depression*. Chapel Hill: University of North Carolina Press, 1990.

Kempton, Murray. *The Briar Patch*. New York: Da Capo Press, 1973, 1997.

Killian, Lewis. *The Impossible Revolution? Black Power and the American Dream.* New York: Random House, 1968.

Kunen, James. *The Strawberry Statement: Notes of a College Revolutionary.* St. James, NY: Brandywine Press, 1995.

Litwack, Leon. *North of Slavery: The Negro in the Free States, 1790–1860.* Chicago: University of Chicago Press, 1961.

Major, Reginald. *Justice in the Round: The Trial of Angela Davis.* New York: The Third Press, 1973.

Marine, Gene. *The Black Panthers: The Compelling Study of the Angry Young Revolutionaries Who Have Shaken a Black Fist at White America.* New York: Signet Books, 1969.

Meir, August, ed. *Black Protest in the Sixties: Articles from the New York Times.* New York: Markus Wiener, 1991.

Meir, August and Elliot Rudwick. *CORE: A Study in the Civil Rights Movement, 1942–1968.* New York: Oxford University Press, 1973.

_____. *Along the Color Line: Explorations in the Black Experience.* Urbana: University of Illinois, 1976.

Moore, Gilbert. *A Special Rage.* New York: Harper and Row, 1971; reprinted as *Rage* New York: Carroll and Graf, 1993.

Morris, Aldon D. *The Origins of the Civil Rights Movement: Black Communities Organizing for Change.* New York: Free Press, 1984.

Morse, Jarvis. *A Neglected Period of Connecticut's History, 1818–1850.* New Haven, CT: Yale University Press, 1933.

Myrdal, Gunnar. *The American Dilemma: The Negro Problem and Modern Democracy.* New York: Harper, 1944; New York: Pantheon Books, 1962.

Newton, Michael. *Bitter Grain: Huey Newton and the Black Panther Party.* Los Angeles: Holloway House, 1991.

O'Reilly, Kenneth. *"Racial Matters": The FBI's Secret File on Black America, 1960–1972.* New York: Free Press, 1989.

Oudes, Bruce, ed. *From: The President: Richard Nixon's Secret Files.* New York: Harper and Row, 1989.

Pearson, Hugh. *The Shadow of the Panther: Huey Newton and the Price of Power in America.* Reading, MA: Addison-Wesley, 1994.

Platt, Anthony, ed. *The Politics of Riot Commissions, 1917–1970: Official Reports and Critical Essays.* New York: Macmillan, 1971.

Pohlmann, Marcus. *Black Politics in Conservative America.* New York: Longman, 1999.

Powers, Richard. *Secrecy and Power: The Life of J. Edgar Hoover.* New York: The Free Press, 1987.

Powledge, Fred. *Model City.* New York: Simon and Shuster, 1970.

_____. *Free at Last? The Civil Rights Movement and the People Who Made It.* Boston: Little and Brown, 1991.

Richards, Leonard. *Gentleman of Property and Standing: Anti-Abolition Mobs in Jacksonian America.* New York: Oxford University Press, 1970.

Robinson, Armstead L. and Patricia Sullivan, eds. *New Directions in Civil Rights Studies.* Charlottesville: University Press of Virginia, 1991.

Roth, David M. *Connecticut: A History.* New York: W.W. Norton, 1979.

Rout, Kathleen. *Eldridge Cleaver.* Boston: Twayne, 1991.

Sales, William. *From Civil Rights to Black Liberation: Malcom X and the Organization of Afro-American Unity.* Boston: South End Press, 1994.

Scott, Claudia. *Forecasting Local Government.* Washington, DC: The Urban Institute, 1972.

Silver, Christopher and John B. Moeser. *The Separate City: Black Communities in the Urban South, 1940–1968.* Lexington: University of Kentucky Press, 1995.

Skolnick, Jerome H. *The Politics of Protest.* New York: Ballantine, 1970.

Tyler, Alice. *Freedom's Ferment: Phases of American Social History from the Colonial Period to the Outbreak of the Civil War.* Minneapolis: University of Minnesota Press, 1944.

Van Dusen, Albert. *Connecticut.* New York: Random House, 1961.

Warner, Robert A. *New Haven Negroes.* New York: Arno Press, 1969.

Warren, Robert. *Who Speaks for the Negro.* New York: Random House, 1965.

Woodward, C. Vann. *The Strange Career of Jim Crow*. Oxford: Oxford University Press, 1974.

Articles

Abron, JoNina. "The Legacy of the BPP." *The Black Scholar* 17 (November/December 1986), 33–36.
Arlen, M. J. "American Verdict." *Atlantic Review*, October 1973, 117–118.
Baker, R. K. "Putting Down the Gun: Panthers Outgrow Their Rhetoric." *Nation* 217, 16 July 1973, 47–51.
Brown, Scott. "The US Organization, Maulana Karenga, and Conflict with the Black Panther Party." *Journal of Black Studies* 28 (November 1997) 157–169.
Cheney, Ruth and Peter Green. "New Haven: Model City?" *Progressive Architecture*, January 1968, 131–147.
Daniels, Robert V. "The Sixties: How Near Was Revolution?" *Journal of the Institute of Socio-Economic Studies* 4 (Winter 1979), 46–57.
Donner, Frank. "Electronic Surveillance: The National Security Game." *Civil Liberties Review* 2 (Summer 1975), 15–17.
_____. "How J. Edgar Hoover Created His Intelligence Powers." *Civil Liberties Review* 3 (February/March 1977), 34–51.
_____. "Hoover's Legacy: A Nationwide System of Political Surveillance Based on the Spurious Authority of a Press Release." *Nation*, 1 June 1974, 34–51.
_____. "Intelligence on the Attack: The Terrorist as Scapegoat." *Nation*, 20 May 1978, 590–594.
Goldberg, A. "Panthers after the Trial." *Ramparts*, 10 March 1972, 24–27.
Harris, Richard. "Reflections: Crime in the FBI." *The New Yorker*, 8 August 1977, 30–42.
Houlding, Andrew. "The Wiring of New Haven." *Nation*, 7 June 1980, 668–670.
Newman, C. "Trials of the Black Panthers." *Harpers*, November 1973, 116–120.
"Protest in the 60s," *Annals of the American Academy of Political and Social Science* 382 (March 1969).
Stern, Sol. "The Call of the Black Panthers." *The New York Times Magazine*, 6 August 1967.
Theoharis, Athan. "Bell Limits FBI Prosecutions." *Nation*, 10 September 1977, 198–199.
_____. "Bureaucrats above the Law: Double-Entry Intelligence Files." *Nation*, 22 October 1977, 383–397.
_____. "Illegal Surveillance: Will Congress Stop the Snooping?" *Nation*, 2 February 1974, 138–142.
_____. "Misleading the Presidents: Thirty Years of Wiretapping." *Nation*, 14 June 1971, 244–250.
"Ice Him." *Newsweek*, 3 August 1970, 25.
"Justice and the Panthers." *Life*, 28 May 1971, 4.
"The Enforcer." *Newsweek*, 17 August 1970, 32–33.
"Trial in New Haven." *Newsweek*, 27 July 1970, 20–21.
"Students and Panthers." *The New Republic*, November 1973, 11–12.
"Who Killed Alex Rackley?" *Newsweek*, 30 March 1970, 22–23.

Dissertations

Cameron, Henry T. "The Story of the Development of the Total Community School in the City of New Haven, Connecticut for the Period, 1962–1971." Ph.D. diss., University of Massachusetts, 1973.
Abraham, Cleo. "Protests and Expedients in Response to Failures in Urban Education: A Study of New Haven, 1950–1970." Ph.D. diss., University of Massachusetts, 1971.
Hopkins, Charles W. "The Deradicalization of the Black Panther Party, 1967–1973." MA thesis, University of North Carolina at Chapel Hill, 1978.
Murphy, David Russell. "Policy Innovation and Political Strategy in an American City: The Formative Years of New Haven, Connecticut's Anti-Poverty Project." Ph.D. diss.,Yale University, 1969.
Newton, Huey P. "A War Against the Panthers: A Study of Repression in America." Ph.D. diss., University of California, Santa Cruz, 1980.
Peel, Mark Steven. "A Reform Strategy in Urban Education: Community Action and Edu-

cation in New Haven, Connecticut, 1962–1972." Ph.D. diss., University of Massachusetts, 1973.

Piccrillo, Martin Louis. "Organizational and Personal Dimensions of the New Haven Police Service." Ph.D. diss., Fordham University, 1973.

Stewart, Helen L. "Buffering: The Leadership Style of Huey P. Newton, Co-Founder of the Black Panther Party." MA thesis, Brandeis University, 1980.

Willis, Daniel Joseph. "A Critical Analysis of Mass Political Education and Community Organization as Utilized by the Black Panther Party as a Means for Effecting Social Change." Ph.D. diss., University of Massachusetts, 1977.

ACKNOWLEDGMENTS

The completion of this book would not have been possible without the assistance of numerous people who generously gave of their time, knowledge, and resources to aide me in my research. First and foremost I am forever indebted to the History Department at Howard University for awarding me the Williston Lofton prize which allowed me to complete the dissertation. In addition, I would have been lost without the advice, encouragement, and constructive criticism of my dissertation advisors Dr. Emory Tolbert and Dr. David Deleon. I would also like to thank Dr. Sharon Harley who was my outside reader and in that capacity provided numerous suggestions which greatly enhanced the book.

Various individuals, in particular Mr. George Edwards, Attorney Michael Koskoff, Attorney Earl Williams and Professor Richard Dowdy, allowed me access to their personal papers as well as interviews which helped to complete the narrative of civil rights protest in New Haven. I wish to thank them, as well as all of my other interview subjects, for contributing to this study.

Next, I would like to recognize two of my colleagues at Delaware State University, Dr. Akwesi Osei and Dr. Bradley Skelcher, who despite considerable projects of their own, found time to read and comment on numerous drafts of the final manuscript and offer valuable insight and criticism. I am also grateful to Mr. Richard C. Carlson who read several earlier drafts. To my close friends Ms. Tamara Brown, Ms. Ericka "Nia" Watkins, and Dr. Rodger Davidson, a heart felt thanks for your advice, encouragement, and gentle haranguing throughout this process. I would also like to thank Dr. Steven Newton who offered some critical advice on avoiding the perils of publishing. Finally I would like to credit the support of my publisher Dr. David Burner and my editor Dr. Thomas West whose thoughtful critique and careful editing of the manuscript was greatly appreciated.

Several manuscript and archive collections were indispensable in the completion of this work. It is with much gratitude that I acknowledge the staff at the Manuscripts and Archives division of the Yale University Library and the staffs of the New Haven Public Library and the Bridgeport Public Library. The librarians who steward the vast documentary collections at the Library of Congress and the FBI Reading

Room in Washington, D.C., were also extremely helpful. I would like to thank the staff at the Moorland Spingarn Research Center at Howard University, especially Mrs. Leida Torrres, who took an active interest in my research. In addition I would like to thank Mrs. Mary Ternes at the Washingtoniana Collection of the Martin Luther King Public Library in Washington, D.C., for her speed and attentiveness to my numerous requests for assistance.

Two impressive undergraduates, Mr. Ben Hatton and Ms. Apryl Walker, further deserve mention. Both aided in the research of the book and Ms. Walker also suffered cheerfully through the completion of the final manuscript. Finally, I would like to thank my parents, Ralph and Elizabeth Williams, for encouragement and financial support during my numerous trips to New Haven, my brother, Mr. Yotisse Williams, who never seemed too tired to take a late night call from a sibling in distress, and my sister, Ms. Yohanna Williams, who spent lots of quality time in the New Haven Library searching through microfilm with me and reminding me to have fun. Most importantly I want to thank my wife Karlyn and my son Mason, both of whom have been blessings from God in my life. Their love, support, assistance, and encouragement was unquestionably the greatest contribution to my ability to complete this work.

INDEX

183

Printed and bound by CPI Group (UK) Ltd, Croydon, CR0 4YY

09/06/2025

14686098-0001